The Franco-Algerian War through a Twenty-First Century Lens

War, Culture and Society

Series Editor: Stephen McVeigh, *Associate Professor, Swansea University, UK*

Editorial Board

Paul Preston *LSE, UK*
Joanna Bourke *Birkbeck, University of London, UK*
Debra Kelly *University of Westminster, UK*
Patricia Rae *Queen's University, Ontario, Canada*
James J. Weingartner *Southern Illinois University, USA (Emeritus)*
Kurt Piehler *Florida State University, USA*
Ian Scott *University of Manchester, UK*

War, Culture and Society is a multi- and interdisciplinary series which encourages the parallel and complementary military historical and sociocultural investigation of twentieth and twenty-first century war and conflict.

Published

Filming the End of the Holocaust: Allied Documentaries, Nuremberg and the Liberation of the Concentration Camps, John J. Michalczyk (2014)

South Africa's "Border War": Contested Narratives and Conflicting Memories, Gary Baines (2014)

The Testimonies of Indian Soldiers and the Two World Wars: Between Self and Sepoy, Gajendra Singh (2014)

The British Imperial Army in the Middle East: Morale and Military Identity in the Sinai and Palestine Campaigns, 1916–1918, James E. Kitchen (2014)

The Japanese Comfort Women and Sexual Slavery during the China and Pacific Wars, Caroline Norma (2015)

Cultural Response to Occupation in Japan: The Performing Body During and after the Cold War, Adam Broinowski (2016)

Second World War British Military Camouflage: Designing Deception, Isla Forsyth (2017)

Jewish Volunteers, the International Brigades and the Spanish Civil War, Gerben Zaagsma (2017)

Women, Warfare and Representation: American Servicewomen in the Twentieth Century, Emerald M. Archer (2017)

Prisoners of the Sumatra Railway: Narratives of History and Memory,
Lizzie Oliver (2017)
The Franco-Algerian War through a Twenty-First Century Lens: Film and History,
Nicole Beth Wallenbrock (2020)
Picturing Genocide in the Independent State of Croatia: Atrocity Images and the Contested Memory of the Second World War in the Balkans, Jovan Byford (2020)

Forthcoming
The Lost Cause of the Confederacy and American Civil War Memory,
David J. Anderson (2020)
The Irish Myth of the Second World War, Bernard Kelly (2020)

The Franco-Algerian War through a Twenty-First Century Lens

Film and History

Nicole Beth Wallenbrock

BLOOMSBURY ACADEMIC
LONDON • NEW YORK • OXFORD • NEW DELHI • SYDNEY

BLOOMSBURY ACADEMIC
Bloomsbury Publishing Plc
50 Bedford Square, London, WC1B 3DP, UK
1385 Broadway, New York, NY 10018, USA
29 Earlsfort Terrace, Dublin 2, Ireland

BLOOMSBURY, BLOOMSBURY ACADEMIC and the Diana logo are trademarks of
Bloomsbury Publishing Plc

First published in Great Britain 2020
Paperback edition published 2021

Copyright © Nicole Beth Wallenbrock, 2020

Nicole Beth Wallenbrock has asserted her right under the Copyright, Designs and Patents
Act, 1988, to be identified as Author of this work.

Series design: Clare Turner

Cover image © Malek Bensmaïl, from the film *China Is Still Far* (2008)

All rights reserved. No part of this publication may be reproduced
or transmitted in any form or by any means, electronic or mechanical,
including photocopying, recording, or any information storage or retrieval
system, without prior permission in writing from the publishers.

Bloomsbury Publishing Plc does not have any control over, or responsibility for,
any third-party websites referred to or in this book. All internet addresses given in this
book were correct at the time of going to press. The author and publisher regret any
inconvenience caused if addresses have changed or sites have ceased to exist,
but can accept no responsibility for any such changes.

A catalogue record for this book is available from the British Library.

A catalog record for this book is available from the Library of Congress.

ISBN: HB: 978-1-4742-6280-4
PB: 978-1-3502-4680-5
ePDF: 978-1-4742-6281-1
eBook: 978-1-4742-6282-8

Series: War, Culture and Society

Typeset by Newgen KnowledgeWorks Pvt. Ltd., Chennai, India

To find out more about our authors and books visit www.bloomsbury.com
and sign up for our newsletters.

Contents

List of Illustrations		viii
Acknowledgments		x
Introduction		1
1	The Twentieth-Century Screen Geography of the Franco-Algerian War	11
2	The Algerian Revolution in Three Transnational Documentaries: *Algérie Tours/detours* (Oriane Brun-Moschetti and Leïla Morouche, 2006), *La Chine est encore loin* (*China Is Still Far*, Malek Bensmaïl, 2008), and *Fidaï* (Damien Ounouri, 2012)	41
3	The Specter of Torture and Atomic Bombs: *L'Ennemi intime* (*The Intimate Enemy*, Florent-Emilio Siri, 2007) and *Djinns* (*Stranded*, Hughes and Sandra Martin, 2010)	61
4	Reclaiming the Screen Algerian Revolution: *Cartouches Gauloises* (*Summer of '62*, Mehdi Charef, 2006), *Hors-la-loi* (*Outside the Law*, Rachid Bouchareb, 2010), and *Les Folles Années du Twist* (*The Crazy Years of the Twist*, Mahmoud Zemmouri, 1986)	89
5	A Scission in the Memory of the Franco-Algerian War: *Mesrine Part I: L'Instinct de Mort* (*Killer Instinct*), *Part II: L'Ennemi Public No. 1* (*Public Enemy No. 1*) (Jean-Paul Richet, 2008)	111
6	The Revolution through Utopian Dialectics: *Une si jeune paix* (*So Young a Peace*, Jacques Charby, 1965) and *Loubia Hamra* (*Bloody Beans*, Narimane Mari, 2013)	131
Conclusion		155
Appendix Timeline: Algeria and France, 1827–2019		159
Notes		163
Selected Bibliography		185
Filmography		195
Index		205

Illustrations

2.1	*Algérie Tours/détours* (Oriane Brun-Moschetti and Leïla Morouche, 2006)	46
2.2	*The Battle of Algiers* (Gillo Pontecorvo, 1966)	47
2.3	*I Am 8 Years Old* (Les Graines de Sable, 1961)	50
2.4	*I Am 8 years Old* (Les Graines de Sable, 1961)	51
2.5	*China Is Still Far* (Malek Bensmaïl, 2008)	51
2.6	*Fidaï* (Damien Ounouri, 2012)	56
2.7	*Fidaï* (Damien Ounouri, 2012)	56
3.1	*The Intimate Enemy* (Florent-Emilio Siri, 2007)	64
3.2	*The Intimate Enemy* (Florent-Emilio Siri, 2007)	66
3.3	*The Intimate Enemy* (Florent-Emilio Siri, 2007)	68
3.4	*The Intimate Enemy* (Florent-Emilio Siri, 2007)	69
3.5	*The Intimate Enemy* (Florent-Emilio Siri, 2007)	72
3.6	*Djinns* (Hughes and Sandra Martin, 2010)	77
3.7	*Djinns* (Hughes and Sandra Martin, 2010)	84
4.1	*Chronicle of the Years of Fire* (Mohammed Lakhdar-Hamina, 1975)	92
4.2	*The Battle of Algiers* (Gillo Pontecorvo, 1966)	92
4.3	*Summer of '62* (Mehdi Charef, 2007)	97
4.4	*Summer of '62* (Mehdi Charef, 2007)	97
4.5	*Outside the Law* (Rachid Bouchareb, 2010)	107
4.6	*The Crazy Years of the Twist* (Mahmoud Zemmouri, 1986)	108
5.1	*Killer Instinct* (Jean-Paul Richet, 2008)	118
5.2	*Killer Instinct* (Jean-Paul Richet, 2008)	118
5.3	*Killer Instinct* (Jean-Paul Richet, 2008)	120
5.4	*Public Enemy No. 1* (Jean-Paul Richet, 2008)	125
5.5	*Public Enemy No. 1* (Jean-Paul Richet, 2008)	127
6.1	*So Young a Peace* (Jacques Charby, 1965)	136
6.2	*So Young a Peace* (Jacques Charby, 1965)	138
6.3	*So Young a Peace* (Jacques Charby, 1965)	139

6.4	*So Young a Peace* (Jacques Charby, 1965)	139
6.5	*So Young a Peace* (Jacques Charby, 1965)	140
6.6	*So Young a Peace* (Jacques Charby, 1965)	141
6.7	*So Young a Peace* (Jacques Charby, 1965)	142
6.8	*Bloody Beans* (Narimane Mari, 2013)	147
6.9	*Bloody Beans* (Narimane Mari, 2013)	148
6.10	*Bloody Beans* (Narimane Mari, 2013)	149

Acknowledgments

This book comes from a belief in healing collaborations and in solidarity with the individuals who persist in transgressing accepted norms. In this spirit, I declare my awe and appreciation to the following directors who offered me their honest opinions and valued time: Merzak Allouache, Malek Bensmaïl, Florent Emilio-Siri, Oriane Brun-Moschetti, Salem Brahimi, Philippe Faucon, Laurent Herbiet, Narimane Mari, Damien Ounouri.

I must express my overwhelming gratitude to the National Endowment for the Humanities, and more specifically to Joseph Krauss and Nabil Boudraa of Oregon State University in Corvallis, who with professionalism and generosity organized two summer institutes on the Maghreb in the arts. The enlightening lectures and conversations in these weeks generated intellectual projects and supportive friendships that increased the comprehension, subtlety, and rigor of my own research. My profound thanks to each of the scholars who contributed to this community and particularly Marie-Pierre Caquot-Baggett, Angelica DeAngelis, Patricia Goldsworthy-Bishop, Névine El Nossery, Amadou Fofana, and Bennet Schaber, who have been encouraging at all stages of this project. This monograph reveals the influence of Réda Bensmaïa, whose creativity and expertise will continue to inspire my research. Julia Clancy-Smith's vast knowledge and nonhierarchical lecture style revealed alternative approaches to me. James Le Sueur offered me advice and encouragement; these pages cite his incisive writing. Ahmed Bedjaoui holds a unique place in Algerian film history and his illuminating words provided privileged information that I could not otherwise access.

I taught at the University of Tennessee Knoxville for the majority of time spent writing this book and benefitted enormously from membership in a unique community of scholars who encourage one another. These professors instilled in me the self-confidence necessary to complete (not to mention begin) a book project, and I count myself extremely lucky to have profited from their interest, time, and genuine friendship. Christine Holmlund welcomed me warmly to a world of academic film scholarship, and Dan Magilow inspired my decision to work with Bloomsbury Books. Maria Stehle remains an example: her strength and joy comes from juggling all aspects of a complete life. Megan Brynson, Matt Bueler, Manuela Cebellos, Elodie Dabbagh Bueler, Noriko Horiguchi, and Anne-Hélène Miller listened compassionately to my mundane but real struggles during this time, and offered keen advice from their own successful endeavors. My friendship with Drew Paul comes from our shared scholarly interest in Middle Eastern cinema; our exchanges continue to shape my understanding of politics and film. I am also thankful to the University of Tennessee for funding several of my trips to France and Africa; Adrian Del Caro's belief in my scholarship's relevance made this possible.

My fascination with film's relationship to Algeria and France derives from my contact with the outstanding scholars at the Graduate Center in New York City. The wisdom and advice of Jonathan Buchsbaum, Amy Herzog, Marnia Lazreg, and Julia Przybos maintained my focus and grounded my efforts. I am truly grateful to Jerry Carlson whose belief in my abilities exceeded my own; his support has been unwavering.

Herrick Chapman read an earlier version of Chapter 2 for *French Politics, Culture, and Society*; his comments enhanced the complexity of my argument, and I am grateful to have had the journal's viewpoint. Mani Sharpe's wit and research shed light on new paths in French film scholarship; his suggestions to my manuscript were taken and I appreciate his time. My expression profits enormously from the film stills illustrating the chapters, and I thank the filmmaker Vasilios Papaioannu for perfecting these images. The exceptionally patient Bloomsbury Books offered me outstanding support. I would like to especially thank Laura Reeves—your confidence in the project made my work possible. It was a true pleasure to teach the inquisitive students of Syracuse University in a Spring 2018 seminar on the Algerian Revolution in literature; the class revealed a comprehension of the war's complexity and the importance of teaching the era, which urged me to complete the manuscript.

As the last paragraphs demonstrate, the personal and the professional for me have in many ways merged. I cannot express the depths of my gratitude to my mother Colleen Beth Hays; her research intersects with my own and our linked curiosity has inspired countless lengthy conversations and debates. How amazing that I can share this passion for knowledge with my mother. I am also fortunate to have the continued love and support of Erika Suffern and Sophie Saint-Just, friends that have, by extension, loved and supported my book. I thank my dad, Mark Wallenbrock, for his consistent confidence in this lengthy endeavor. Finally, the tenderness and innocence of my 7-year old son Guy maintained my faith in humanity throughout the entire process. I thank Guy for the fun that punctuated hours of quiet contemplation.

Introduction

Cinema reveals the contradictions and the ambivalence with which one finds the memory of the Algerian Revolution (1954–62), the last French war of decolonization. Twenty-first-century films depicting and alluding to the Algerian Revolution seek to fill gaps in the public imaginary that were dug by public and government censors. The films that this book discusses determine that the war be associated with independence group fratricide, napalm bombing, atomic bomb tests, French police and military torture, in addition to massacres. As a discourse, the films declare that these facts should not be elided either from film history or from the public imagination. In this way, recent Algerian and French films concerning the war both symbolize and overtly represent an international memory process. Such a cinematographic approach to international history confuses what are distinct and yet collapsing borders in time and space.

Two highly publicized statements from 2017 introduce our film corpus by exposing a current of both judgment and exoneration in today's memory of the Franco-Algerian War. In a publicity tour for a collection of his articles, Algerian journalist and Goncourt-winning novelist, Kamel Daoud revealed his modern approach toward Algerian history: "I have enormous respect for the martyrs, for our elders, those who fought so that I would be free, free to speak, but we must also exit History to assume our present. To honor them, we must exercise our liberties."[1] Daoud's statement reverberates with that of the soon-to-be president of France, Emmanuel Macron, who apologized for colonization and noted its paradoxical rapport with the foundational French government document, the Declaration of the Rights of Man and of the Citizen: "Colonization is part of French history. It's a crime, it's a crime against humanity, it's a real barbary. And that is part of this past that we must look at directly, presenting our apologies in regard to those against whom we have committed these acts. But at the same time, we cannot sweep away all of this past. And I don't regret that because there is a nice formula that describes Algeria: France instated the Rights of Man in Algeria. Only it forgot to read them."[2]

In these statements, both public figures attempt and fail to escape the prism of history. The quotes above, delivered during France's 2017 presidential election turmoil, describe and encourage a larger international ambivalence that includes all media that seek to recover the horrific past of the Algerian Revolution. Whether it be the once censored October 17, 1961 Paris Massacre as found in *Caché* (Michael Haneke, 2005)[3] and *Hors-la-loi* (*Outside the Law,* Rachid Bouchareb, 2010), or the psychological turmoil of the French soldiers who did in fact torture and kill in Algeria as in *Djinns* (*Stranded,* Hughes and Sandra Martin, 2010) and *L'Ennemi intime* (*The Intimate Enemy,* Florent-Emilio Siri, 2007), a paradoxical confrontation with past representations dominates visual texts that seek to admit and admonish national myths. As Daoud resolves "to assume the present" and Macron "to apologize," the public figures seek new partnerships between Algeria and France, an approach that governs many of these twenty-first-century films—not only do transnational production details demonstrate this tendency, but also the plots evoke severed friendships between Algerians and the French during warfare as shown in *Cartouches Gauloises* (*Summer of '62,* Mehdi Charef, 2007) and *Loubia Hamra* (*Bloody Beans,* Narimane Mari, 2013). By parsing wide-ranging film matter (from documentary, to gangster, to experimental) made within the same seven-year period, *The Franco-Algerian War through a Twenty-First Century Lens: Film and History* illustrates film's cultural currency, a format of exchange and dialogue between the young nation and its former oppressor. As such, this post-postcolonial film discourse locates a tenuous reliance on a tumultuous past, a notion that can be extrapolated to understand more generally the negotiations made in media between former colonies and their once empires.

"France Instated the Rights of Man in Algeria. Only It Forgot to Read Them"

The paradox within Macron's description of France's relationship to Algeria adheres directly to this body of cinema, namely films that seek to deny their ineffaceable affiliation and aim to expose the hypocrisies of Algeria's war of independence. Undeniably, Macron's campaign speech in Algeria belies a political maneuver; the future president wished to distinguish himself from his predecessor, François Hollande, who had made significant progress with Algeria after Nicolas Sarkozy, but who did not apologize for France's behavior. However, in consideration of his ultimate victory, Macron's strong anticolonial statement signifies the growth of a discourse within French mainstream thought and media (eclipsing but not eradicating the significant extremist right-wing movement). Macron posits that *liberté égalité et fraternité,* precepts of the Declaration of the Rights of Man and of the Citizen, signify universal values. Yet in the same sentence, Macron employs barbary, a word laden with classical etymology, to describe France's actions that were disguised with such global truths. *Barbar,* the word used by Romans to describe the foreign and the uncivilized, has specific resonance in France's conquer of Algeria; in fact, in 1833, after visiting Algeria, a member of the investigating committee reversed the term's once intended subject, "we have gone further than the barbary of the *Barbares* that we came to civilize."[4] To this extent, Macron's call to study France's past crimes from the present demands an unearthing of the atrocity of historical acts, without forgetting the Republican ideals mislaid at its core. This understanding of the French colonization of Algeria and the French military's participation in the Algerian Revolution begs the public to balance such errors with a broader view of civilization. Macron thus advances colonization as an aspect of French history, but fails to address its specific legacy in Algeria. Such an interstitial space lodged between recognition and denial of the Other, which reads the present and past simultaneously, suggests the unique French productions analyzed in Chapter 3, The Specter of Torture and Atomic Bombs: *L'Ennemi intime* (*The Intimate Enemy*, Florent-Emilio Siri, 2007) and *Djinns* (*Stranded,* Hughes and Sandra Martin, 2010), as well as in Chapter 5, A Scission in the Memory of the Franco-Algerian War: *Mesrine Part I: L'Instinct de Mort* (*The Killer Instinct*), *Part II: L'Ennemi Public No. 1* (*Public Enemy No.1*, Jean-Paul Richet, 2008). These overtly male-centered French films proffer an explanation for the military violence and lessen the severity of blame by presenting the trauma of war on the French psyche.

"We Must Also Exit History to Assume Our Present"

By situating Kamel Daoud's statement next to that of Emmanuel Macron, we find a revision of the Algerian Revolution's symbolism and the need to free individual expression from the tropes of the Algerian government's sponsored and controlled depictions. Daoud promotes an exercise of liberties, which he has won through Francophone expression and a rapport with the French canon. In fact, his novel *Meursault contre-enquête* (*The Meursault Investigation*), which won the most celebrated French literary prize, the Prix Goncourt,[5] responds and references *L'Etranger* (*The Stranger*) by the French-Algerian author,[6] Albert Camus.[7] Following *The Meursault Investigation*'s publication, a Salafist imam in Algeria issued a fatwa against Daoud because of his protagonist's critique of Islam.[8] Like Macron, Daoud speaks of departing from a historical legacy, yet invokes the Algerian-French past in his writing and interviews, demonstrating colonial history's inescapability. A similar temporal dynamic predominates the films covered in Chapter 2, The Algerian Revolution in Three Transnational Documentaries: *Algérie Tours/detours* (Oriane Brun-Moschetti and Leïla Morouche, 2006), *La Chine est encore loin* (*China Is Still Far*, Malek Bensmaïl, 2008), and *Fidaï* (Damien Ounouri, 2012), as these features expose contemporary Algeria's struggle with the fading past, a state-led mythology entangled in a web of memory that film documents. Chapter 4, Reclaiming the Screen Algerian Revolution: *Cartouches Gauloises* (*Summer of '62*, Mehdi Charef, 2006), *Hors-la-loi* (*Outside the Law*, Rachid Bouchareb, 2010), and *Les Folles années du twist* (*The Crazy Years of the Twist*, Mahmoud Zemmouri, 1986), also finds Algerian cinema within a broader transnational compromise that aligns with Daoud's ambiguous statement; respect for the atrocity of the Algerian Revolution does not prevent revolt against the tropes of its national representation. Finally, the monograph's last chapter, Chapter 6, The Revolution through Utopian Dialectics: *Une si jeune paix* (*So Young a Peace*, Jacques Charby, 1965) and *Loubia Hamra* (*Bloody Beans*, Narimane Mari, 2013), illustrates the magnitude of ways in which the two quotes conceivably intermingle by pairing an artfilm starring children on the Algerian beach with the first fiction Algerian film that stars Algerian orphans. *Bloody Beans*' utopian portrayal of Algeria relies on a symbolic representation of the Revolution, and historical signage empowers and liberates such a futuristic vision. In this way, the Algerian contributions to the corpus suggest what the work of Malika Rahal also determines in Algeria: "the confusion between 'history' and 'the history of independence.'"[9] However, the Algerian-French coproductions mitigate the perception of the war, even when upholding the official history. Furthermore, my final chapter proffers *Bloody Beans* as a creative lens through which to view the Algerian Revolution, arguing that cinema projects possibilities from the present on past wars.

As this brief investigation of such rich quotes indicates, Emmanuel Macron and Kamel Daoud, political icons in varying degrees, tap into a powerful historical query that cannot be extracted from its contemporary context. The Mediterranean Sea that separates Algeria from France cannot be crossed without traversing the historical warring that for so many years defined their distance and proximity. For this reason, I often employ the vocabulary of Gilles Deleuze and Félix Guattari (deterritorialization and reterritorialization, the rhizome, and the body without organs) as well as the work of Réda Bensmaïa that reveals the Algerian significance of these post-structural theories.[10] David Harvey's *Spaces of Hope* also geographically informs my final chapter,[11] for through the study of an experimental film I perceive of the war's representation. These concepts facilitate our navigation through the portrayal of a past war that demands fluid travel in time and space. Varying gradations of cinematic groundlessness reveal and secure an evolution in historical comprehension, demonstrating the weight of the Algerian Revolution on the contemporary consciousness, and the new efforts to visually purge and alleviate the toll of this load.

The Algerian Revolution remains a potent symbol in cinema, as it does in Algerian-French relations and their portrayal in the press. However, the twenty-first century brings significant changes to such symbolism of pain, loss, and power. Over half a century later, post memory, multidirectional memory, and immigration transport a once national discourse into a realm of international memories, a field that blurs the once easily read chronology and geographic borders. Cinema participates, reflects, and encourages such paradigm shifts in the popular comprehension of history. Most of the films I have included represent such international undertakings that parse the growing distance from the particular traumatic memory of the Algerian Revolution with the flashback device, documentary footage of the war, and/or verbal descriptions of witnesses filmed in the present day. Cinema remains an expensive art form, as such productions and their reception demonstrate cultural tastes as well as economic interests. Scholars thus may view war in the popular imagination through film—a particularly challenging task when concerning Algeria, whose government still controls most aspects of cinema. It is important to note that this monograph does not undertake the Algerian state–produced biopics of revolutionary generals.[12] Instead my monograph exposes films that challenge a previous, national narrative—whether they are French films that emphasize the post-trauma of veterans or are coproductions that present Algerian-French friendships. In fact this corpus reflects a multitude of revelations in the popular understanding of the war's history.

For this reason, it is imperative to begin any study of twenty-first-century Algerian-French relations with a review of the past. As a reference, I have included a timeline that briefly describes events in Algerian and French history that can be and are referred to in the films and in my writing. This document may be helpful when considering the years of the Algerian Revolution, but equally important when probing the specific time-period of a film's production. The first chapter then outlines the general currents of twentieth-century film's relationship to the memory of the Algerian Revolution in order to better contextualize a contemporary dialogue in the subsequent chapters, as well as its transgressive nature.

Until very recently, many scholars suggested that French cinema of the 1950s ignored the "events" or "*événements*" taking place abroad and thus failed to chart the new wave's involvement with its political historical surroundings. In fact, the environment of the censor and the unsaid bred an underground film culture that confronted the logic of the status quo. Furthermore, what became known as *le cinéma parallèle* with clandestine screenings played an essential role in building antiwar sentiment in France. Many French filmmakers (such as René Vautier, Yves Boisset, Pierre Clement, and Jacques Panijel) identified their work with the ideological plea argued by theorists such as Jean-Paul Sartre and Frantz Fanon. In this way, I argue that the work of James Le Sueur and Robert Malley,[13] which demonstrates the influence of French thought on Algerian patriotism, can be extrapolated and applied equally to the militant films of the period. This first chapter thus demonstrates that cinema was indeed part of a political machine whose ideology was determined by the French-trained theorists.

In Chapter 1, I amend Paul Silverstein's term "transpolitics"[14] (the ways in which events and grassroots activism in one country influence the history of another) as "transcinema" in order to discuss twentieth-century depictions of the war. While transcinema largely dominates depictions of the Algerian Revolution in the twentieth-century cinema of Algeria and France, the twenty-first century brings a new era of collaboration and partnership that reviews the painful past and its representations. Although the following chapters do not chronologically study the films of 2000–2015, the films as a grouping exemplify the shift from nationalist portrayals of war toward the transnational, an interest facilitated by immigration and travel between the former colonizer and the former French territory, a virtual impossibility in the 1990s.

The work of Nicolas Bancel and Pascal Blanchard, in particular their chronological categories for the French memory of the Algerian Revolution, situate the French films and their viewers within a particular episteme of confrontation with the absence of past representations—they write that post-2002 the war is "visible and recurrent at the core of French society."[15] Yet despite this chronological understanding of the memory, I have not chosen each of Chapter 2 through Chapter 6's pairings for their seven-year enclosure (2006–13). Rather I have selected counterparts that reveal one another as filmic forces of memory and invention. In fact, I initially conceived of the project as an exposure of the discourse that followed the trial of Maurice Papon (1997) and the historical reflection of the torture during the Algerian Revolution made public again by Benjamin Stora (1991)[16] and Raphaelle Branche (1998),[17] as well as by General Paul Aussaresses who defended his use of the technique in 1999.[18]

Despite the unintentionality in my process, my corpus' film-production years present a challenge to Article 4 of the 2005 law that asked French teachers to promote a more positive image of North African colonization, a dismissal that is most radically upheld by Algerian-French coproductions that present the Algerian Revolution with what may be perceived as pedagogical aims, for example, *Summer of '62* (2007) and *Outside the Law* (2010). The riots of 2005 in France, which reestablished the state of emergency (which had not been imposed in France since the Algerian Revolution), exposed the economic and educational disparity for those of African origin in France. With the reopening of Algeria to French visitors after a gruesome civil war referred to by many as the Black Decade (1991–9), Algerian-French coproductions are again viable. A collaborative cinematic investigation of the Revolution became possible, and *La Trahison* (*The Betrayal*, Phillippe Faucon, 2005) was the first Algerian-French picture filmed in Algeria to follow the Black Years. The aging Algerians who fought and/or who were subjected to abuse during the Revolution as well the French veterans who had battled, tortured, and/or been imprisoned were then mediatized in reports and documentaries. My study of the individual films demonstrates that the public interest in France supported productions, while box-office support was less favorable. Nonetheless, the entrance of the Franco-Algerian War as a current of twenty-first-century viewership represents a grappling with history and post-trauma. The specific years (2006–13) of my corpus emblematize the Franco-Algerian War in transnational partnerships and genre films and a specific interest in depicting post-trauma. However, references to documentaries and films that were made at the end of the twentieth century and at the beginning of the twenty-first century (before 2006) also provide insight and indicate an international memory process.

In many ways, the first two chapters are companions, the three experimental documentaries, *Algérie Tours/detours* (2006), *China Is Still Far* (2008), and *Fidaï* (2012), analyzed in Chapter 2, directly reference films from the Algerian Revolution era. Each documentary pivots on the question of the transnational, all three documentaries have funding from both Algeria and France, and *Fidaï* has additional funding from China and Qatar. Furthermore, all three indicate the negotiations and challenges of filming for a largely European public with the consent of the governmental authority, largely built on the Revolution and the invocation of its memory. In this way, the three films together demonstrate the distinct limitations of such Algerian-French coproductions; we find history exposed and questioned and a boundary line drawn. The experimental nature of the films and their individual interest in locating the Revolution of nearly fifty years past in contemporary Algeria easily suggests the rhizome, a term taken from plant life by Gilles Deleuze and Félix Guattari to define a formless being or object. Each film slips between Algeria and France either in funding and/or in narrative, and all three expose the task of elderly veterans and witnesses who educate a largely ignorant and growing youth populace. These three experimental documentaries with transnational funding evoke a unique early twenty-first-century perspective of the war, rhizomatic in its blurring of chronology and geographic space.

Chapter 3 shifts to study two uniquely French productions set during the Franco-Algerian War, but filmed in Morocco. The chapter negotiates the general knowledge of military policy in France in the twenty-first century with forgiveness for the young soldiers who committed criminal behavior under orders and duress. The films narrativize the descent from altruism into torture and/or murderous activity, but also evoke the psychological turmoil that torments soldiers after committing such heinous acts (excused to an extent by grief, alcohol, and/or previously being tortured in Indochina). In the case of *Djinns*, the French atomic bomb tests in the Sahara weigh heavily and abstractly on the actions of the soldiers.[19] While the soldiers of the film remain ignorant of the government's secret plans, dreams and intercuts preview what will occur. The same post-traumatic stress disorder that affects the torturing soldiers of *The Intimate Enemy*, here transforms into a ghostly presence. These jinns, created through digital animation and who appear as smoky outlines, rewrite the Franco-Algerian War and the atomic bomb tests as a horror film. The legacy of the bombs and Franco-Algerian War guilt then cinematically translates into the fantasy-horror genre, indicating popular culture's discomfort with this history, which results in an ambivalent, if distressed, confrontation. Although the film portrays the aura of secrecy surrounding the atomic tests of 1960, few details emerge.

Chapter 4 continues to draw on the theory of Gilles Deleuze and Félix Guattari, previously discussed in Chapter 2. However, as mentioned earlier, I integrate Réda Bensmaïa's discussion of deterritorialization and reterritorialization from *Experimental Nations* to describe the postcolonial Maghreb.[20] French colonial rule had forced the departure of many Algerians from their homes and claimed most ancestral territories. The war of decolonization only compounded the difficulties of Algerians as French troops placed many families in shantytowns and men in prisoner work camps. Such rootlessness became the reason behind reterritorialization; Algerians inhabited what were once French homes and state buildings as an act of reclaiming their land. Furthermore, the dramatic recapitulation of a historic deterritorialization played a powerful, narrative role in the reterritorialization of cinema. Not only did the onset of cinema coincide and bolster an imperial project, the majority of films shown in pre-Revolution Algeria were European and American. Abdelghani Megherbi writes of colonial cinema in Algeria: "Conforming to the implacable logic of colonization, the Algerian is almost absent throughout. Whether it be in the core of the movie theater public, or at the core of the profession itself."[21] Independence demanded that Algerians assert their ownership of their film territory.

A detailed explanation of the deterritorialization and reterritorialization inherent in early Algerian cinema provides a greater understanding of twenty-first-century transnational productions that reference and reestablish their own reterritorializing dynamic. *Summer of '62* by Mehdi Charef departs from the negative portrayals of the French found generally in Algerian cinema and overwhelmingly in Algerian depictions of the Revolution. The tender age of the protagonist of *Summer of '62* permits him access to the French language and French children at school, where he appears to be the only Algerian in attendance. In addition, his employment, delivering groceries and newspapers, further exposes him to French friends and perspectives that have largely been absent from Algerian depictions of the Revolution. In this way, Charef revisits the *moudjahid* cinema with stylistic and thematic impulses that derive from exposure to French cinema and French people. *Summer of '62* presents the trauma of deterritorialization and the Algerian euphoria of liberation, but emphasizes friendships between Algerians and Europeans and their subsequent loss. Made several years later, Rachid Bouchareb's *Outside the Law* begins economically and historically from a different point. Filmed four years after his extremely successful film *Indigènes* (*Days of Glory*, 2006), and starring the same box office stars, the film continues to be the most expensive depiction of the Algerian Revolution. Yet similar themes of deterritorialization and reterritorialization prevail. An analysis of Mahmoud Zemmouri's *The Crazy Years of the Twist* (1986) complements a study of such twenty-first-century works, for the comedy refuses to adhere to previous Algerian cinema aesthetics. Comparing Zemmouri's depiction of the Revolution with his twenty-first-century counterparts (Bouchareb and Charef maintain a residence in France; Zemmouri died in Paris in 2017), we locate a brief moment in which rebellion against the state narrative was possible. *Summer of '62* and *Outside the Law* represent an amended version of the Algerian film revolution, that is, transnational twenty-first-century productions permitting French people and France new cinematic roles in an Algerian partnership.

Chapter 3 concerns uniquely French productions. However, the influence of an Algerian-immigrant sentiment (Abdel Raouf Dafri, a second-generation Algerian, penned the scenario) weighs heavily on the diptych biopic thriller discussed in the chapter. The gangster genre presents France's most famous criminal Jacques Mesrine (1930–79), whose life is molded by his service in the Franco-Algerian War. The gangster-genre formula thus permits an early twenty-first-century perspective of the Franco-Algerian War that reflects and contradicts previous interpretations of the torture and racism surrounding the conflict. For this reason, Jacques Derrida's terms *scission* and *circumcision* provide a useful lens through which to view the cultural changes presented in the films;[22] the diptych depicts the main character's changing relationship to Algeria, a paradigm of the French imaginary.

The last chapter of this volume, Chapter 6, investigates the seldom studied first Algerian fiction film, *So Young a Peace* (Jacques Charby, 1965), before examining the experimental twenty-first-century feature with a similar premise, *Bloody Beans* (Narimane Mari, 2013). Both films star children who reenact the Algerian Revolution. *So Young a Peace* specifically casts orphans and depicts their struggles to overcome their trauma through battles against one another; *Bloody Beans* finds a group of Algerian children dwelling on the beach, before they steal food from the French military in order to assuage their hunger. Whether the children are on the soccer field, at the orphanage, in the cemetery, or in the forest, *So Young a Peace* frames the child cast within borders that limit their exploration. Thus, the geographical concept of heterotopia describes early independent Algerian visual aesthetics, in which the children's interactions represent a micro society. On the other hand, *Bloody Beans* explodes such notions of enclosed space and instead reveals what geographer David Harvey labels spatiotemporal utopian dialectics. For example, the memory of such fixed notions of time and space present in allusions *So Young a Peace* now dialogues with the broad expanse of ocean and beach. To this extent, Chapter 6 provides a very optimistic ending to my study: by concluding my film analyses with a low-budget, transnational, experimental film, I indicate the vast future of Algerian Revolution representations. When filmmakers employ symbols previously wrought with pain to represent nature and freedom, the cinematic possibilities are endless.

I chose these specific films for their confrontation of history and their criticism of a previous nationalist discourse. The renewed representation of torture during the Franco-Algerian War reflects the twenty-first century's understanding of post-trauma and a French nation grappling with the results of what we can now label criminality. Algerian-French transnational cinema proffers a judgment partnership, finding the nations united in an attempt to bring the truth of the war to a shared public. Nevertheless, we find an inherent compromise in all revelations concerning history. Cinema with its endless possibilities also suffers from the constraints of the screen and financing—big budget pictures that pursue a large public may have very different goals than independent features, while films aiming for Algerian government funding also may make negotiations. Taking these differences into account, *The Franco-Algerian War through a Twenty-First Century Lens: Film and History* generally exposes brave confrontations with past myths as well as the paradoxes that occur when visualizing the past from the present. As my final words of introduction, and in consolidation of the two opposing opinions that opened the book, each of the ten early twenty-first-century films studied in this monograph assumes the present while looking at the past. However, this light from the present both elucidates and obscures our direct view of history.

1

The Twentieth-Century Screen Geography of the Franco-Algerian War

There has been considerable academic reflection on cinematic depictions of the Algerian Revolution in the twentieth century (largely in association with the historical interest in the time period and its consequences in contemporary France).[1] However, Algerian and French depictions of the shared war have been studied separately. Generally speaking, Algerian cinema and French cinema have been critiqued as independent entities, in large part because they did work autonomously in the twentieth century. The Algerian government pursued the *moudjahid* or freedom-fighter cinema and filmed in Algeria, while the most well-known features by French new wave directors that addressed the Algerian Revolution—Jean-Luc Godard's *Le Petit Soldat* (*The Little Soldier*) filmed in 1959 and censored until 1963 and Alain Resnais's *Muriel ou le temps d'un retour* (*Muriel or the Time of Return*) also released in 1963—were filmed and set in Europe with European actors. In league with both governments' postcolonial Mediterranean maps, one finds few efforts to locate the ties between the two countries' portrayals, and little exploration of a latent awareness of one another's cinematic presence.

Yet on closer examination we find a history of productions between Algerian and French people: René Vautier's and Pierre Clément's leadership in the FLN's (Front de libération nationale) early cinematic endeavors, 1980s' *auteurs* living in France and yet funded by the FLN—such as novelist and filmmaker Assia Djebar, and actor and director Mahmoud Zemmouri—are just a few examples this chapter explores. Such twentieth-century films elude a coproduction label, as their funding, target audience, and/or cast and crew were national. Nonetheless, these films represent an effort to expose the complications of the revolutionary era and/or employ the apparatus to include the ideas and opinions of the Other. In brief, this chapter reviews the various ways in which the Franco-Algerian War was cinematically depicted before 2000. However, in coalition with the following chapters' emphasis on coproductions, I underline the ways in which the two nations' vision of the war era reveals partnerships and, even when antagonistic, a cinematic conversation.

Consequently, the term "transpolitics," coined by Paul A. Silverstein, applies to the relationship between the nations' cinemas in the twentieth century. Silverstein's 2004 sociological study *Algeria in France: Transpolitics, Race, and Nation* reveals how activities that take place exclusively in one nation reverberate and extend to political events in the other—the shared history and geographic proximity of Algeria and France exemplify such tensions. During Silverstein's period of study, the Algerian Civil War (roughly 1992–2002) notably affected opinion and policy toward Islam and immigrants in France—the Islamic headscarf, the construction of mosques, and the like. Reversing this power dynamic, Silverstein also finds the Algerian communities in France largely inspired the Berber movement in Algeria (and the Berber Spring of 1980 in particular). Silverstein writes, "The processes of collusion and contention, of appropriation and transformation, that link Algeria and France—Algerians and Franco-Algerians—constitute what I refer to as *transpolitics*."[2] Such a concept transcends the transnational, for in these historic examples, Algerians and French citizens are not obviously partnering a final project that blurs their national distinctions. Instead the brutal legacy of colonization and its memory link the two nations' consciousness, resulting in distinct political acts that evoke an internalization of events abroad.

As we consider films as political acts in and of themselves, we find an awareness of the former colony/of the former colonizer bleeding into the national imaginary, and integral to both nations' portrayals of their shared war. In the struggle to cinematically depict the eight years of warfare in the twentieth century, Algeria and France assessed one another's cinematic output. The damning insider portraits of the French military, *Avoir 20 ans dans les Aurès* (*To Be 20 in the Aurès*, René Vautier) and *R.A.S.* (*Nothing to Report*, Yves Boisset) were released respectively in France in 1972 and 1973 in part refuting the war-era censor. These small productions prepared Europe for an Algerian film, Mohammed Lakhdar-Hamina's *Chronique des années de braise* (*Chronicle of the Years of Fire*, 1975); although financed and produced by the Algerian state, the film garnered a European public by entering the festival circuit and winning the Palme d'Or at Cannes Film Festival. Such lightly sketched examples illustrate transcinema, citing Silverstein's transpolitics as a point of departure. This twentieth-century international film-dialogue between Algeria and France can be read as epistolary—space and exclusion inform national responses. Nevertheless, both Algerian and French films concerning the Algerian Revolution depend on one another for contestation and/or motivation, revealing traces of one another even when scarcely touching. Again, when reading films as political acts, we expose cinema's pivotal role in the transpolitical realm, most obviously in concerns of immigration; both the growing Algerian population of France and the departed European population of Algeria find significant expression in national cinemas that cross and contaminate. Undoubtedly, the transcinema between Algeria and France in the twentieth century and its evolution toward the twenty-first merit their own book-length investigation. Nonetheless, this chapter's investigation of Franco-Algerian transcinema (or the ways in which films of one nation affect the mood and portrayals by the other) imparts a chronological outline that introduces the following chapters' study of early twenty-first-century films.

This chapter unearths a foundation of both exchange and dissidence, one that hints at the broader revelations that soon advance and consume the Franco-Algerian War in the popular imaginary. During this half-century, cinema's mapping of the Algerian Revolution guards a Mediterranean border, while the films' existence and response to one another simultaneously suggest a courier passage. In order to situate transcinema within an ideological history, we will first view Jean-Paul Sartre's influence on understandings and portrayals of the Revolution. I then move from the beginnings of independent Algerian cinema to chronologically expose productions key to the exchange and evolution of the symbolic Algerian Revolution. The few exceptional productions and individuals of the twentieth century that bridge national barriers (either through funding, setting, or casting) pave the way for the war's twenty-first-century screen cartography, a grouping largely determined by immigration that seeks to merge memories and terrains.

During the War

The SCA and the Censor

France's military provided television and news reel coverage through the SCA (Service cinématographique de l'armée), in both French-Algeria and France.[3] The SCA created propaganda films in order to present the draft as pacific—footage of soldiers offering food and health care services to Algerian children was common. The SCA films denied the violence of the French military by singularly representing the French military's benevolence toward Algerians. As Benjamin Stora stresses by employing the second-person pronoun, a personal interaction with the French public took place in these moving images that sought to bolster French national identification and pride: "French soldiers had but the uniform of the soldier ... one always sees them caring, constructing, teaching ... The legend explains: 'You are the best elements of contact with the population.'"[4] Through carefully constructed and selected footage, the French government largely controlled the warfare from reaching global mainstream media circuits; as ambassadors of goodwill, the young French men appeared as the viewers' idealized likeness, in stark contrast to the blurred Algerian population, who appeared poor and foreign, virtual props for the French military. The films were not only produced for French consumption, they also aimed to indoctrinate Algerians. Equipped *cinébuses* (discussed in Chapter 2) would tour the Algerian countryside projecting appropriate SCA films to educate and tame the rural population.

In this manner, the SCA reinforced *la commission de contrôle* (or censor), which helped to ensure French public support by banning any media that exposed or questioned the violence of French involvement, and whose decrees became increasingly strict when General Charles De Gaulle returned to presidency in 1958.[5] In fact, during the conflict, Fox Movietone diffused the only moving images of warfare in Algeria, but exclusively for an American public.[6] Although the censor always aimed to control straying French morals and youth culture, its primary goal after World War II was to eradicate any trace of Vichy support. While the Fifth Republic created a ministry of culture headed by author André Malraux that encouraged the new wave financially by basing government funding less on box office receipts, the *commission de contrôle* restricted the new artists' creative impulses, as a pre-censor review of scripts banned any possible portrayal of the recent events in Algeria. Metaphor also incited censorship, as in the case of *Moranbong, une aventure coréenne* (*Moranbong, a Korean Adventure,* Jean-Claude Bonnardot, 1959), which was banned until 1963. The censor also banned two films set during World War II due to parallels to the contemporary draft and desertion: *Les Honneurs de la guerre* (*The Honors of the War*, Jean Dewer, 1960) and *Tu ne tueras point* (*Thou Shalt Not Kill*, Claude Autant-Lara, 1961).[7]

An underground press ignited the French movement for Algerian independence, and the cinema linked to such literary currents and against the censor emerged as part and parcel of the anticolonial French voice. Perhaps the most successful of such literature was *La Question*[8] a pro-independence journalist's account of torture (and survival) at the hands of the French military in Algeria.[9] The shocking truth of French military torture sold over 60,000 copies in its first two weeks before being banned and confiscated, an act that only increased public interest in the short book.[10] Nevertheless, by the end of 1958, many French homes owned copies of *La Question*, while the scandal had made the text and its claims familiar to the general public. Journals such as *Les Temps modernes* and *Vérité liberté* as well as *El Moudjahid* (the smuggled French language FLN newspaper in which the psychoanalyst from Martinique turned theorist Frantz Fanon wrote) inspired many *porteurs de valises*—the term commonly employed for the French who secretly transported money to the FLN. Furthermore, the reports depicting the French military's heinous behavior abroad posed larger questions to French history, interrogating the roots and reasoning of colonialism. Such a clandestine press through its printing, distribution, and purchase represented a cluster of anticensor/antistate acts.

A French philosophical approach largely influenced by Jean-Paul Sartre informed the Algerian independence position and permeated the clandestine press, and thus a brief investigation into their legacy informs our reading of Algerian twentieth-century film and its dialogue with French productions depicting the war. In *Uncivil War: Intellectuals and Identity Politics during the Decolonization of Algeria*, James Le Sueur demonstrates that French thought's contribution to the Algerian independence movement and the eventual government ideology did not in fact represent all aspects of the Algerian population. (Although Frantz Fanon was from Martinique, Le Sueur includes him in this grouping; Fanon's work displays the influence of Jean-Paul Sartre and Fanon received his doctorate in psychology in France.) Jean-Paul Sartre first developed his use of the term the Other in his seminal philosophical work *L'Être et le néant: essai d'ontologie phénoménologique* (*Being and Nothingness*). According to Sartre, the Other's differences from the Self in part construct one's self-image. For example, Sartre writes in consideration of the Other's body, "The Other moves within limits which appear within immediate connection with his movements and which are the terms within which I cause the meaning of these movements to be indicated to myself."[11] In this citation, the Self formulates the meaning of the Other's actions, and those interpretations then color one's self-view.

A few years later, the concept of the Other and Self transferred easily to questions of racism in *Réflexions sur la question juive* (*The Anti-Semite and the Jew*, 1946), a model that could then be adapted to refer to Algeria. Le Sueur describes this transfer, "Finally, the unsuccessful attempt to achieve reconciliation between the French and Algerian people encouraged French intellectuals such as Sartre to use the most radical notion of identity, the concept of the Other, as both an analytical tool and political ploy."[12] In these essays by Sartre, as well as in the work of Frantz Fanon and the Tunisian author

Albert Memmi, a binary of colonizer/colonized dominates, a division that sought to inspire political action. Sartre's essays directly aim to convince a French public, and thus employ *nous* or we, establishing a colonizer within the Self to be eradicated;[13] the decolonization of colonies thus imparts a decolonization of the colonizer.[14] On the other hand, Fanon identifies himself as a colonized, and his use of *nous* demonstrates his solidarity with Algerians. One easily locates Sartre's philosophical approach in Fanon's call to action. In *L'An V de la Révolution Algérienne* (*A Dying Colonialism*), Fanon's reference to the "conscience of the colonized," and "his perception of the colonizer,"[15] evoke the previous description of the movements of the Other in *Being and Nothingness*. Sartre often combines the entrepreneurs of the metropole and French-Algerians as a counter to Algerians, which he and Fanon term "*le peuple*," throughout their anticolonial texts concerning Algeria. For example, Sartre writes in consideration of the imminent Fifth Republic, "Parisian capitalists, land owners of Algeria … Still agree on one point: muzzle the people."[16] In summary of Le Sueur's thesis, the theorists virtually ignore the multiplicity of voices and cultures within Algeria and the Revolution. To this extent, Le Sueur writes that the theorists disregard the majority of violence done by the Algerian nationalists as such acts "could be interpreted (and therefore justified) as a legitimate response to the capitalist West."[17]

The focus of *Uncivil War* remains most obviously in the print discourse surrounding the Revolution and the ways in which the former colony and colonizer affected Algerian mood and action. However, film contributed and proved relevant; films made in war, often developed at laboratories in East Germany and Yugoslavia, attracted local and international support.[18] Like the whole of the independence movement, Algeria's burgeoning film industry adopted French theory as a tool to awaken the revolutionary spirit—both in the early short, galvanizing, films and later in the Algerian state films that enforced a patriotic memory of the Revolution. The contribution by French individuals to such pro-Algerian independence films, as well as their clandestine screenings, reveals the interlacing of French and Algerian efforts.

Jean-Paul Sartre and René Vautier

Highlighting the similarities between perhaps the twentieth century's best-known theorist and the lesser-known first anticolonial filmmaker reveals the underground French cinema as the filmic embodiment of the era's anticolonial ideology. Indeed, such a comparison is not superfluous; both Franco-French men from the metropole were celebrated as African due to their cross-continental involvement and influence. Though Sartre's collaborative work with Frantz Fanon is well known, he contributed largely to the recognition of Leopold Senghor and other African writers in France through his association with the press, *Présence Africaine*.[19] The novel *La Nausée* (*Nausea*, 1938) and the play *Huis clos* (*No Exit*, 1944) best represent Jean-Paul Sartre's place in the canon. However, V. Y. Mudimbé the celebrated Congolese poet and philosopher refers to Sartre's *Orphée Noire* (*Black Orpheus*, 1948) that publicized and extolled the *négritude* movement,[20] as the shroud.[21] In fact, Mudimbé went as far as to call Sartre an African philosopher.[22] Likewise, Vautier became known as the *papa du cinema algérien* for his pioneering role in the nation's cinema, though he made over twenty films that promote causes as diverse as the decolonization of Africa, Breton identity, feminism, and labor rights.[23] Vautier played a formative role in Algeria, not only by directing films concerning the country's Revolution (*Une nation Algérie* [*A Nation Algeria*], 1954;[24] *Algérie en flammes* [*Algeria in Flames*], 1958) but also by heading the first cinema agency (Groupe Farid) of GPRA (Gouvernement Provisoire de la Révolution Algérienne), which among other tasks trained Algerians who lacked previous film experience. These two activists should be considered together for their influence and investment in Third-World *auteurs*. However, most importantly, the pairing emphasizes that a film movement developed in tandem with the intellectual rebellion in print, and both mediums were dependent on clandestine trade. In addition, a French education informs the anticolonial philosophical stance integral to works by Sartre and Vautier that influenced Algeria (and other emerging nations). In such a way, we locate the colonizer's thought and culture within the cry of independence. In spite of their age difference of twenty-three years (Sartre [1905–80], Vautier [1928–2015]), biographical details also reveal similarities, demonstrating that those attending and participating in the underground cinema movement functioned as part of the same anti-colonial current.

Michael Rothberg's *Multidirectional Memory: Remembering the Holocaust in the Age of Decolonization* demonstrates that the wars of decolonization drew parallels to the recent wounds of the Holocaust, as the events in Algeria further deepened scars caused by racism and nationalism. This generation, which had lived through both eras, disclosed both directly and indirectly the commonalities in war techniques and philosophical queries. A consideration of René Vautier's life and films equally presents such a network of memories; he began photographing as a fervent resistant during World War II. When filming an educational short for the French government on the Ivory Coast, Vautier by chance witnessed the French military's suppression of a liberation rally and recalled the Nazi Army he had fought against several years earlier; filming appeared as an ethical imperative.[25] The French government arrested Vautier who then served a year in prison, and banned *Afrique 50*, which was not the genre of educational footage that they had commissioned. Sartre also was active in the Resistance; a war prisoner during the Holocaust, he wrote articles for *Combat*, which Albert Camus edited. Like Vautier, Sartre positioned this moral foundation and witness account as the root of his theoretical and concrete engagement with decolonization, most notably in his essay "Une Victoire." In this essay, Sartre compares the position of France under censor to that of the Nazis, and when opposing the torture techniques enacted by the French military, he describes Hitler as but a precursor.[26] While Sartre's profile demanded that attention be paid to his analogies, Rothberg cites and refers to many others who recognized the torture in Algeria as similar to the techniques practiced by the Nazis, the use of concentration camps in Algeria also drawing comparisons.

In fact, a number of directors and films draw parallels between the Holocaust and the Franco-Algerian War. Rothberg focuses on Marceline Loridan in the documentary *Chronique d'un été* (*Chronicle of a Summer*, Edgar Morin and Jean Rouch, 1961) as the revelation of a Holocaust survivor—the pan to the serial number on her arm and her description of deportation merge with the film's brief discussions (and headlines) concerning Algeria and African decolonization. Perhaps the experience in film inspired Marceline Loridan to relay such connections through documentary, for after Algerian independence with Jean-Pierre Sergent (also in *Chronicle of a Summer*) she filmed *Algérie année zero* (*Algeria Year Zero*) a title that invokes Roberto Rossellini's *Germania anno zero* (*Germany Year Zero*, 1948), a neorealist fiction concerning German children in the aftermath of World War II. Loridan-Ivens admitted later to a high degree of self-censorship that would protect the rural Algerians from a European critique of their violence, implying an incongruous relationship to those French (René Vautier and Pierre Clément) working with GPRA. Ultimately, the peasants' squalor, unrest, and testimonies incited the censor of both Algeria and France. The first Holocaust survivor in French cinema thus also represents a candidness in exposing a mitigated portrait of Algerian independence, proof of her complicated relationship to nation and truth.[27]

Jacques Panijel, director of *Octobre à Paris* (*October in Paris*, 1962), witnessed "the same technique that the Nazis used with their prisoners"[28] at the Paris Massacre of 1961, while the metaphors of World War II to the Franco-Algerian War found significant expression (and censor) that the previously mentioned *The Honors of the War* (1960) and *Thou Shalt Not Kill* (1961) exemplify. Although Alain Resnais's *Nuit et brouillard* (*Night and Fog,* 1956) objectively addresses the Holocaust by visiting former Nazi concentration camps and uncovering archived footage, the director later claimed that his documentary short warns and protests against the then contemporary French activity in Algeria—though the narration never mentions Algeria directly. In fact, Cynthia Marker[29] and Virginia Bonner respectively suggest that Cayrol and Resnais maintained a general approach to war in *Night and Fog* in order to allude to the then current crisis in Algeria while avoiding the censor.[30] Nonetheless, *la commission de contrôle* still censored an image of a policeman working at a Nazi prison camp, whose cap identified him as French, demonstrating the degree to which the reputation of the French army connected and befuddled the wars. Representative of a larger intellectual French approach, René Vautier and Jean-Paul Sartre were first active in a movement to free France from Nazi oppression, and these memories of the not so distant world war served their argumentation for the French involvement in the Algerian independence movement.

The East German state film studio DEFA (Deutsche Film-Aktiengesellschaft) provided postproduction assistance for the nationalist short by René Vautier titled *Algeria in Flames*, and although the film could not be screened within Algeria,[31] DEFA made 800 prints that the FLN distributed.[32] The film was part of the FLN's turn to international propaganda,[33] to which it devoted nearly half of its efforts in 1958 in preparation for a 1959 United Nations debate. Among others, DEFA produced a fiction film *Fluct aus der Hölle* (*Escape from Hell,* Hans-Erich Korbschmitt, 1960) for East German television in which a West German serving in the Foreign Legion seeks to desert his post in Algeria. DEFA also produced *Allons les enfants ... pour l'Algérie* (*Let's Go Children ... for Algeria,* Karl Gass, 1962) a forty-minute documentary that exposed French and West German interest in nuclear weapon research and oil reserves in the Sahara. Such films confirm the political opportunity that Algeria represented for socialist countries, and the ways in which GPRA's film involvement further situated Algeria globally against France.[34]

In fact, when locating Sartre in the cinema of decolonization, Vautier's films concerning Algeria advance a simplistic but unifying vision, as there is no mention of disagreement between the independence factions of the FLN and the MNA (Mouvement National Algérien)—a battle for power that resulted in many deaths (a subject explored in Chapter 4).[35] Furthermore, in spite of his own voice's French narration,[36] Vautier never verbally suggests the possibility of a French or European ally, nor does he imply that Algerians served in the French army. In reality, the French military relied on *harkis*, and even designed an inner Algerian network the *bleuite* (discussed in Chapter 6), while the GPRA also depended financially on French *porteurs de valises*. In *Algeria in Flames*, Vautier narrates that "the army is the people as the people are the army,"[37] reinforced by images of male and female soldiers (or nurses dressed as such) preparing to battle.[38] In another sequence, the soldiers also smile and give food to children—emphasizing children just as the previously addressed SCA propaganda reels. Other such short documentary films made under duress (four Algerian filmmakers that Vautier trained died in combat) similarly reflect the emerging nation's agenda to strengthen and impart a resilient nation.[39] Vautier's cinema visually reenforced a central binary in the anticolonial theory that Sartre and others circulated in press.

Nevertheless, Vautier's films made during the Algerian Revolution, his arrest and the confiscation of his films (the destruction of others later in France), and his work for the FLN as head of a film unit and as a teacher of emerging Algerian filmmakers confuse the Algerian/French binary that such films dictate. Do we label these films Algerian if they were made through the growing independence collective as international propagandistic devices? How is the DEFA's support and/or the director's education and history inflected in the film's purpose? Refracting his national status, René Vautier was awarded a *croix de guerre* by Charles de Gaulle for his service in World War II, though Vautier later opposed de Gaulle's government. Younès Dadci critiques Vautier's stature in Algerian cinema, stating that Vautier might have in fact worked for a tourism network, *France-colonie*—a hypocrisy that, if true, pierces the legend surrounding Vautier, and which Guy Hennebelle's biography of Vautier does not address.[40] In all cases, the European influence surrounding Vautier confers a problematic search for authenticity.

René Vautier's French collaborator Pierre Clément, who directed the documentary *Sakiet Sidi Youssef* (1958) in Tunisia for GPRA to draw attention to the French massacre of the Tunisian refuge for the ALN (Armée de la Libération Nationale), inspires similar questions.[41] The French government imprisoned both filmmakers in Tunisia for their filmmaking practices and collusion with the FLN (Clément's sentence was ten years in 1958, but he was released after independence in 1962). In this way, the French Vautier and Clément were enemies of the state. Further confusing their works' national status was the fact that after Clément's film was confiscated, he reportedly viewed his own anticolonial footage, now edited and incorporated into the French government's SCA reel.[42] Thus, through the claw of censor and prison, the filmmakers were simultaneously enemies and servants of the state. Prison further complicates Vautier's national identity; in addition to his prison term in Tunisia for anticolonial work (1952), he was imprisoned by the new Algerian state (GPRA) for conspiring with Egyptians (allies of France)—a falsity for which he was released two years later. Therefore, Vautier was a prisoner of both Algeria and France, albeit in different instances, blurring his national affiliation. Despite the severity of such an error, Vautier became director of Algeria's audiovisual center and the leader of ciné-pops (short for *cinéma populaire*), a travelling unit not unlike the SCA *cinébuses*, whose function was to encourage cinema culture in the new nation.[43] The careers of both Clément and Vautier relate not only the hardships and courage of war, but the inner contradictions that obfuscate their intentions and bias.

In fact, Vautier finds his French roots as the impetus for his political determination. In a 1976 essay, he writes, "I was not doing it for the Africans, for the Tunisians, for the Algerians. I was doing it against the colonial system built in my name."[44] The intersection of belonging to the imagined French community while ferociously critiquing nation and the personal appropriation of such a legacy (my name) rebounds when Vautier quotes in his 1998 memoir the "Declaration of the Rights of Man." The 1789 document that states that "all citizens can thus speak, write, print freely"[45] serves as a source of inspiration in the fight against colonialism; here Vautier also incisively compares the demise of his regional Breton culture with that of the colonized. Vautier fiercely believed in training Africans so that their point of view might replace that of Europeans directing from an anthropological perspective (as he argues Jean Rouch does in *Moi un noir* [*Me a Black Person*], 1958).[46] However, Vautier perceives the universal values that inform this position as French; this need to patronize and validate the Other's construction of the Self also reveals the sphere and influence of the French philosopher Jean-Paul Sartre.

Cinéma Parallèle

Positif, the left-leaning cinema magazine still in print, published a manifesto for an engaged underground cinema that was written by Yann Le Masson and Olga Poliakof, the directors of *J'ai huit ans* (*I Am 8 Years Old*, 1961) a short discussed in both Chapters 2 and 6. The manifesto, written after Algerian independence was declared, especially condemns the censor and the national cinema financing mode through which these directors personally suffered. While *Vérité liberté* published the manifesto in the months after the Evian Accords, it relates aspects of the *cinéma parallèle* that were already in place:

> France of 1962 buzzes with cultural organizations: *ciné-clubs*, committees of friendly businesses, union sections, committees of defense, groups, smaller groups, and chapels. These organizations are private. They are free to say and see what they want. They are placed outside of the money circuit, from the state of profit, and in this way escape if only partially, the constraints that strangle the freedom of expression.[47]

As screens and spectators are intrinsic to the cinematic apparatus, the *ciné-clubs* and union screenings as described were essential in valorizing pro–Algerian independence films. This is not to say that French filmmakers in North Africa were the only ones rebelling against the draft and the censor. Perhaps, obviously, the films made in

France primarily concerned the draft and the resulting traumatized veteran. Two films addressed the post trauma of returned veterans, *58.2/B* (Guy Chalon and the Groupe Jean Vigo, 1958) and *Secteur postal 89098* (Philippe Durand, filmed in 1959 screened clandestinely in 1961) when no such films about the detrimental mental effect of Franco-Algerian war on French soldiers had previously been made. Eight short films made in France about the Franco-Algerian War that were banned, screened in underground spaces via the circuit of *cinéma parallèle*.[48] The already mentioned *Thou Shalt Not Kill* (Claude Autant-Lara, 1961) screened through *cinéma parallèle*'s circuit that relied on the underground press –the satiric left-wing *Le Canard Enchaîné* gathered 800 spectators to see the film abroad.[49] As the films were illegal and often confiscated, such activities and groups associated with activism and the intellectual left maintained the small but significant community.

Jacques Panijel's documentary *Octobre à Paris* (1962) survives as a testament to the *cinéma parallèle* and demonstrates transcinema activity; the reflection and commentary on the brutal massacre of those protesting a racist curfew by Parisian police cinematically expressed the French intellectual left, while the production process also reveals interaction with the FLN. After approaching numerous well-known directors who rejected the challenge to the censor, Panijel resolved to direct a vision of what he had witnessed—a massacre committed by the police. Signaling that cinema was indeed a tool of the intellectual left, the journal *Vérité liberté* contributed significantly to its funding; however it was Panijel's own mother who donated the final funds needed. The Comité Maurice Audin (named for a mathematician and activist tortured to death by the French military in Algeria) also organized underground screenings. In an interview, Panijel reiterates his refusal to work under an Algerian agency, superficially guarding his film's geographic, and national status. He explains that in contrast with the *porteurs de valises* working with the Francis Jeanson network: "We weren't and didn't want to be substitutes for Algerian militants." Nevertheless, the filmmaker frequently contacted the FLN in France for permissions calling such interactions "*la camaraderie franco-algérienne.*"[50] Unsurprisingly, the French government confiscated *Octobre à Paris* at its first underground screening October 9, 1962. However, demonstrating the organization of the *cinéma parallèle*, twenty-six copies of the film still existed and were screened clandestinely reaching 30,000 viewers by 1963.[51] Jacques Panijel's documentary in the context of various censored political shorts reveals a network of courageous anticolonial individuals; cinema culture fought against the French draft and for Algerian independence shortening the distance across the Mediterranean by projecting Algeria's independence trajectory. *Octobre à Paris* evoked the distant war's French locale, and the featured Algerian survivors of police violence frequently name their attackers "*harkis*" a term originally and principally used to describe Algerians working in the French army in Algeria during the Revolution. This signifier in colloquial speech troubles the French/oppressor, Algerian/victim binary as it reveals that the Algerians working for the French police also contributed to the massive violence against their fellow immigrant countrymen.

As my emphasis on René Vautier indicates, the emerging Algerian government envisioned and promoted cinema as a publicity force largely inspired by the theory of the Other. Film could establish a national mythology that would adhere to a communist-twinged, anticolonial interpretation of history in which Frantz Fanon's new man would dominate.[52] Reasonably, Mohammed Lakhdar-Hamina, who soon became Algeria's most recognized director, repeatedly depicted the Revolution. Before his epics *Le Vent des Aurès* (*The Wind of the Aurès*, 1967) and *Chronique des années de braise* (*Chronicle of the Years of Fire*, 1975) that I discuss as examples of *cinéma moudjahid*'s reclaiming of Algeria (Chapter 3), Lakhdar-Hamina employed his Czech film training and aesthetics to depict the surrounding revolutionary warfare in shorts filmed in Tunisia where he (and the GPRA headquarters) sought refuge. One short, *Yasmina* (1961), portrays a young woman faced with the destruction of her village. Yasmina overtly symbolizes the young nation, a motif that returns with *The Wind of the Aurès* in which a mother represents Algeria. Chapter 4 also presents Lakhdar-Hamina's importance in Algeria's film industry—his early presence in the OAA (Office des Actualités Algeriennes), which began to dominate film production, awarded him the powerful position of director in 1967. When the OAA and the CNCA (Le Centre National du Cinéma de l'Audiovisuel de l'Algérie) became the ONCIC (Office national pour le commerce et l'industrie cinématographique), Lakhdar-Hamina chaired the new organization that now held a monopoly over all film production. Algerian film historian Lofti Maherzi described Lakhdar-Hamina as a "powerful symbol of evil in Algerian cinema"[53] because of his control and favoritism, which denied many opportunities, while ensuring the budgets of his own films.

La nouvelle vague

The new wave of French cinema is traditionally viewed as a postwar phenomenon, shaped in large part by new access to American films banned during World War II and technological progress. However, the movement equally developed with the Franco-Algerian War. Born of *cinémathèques* and film criticism, the new wave questioned form as much as content, resulting in a confrontation with the French establishment. François Truffaut's ideological declaration of the *auteur* theory and a new French cinema "Une certaine tendance du cinéma français" appeared in the January 1954 issue of *Les Cahiers du cinéma*, the same year that the FLN launched attacks against French colonists. Though many associated particular directors' with the new wave throughout their long careers, the heart of the movement is frequently understood as ending in the early 1960s. In fact, Michel Marie claims 1963 as the last year of the new wave, indicating the movement's proximity to the Evian Accords (March 18, 1962) and the declaration of Algerian independence (July 5, 1962).[54] The cover of the December 1962 issue of *Les Cahiers du cinéma* pictures Jean Seberg of *À bout de souffle* (*Breathless*, Jean-Luc Godard, 1960) with the headline, "La nouvelle vague: une légende en question." The end of the year cover demonstrates the founding new wave magazine relegating the movement's pertinence to the past while debating its uncertain future. As young men served the required eighteen months in the military (which became twenty-seven months in April of 1958)[55] and as many were then recalled for six months and crossed the Mediterranean again, young directors at home experimented with narrative form and garnered international accolades. While *les événements d'Algérie* escalated, the two most famous new wave films premiered in France: *Les Quatre cents coups* (*400 Blows*,

November 1959) and *Breathless* (March 1960). At this time, 60,000 *harkis* or *soldats supplétifs* served France with over 440,000 French soldiers in Algeria—seven times the number of soldiers there in 1954.[56] While Truffaut and Godard were never soldiers, the cinematographer of many Truffaut and Godard films of the period including *Breathless* and *The Little Soldier* was Raoul Coutard, who had previously worked as a photographer for the SCA in Indochina. This experience influenced the films' style, which relied on his abilities to film without lighting by using high speed film for stills and the handheld Cameflex.

Contemporary scholarship discloses the importance of the war abroad to new wave film. Sam Di Orio argues that André Bazin's theory of total cinema (that film and its advances derive from our mimetic impulses) was but an aspect of a larger "discourse of 'truth'" taking place with lighter cameras and live sound that reacted to the Algerian Revolution and the simultaneous state censor.[57] Yet the *cinéma verité* documentary *Chronicle of a Summer*, which many categorize as new wave, only broaches the conflict; editing obscures any clear anti-French-Algeria sentiment. Matthew Croombs proves the ways in which the enormously influential science-fiction short *La Jetée* (Chris Marker, 1962), set in the future and in Paris, draws directly from the torture exposed in Henri Alleg's *La Question* and still never mentions Algeria.[58] Mani Sharpe also finds that a self-censor permeated the new wave, arguing that erotophilia acts as political sublimation, or sexorship—*Les Distractions, Paris nous appartient* (*Paris Belongs to Us*, Jacques Rivette, 1962), *Le Feu follet* (*The Fire Within*, Louis Malle, 1963)—and that an obsession with domesticity distracts characters and the public from the war abroad—*Adieu Philippine* (Jacques Rozier, 1963) and *La Belle Vie* (*The Beautiful Life*, Robert Enrico, 1964).[59]

After the Evian Accords, we find more direct cinematic expression of the war and trauma: in fact, Chris Marker's *Le joli mai* (*The Pretty May*, 1963) responds to *Chronicle of a Summer*. Marker questions citizens outside the courthouse where Raoul Salan, the leader of the pro-*Algérie-française* terrorist group the OAS (Organisation Armée Secrète), is on trial and the film focuses on political topics that include the massacre at the Charonne metro station for which the OAS was responsible. Befitting their chronology, Agnès Varda's *Cléo de 5 à 7* (*Cléo from 5 to 7*, 1962) (released one month before the Evian Accords) depicts the war-abroad in the present tense, a fate that will separate her protagonist (Cléo played by Corinne Marchand) from a possible love interest in uniform (Antoine Bourseiller). Jacques Demy's *Les Parapluies de Cherbourg* (*The Umbrellas of Cherbourg*, 1964) briefly depicts the war, whose primary narrative function is to separate a young couple. In fact Jacques Demy states in *Jacquot de Nantes* (Agnès Varda, 1991) that the true subject of *The Umbrellas of Cherbourg* is the after effects of the war; in the final scene of *The Umbrellas of Cherbourg*, the couple once in love struggle through an empty and sorrowful exchange.

Resnais's *Muriel ou le temps d'un retour* (*Muriel or the Time of Return*), released in 1963, remains the most successful feature to expose the post-trauma of a French veteran of the Franco-Algerian War. However, there is a lesser-known film from the era, *La Belle Vie* (*The Beautiful Life*, 1964), that also relates the post-trauma and isolation of veterans. Robert Enrico had served in the SCA between 1956 and 1959 before drawing on interviews and his own experience to direct his first feature-length film. *The Beautiful Life*'s inventive use of sound represents flashbacks to suggest the mental trauma of a war veteran. Perhaps drawing inspiration from the documentary footage he filmed in the SCA, Enrico included many news sequences credited only as being from the Actualités Françaises—in fact the opening credit sequence appears to be solely footage of Algeria and includes many troubling and controversial shots including a bloody corpse in French uniform. Following the credits, the first narrative shot is a three-fourth angle close-up of Frédéric (Frédéric la Pasquale), who we learn is on a train returning from his military service—this information situates the title sequence of war footage as Frédéric's memories, or thoughts. Other news footage of varied world locations and events (including horrific scenes of the Holocaust with a voice-over text that recalls *Night and Fog* in asking if children will forget) interrupts the narrative, and like the film's introduction, anchors the entire film in the bewildered pained space of a newly returned veteran's mind. An aspect of the film's spatio-temporal confusion must be attributed to the censor that cut many sequences, shots, and dialogue. Nevertheless, as Thomas Simonet notes of Enrico's work generally, the style "simulate(s) those inner life processes that involve abstraction and unfettered movement in time and space." As the film closes, Frédéric wanders the new apartment in the morning while his pregnant wife sleeps; he has closed the door on a military official who has delivered his recall notice. As we study Frédéric's face and posture, sound exposes the mind of a veteran mentally wounded by a war to which he must return—we hear bombs, gun fire, and sirens.

The new wave, a movement of the late 1950s and early 1960s, cannot be extracted from a France struggling to keep its empire. An atmosphere of denial, in which underground organizations fought against censorship and for Algerian independence, is the same environment that created such curious, experimental, narrative films. In a more careful probing of the epoch's content, allusions to the Franco-Algerian War are less rare than commonly suspected, and the censor does not filter the war's presence. The new wave's interrogation of form poses still deeper questions about expectations and trust running parallel to a deceitful government's attempt to hide a war abroad. Proving cinema's participation in the anticolonial literary discourse, new wave directors François Truffaut and Alain Resnais, as well as film journalists, joined Jean-Paul Sartre, Simone de Beauvoir, and other intellectuals to sign the *Manifeste des 121*, a document that denounced torture, asked the war to be named as such, and defended conscientious objectors.[60] (That Jean-Luc Godard did not sign the manifesto, perhaps, reflects his ambivalence; yet his Swiss/foreign status may have prevented his involvement.) Directors resented the *commission de contrôle*'s dictates over their expression, which only increased an antiwar/antigovernment sentiment in their films and encouraged a rebellion that acclaimed film's truth-telling powers.

According to René Vautier, several successful French directors (François Truffaut, Roger Vadim, and Claude Chabrol) envisoned projects concerning the war and veterans, but then abandoned them under the threat of the censor and a lack of production financing.[61] He claims that Alain Resnais's *Muriel* (1963) was such a project, conceived of during the war, but abandoned until the censor on the subject was lifted.[62] Although the French new wave's aesthetics vary by film and director, one often finds a study of technique and form related to literature in new wave works. In particular, Resnais collaborated with authors of the *nouveau roman*, for example Marguerite Duras screenwrote *Hiroshima mon amour* (1959) and Alain Robbe-Grillet penned *L'Année dernière à Marienbad* (*Last Year at Marienbad*, 1960), films that favor enigma to a direct call to action. Vautier's opinion of Resnais's work echoes the previously cited manifesto of the *cinéma parallèle*, which also claims that other filmmakers' silence was an economic strategy. Yet in spite of the contrasts in form and direct address, both the *cinéma parallèle* and the French new wave derive from the same historic milieu of war-abroad, draft, and censor. In the following pages, I will isolate several examples of the Franco-Algerian War's film predicament to elucidate my chapter's primary thesis of transcinema; in these films released after the Evian Accords, Algerian and French cinema operate primarily as separate entities that nonetheless influence one another.

Le Petit Soldat

Although Jean-Luc Godard is Swiss, for many he embodies the French new wave and its surrounding mythology. Godard's outspoken political stance post-1968 perhaps overshadows his elusive position during the Franco-Algerian War, which in many respects mirrors the ambivalence and contradictions of France during the conflict. Jean-Luc Godard's background colored interpretations of his early films; rumors circulated that his family had been Nazi sympathizers, and his friendship with right-wing poet Parvelesco (mentioned in *Breathless*), as well as the previous Vichy employment of his producer Georges Beauregard, merged with his own deliberately ambiguous statements to color his public image.[63] Although Godard originally wanted to film in France, the French CNC (Centre Nationale de Cinématographie) denied his crew a permit because of the subject matter. As such Switzerland was a backup location.[64] Still, *The Little Soldier* evokes an often disregarded Swiss position to the Algerian Revolution.[65] A neutral nation, Switzerland defended neither Algeria nor France and thus Evian, on the French-Swiss border, proved ideal for the peace negotiations.[66] With Brechtian aesthetics, Godard's *The Little Soldier* satirizes both the FLN and the French nationalists that would become the OAS; a deserter that works for a pro-French-Algeria group, Bruno (Michel Subor) changes sides with ease when he becomes enamored with a female FLN spy (Anna Karina). Ultimately, the film mirrors Switzerland's neutrality, for the protagonist's political caprice suggests little to no bias. Furthermore, the plot's tension between the FLN and OAS in Geneva represents an actuality, for Switzerland's geographic territory became highly attractive to both nationalist groups—the FLN and OAS both held meetings there. It is not irrelevant that the action of *The Little Soldier* begins on April 3, 1958 and ends but a month and a half later, for on May 13, four retired generals attempted a putsch in Algeria—Charles de Gaulle returned to restore order in the following weeks. Godard's use of *film noir* thus comments on the French politics of the era in neighboring Switzerland, the secrecy of government, the OAS, as well as the *porteurs de valise* working for the FLN.

A France in confusion and denial of its falling empire emerges, casting a screen mood reminiscent of film noir's postwar America.

The Little Soldier also invokes a contentious position to the torture memoir *La Question*. In the film, Godard reverses the known torture dynamics; it is the FLN who torture Bruno, at this point associated with the French nationalists. Otherwise, Alleg's text provides Godard with a scenario: the specific techniques that Godard films are recorded practices of the paratroopers found in *La Question*, a reference similarly found in Chris Marker's *La Jetée* (1962) as previously mentioned. In addition, Bruno, like Alleg, remains silent in spite of waterboarding, shocks, and "truth" drugs—albeit such cinematic torture can only be described as tame in comparison with that of the soon to be discussed *La Battaglia di Algeri* (*The Battle of Algiers*, Gillo Pontecorvo, 1966) and thus borders on satire (e.g., the FLN shock Bruno's feet instead of his sex).[67] Direct citations from *La Question* read in voice-over illustrate most clearly an ambivalent filmic reaction to the political intellectual left. Post-dubbing, an important element of Jean-Luc Godard's early direction, allowed for a hidden authorial voice—Jean-Luc Godard dubbed his voice reading *La Question*, while on screen the Algerian (played by the Hungarian filmmaker László Szabó) holds the book over his face. Godard thus employs a highly charged symbol (the book cover of *La Question*) to exchange the roles within, and thus declares that the sides are in fact interchangeable, a controversial statement made in a highly politicized climate.

The Little Soldier in no way supports Algerian independence, and in some instances the dialogue accuses Algeria as being culturally and geographically inferior. Yet, the film doubly and directly confronts the censor in France concerning the question of Algeria, a feat unmatched by the rest of the new wave. As such, the director provides a very personal statement, publicizing *La Question* as an anti-censor declaration, and yet denying its meaning.[68] Godard's second film thus surreptitiously debates with Frantz Fanon, Jean-Paul Sartre, and Henri Alleg concerning French-Algeria and torture, but yet joins such thinkers in their combat of the censor. Several years later, Godard returned to the problem of torture in Algeria with a more clear view of the French military—yet the censor cut the few lines in which characters of *Pierrot le fou* claim to have learned waterboarding in Algeria during their military service.[69] When Godard presented a short film *Le Grand escroc* (*The Confidence Man*, 1963) at the Cinémathèque Algérienne in Algiers in 1967, he expressed an evolution in his political thought: "At the time of your liberation I wasn't very aware … *The Little Soldier*, it's the film of a young bourgeois French man with all of the limitations that that brings."[70]

Muriel ou le temps d'un retour

Muriel or the Time of Return premiered a year after the Evian Accords and thus avoided the censor. Six months after *The Little Soldier*, *Muriel* specifically addressed psychological effects of torturing, predicting a theme integral to twenty-first-century depictions and awareness. In this Alain Resnais feature, the memory of assisting in the torture and murder of an Algerian woman disturbs Bernard (Jean-Baptiste Thiérée). Bernard, a young war veteran, speaks of the departed as a present-day girlfriend named

Muriel, a lie that denies her murder, hence his own complicity. Despite *Muriel*'s focus on memory, the film takes place entirely in the present; camera work insists on the now with little to no movement forwards or backwards and although Resnais's previous films reveal a mastery of the tracking shot, *Muriel* has none. Still the past looms large in the present, not only the recent Franco-Algerian War, but also World War II. Jean Cayrol an author whose style anticipated the *nouveau roman* was a Resistant and concentration camp survivor who penned both the narration of *Night and Fog* and the screenplay of *Muriel* for Resnais. The setting of the film, Boulogne-sur-mer, a city with both war remnants and reconstructed neighborhoods, combines with other references to World War II, thus bridging the French post-traumas of 1963.[71]

With no images of the torture and death that constitute the major trauma around which the plot revolves, Naomi Greene poetically describes Muriel as "a black hole."[72] What Resnais and screenwriter Cayrol provide instead of a flashback results in a sequence that is traumatic because of its absence. Bernard's films of his war experience are super-8 reels that French soldiers made for their family members, but that also resemble the SCA's already discussed propaganda (both topics are central to Chapter 3's discussion of *Djinns* [*Stranded*, Hughes and Sandra Martin, 2010]).[73] In fact, Bernard's monologue that describes his observation and possible participation in torture and murder emphasizes the importance of body parts and sight, all while denying the spectator access to the ghastly spectacle ("J'y vois encore ... pourquoi elle m'a regardé?" [I see it still ... Why did she look at me?]). Maria Flood explicates this division of sound and image, "Resnais strives to preserve something of the incommunicability of the experience of torture while registering the precise details in verbal, narrative form."[74] Yet, this valid interpretation still absents an Algerian testimony. In 1971, closer to the Franco-Algerian War era (and during a period of debate surrounding the censor), Claude Bailblé, Michel Marie, and Marie Claire Ropars-Wuilleumier suggested that Resnais in fact invoked the language of the censor in order to critique it.[75] Also in 1971, the Algerian poet and novelist Rachid Boudjedra voiced his resentment of the lack of Algerians, "*Muriel* is not a film about Algeria, but a film where the question of Algeria is but an annoying thought that each (character) tries to forget."[76] Although, Boudjedra correctly identifies a French sentiment of denial and dismissal in *Muriel*, he fails to acknowledge the anti-censor statement produced by this paradox of brutal language and banal images, for a soldier's post-trauma in *Muriel* disrupts the government's agenda—albeit while absenting Algeria and Algerians.

Perhaps such a vision of the Algerian Revolution (from the present, from a French man's perspective in France) results in the muted, ambivalent stance under which the new wave movement similarly falls. In fact, the 1962 manifesto of the *cinéma parallèle* critiques such indirectness as a result of the capitalist economy, suggesting the culture industry: "The Resnaises, the Markers, the Autant-Laras, and the other courageous filmmakers must, to see their films distributed, choose ambiguity." However, the difference in the new wave and the *cinéma parallèle*'s approaches may signify more than an economic convention, for the manifesto's next sentence shows a lack of confidence in the French public to identify metaphor and allusion. The manifesto reads, "Their secret intentions do not, it's the least that one can say, have any chance of being understood by the public."[77] Algerian post-Revolution films agreed with the statement, and produced direct portraits of the war that defended a unified people rather than sympathizing with the French in post-trauma. Demonstrating the extent to which an Algerian awareness of French depictions affected the Algerian portrayal, Rachid Boudjedra, who severely critiqued *Muriel* as previously cited, copenned, with directors Mohammed Lakhdar-Hamina and Tewfik Farès, the most well-known Algerian depiction of the Revolution in 1975, *Chronicle of the Years of Fire*.

La Battaglia di Algeri

The genesis of *The Battle of Algiers* harkened from the nationalist propagandistic gestures of early Algerian documentaries. In fact, René Vautier cowrote the first script with Saâdi Yacef, whose prison journal from 1957 provided a general outline.[78] However, Saâdi Yacef always entranced by cinema (as a boy he was an extra in *Pépé le moko*, Julien Duvivier, 1937) sought international attention and prestige, as well as economic benefits. In fact, he founded Casbah Films in the private domain to attract foreign film productions to Algeria and was successful with *Lo straniero* (*The Stranger*, Luchino Visconti, 1967), and even a French film that was censored by Algeria, *Soleil Noir* (*Black Sun*, De La Palletière, 1966). A year after *The Battle of Algiers*, when the Algerian state created the ONCIC,[79] the possibility of Algerian coproductions with varying perspectives diminished.[80] Still in 1965 a broader fascination and knowledge of European cinema inspired the search for a neorealist director which led to Gillo Pontecorvo, a communist whose first film (*Kapò*, 1960) had received additional aid from the socialist Yugoslavia, just as many Algerian films made during the Revolution.

The often dissimulated consideration of Algeria in 1965 by the established directors of the once new wave was concurrent with Algeria's first features, which strove for national unity by depicting the war and its wounds with melodrama. The European influence on early independent Algerian cinema aligns with the legacy of the colonial film culture (509 movie theaters before independence, and 450 still standing after the war).[81] The *cinéma parallèle*'s influence, its connection to Europe, as well as its socialist bent contributed to the search for an Italian communist director for *The Battle of Algiers*. A confluence of politics, ideology, and technology demanded a larger call to independence and revolution that would surpass geographic barriers. In fact, in the years that followed, the Black Power movement required viewings of *The Battle of Algiers* for members and the Palestinian Liberation Organization's attempted screenings were banned.[82] The FLN supported both groups and the film came to signify global solidarity against the oppression of all peoples.

While much continues to be written on the impact of *The Battle of Algiers* in cinema as the first pseudo-documentary, this monograph emphasizes the film as a historical document whose importance to Algerian culture continues to be unmatched and whose symbolism and reception in France evolves. As *The Battle of Algiers* was made several years after the war, the recent memory of events doubtlessly informed the performances of nonactors, including the Algerian men who played the French military. While filming the remembrance of the Revolution with leagues of former participants, Ben Bella's government suffered a coup d'état led by the defense minister, Houari Boumediene—the mise-en-scène hid the actuality of political upheaval from the common people, as many believed the tanks were set pieces.[83] The sudden coup d'état demonstrated the new state's fragility; although *The Battle of Algiers* represents the people's determination and solidarity, a hidden paradox resulted in an upheaval.

The scandal and fear caused by the idea of *The Battle of Algiers* forced the French memory of the warfare further into the vault; Laurent Garreau's research proves that the commission called for its complete censor in 1966,[84] and Patricia Caillé writes that after the Venice Film festival "there was a consensus in the press as well as in the industry that *The Battle of Algiers* should not be released in France at the time and no distributor ever requested a certificate for its release even after it had received the Golden Lion."[85] Thus, while Boumediene's government (1965–76) produced the most prolific era of Algerian films, many of which revisited the Revolution, French cinema receded from its representation in the same period. One may claim that the results of the war correspond with the national cinemas' interest for the subject matter; the war's outcome announced independence for one and collapsed a dwindling empire for the other. However, the cinemas' reactions following *The Battle of Algiers* also imply a controlled opposition to the former enemy.

Elise ou la vraie vie

After the student and worker strikes of May 1968, the 1970s found youth-driven France reflecting negatively on the past government censor. Algerian immigration posed new questions to cinema,[86] and *Elise ou la vraie vie* (*Elise, or Real Life*, Michel Drach, 1970) was a first to imply if not fully depict a romance between an Algerian and French person in France. Based on the novel of the same title written by Claire Etcherelli (1967), the film version, *Elise, or Real Life*, exposes the anti-Algerian mood of France during the war, as well as the social order in a factory—we see French police suspect and arrest innocent Algerian migrants. In this way, *Elise, or Real Life* bravely confronts and admonishes the recent censor, and in the same breath reproaches labor and immigration regulations. The film also grounds its two stars in a cinematic memory of the Algerian Revolution: Nicole Garcia, a French-Algerian actress who would later star in the French nationalist film *L'Honneur d'un capitaine* (*The Honor of a Captain*, Pierre Schoendoerffer, 1982) and direct her own film concerning the conflict titled *Un balcon sur la mer* (*A View of Love*, 2010) and Mohamed Chouikh, who had already acted in two Algerian classic *moudjahid* features—*The Wind of the Aurès* (Mohammed Lakhdar-Hamina, 1967) and *Les Hors-la-loi* (*The Outlaws*, Tewfik Farès, 1969). In fact, Chouikh would also make an indelible mark as a filmmaker, and concretely questions the Algerian Revolution's symbolism and the new radicalized extremists in *Youssef: la légende du 7e dormant* (*Youssef: The Legend of the Seventh Sleeper*, Mohamed Chouikh, 1994). *Elise, or Real Life*, a rare coproduction, emblematizes the nascent stage of an international filmic discourse in which the memory of the Algerian Revolution confronts contemporaneous questions of immigration and the miscegenation.

R.A.S. and *Avoir 20 ans dans les Aurès*

As Kristin Ross persuasively argues in *May '68 and Its Afterlives*, the Algerian Revolution of six years earlier informed and inspired the 1968 student-worker rebellion. Just as the memory of the Holocaust resounded in the reactions of activists, artists, and the French state, for the young, the Franco-Algerian War now represented the foundation of many French political affiliations. In particular, a new vocal group countered the memory of the French government censor—*Positif* published several articles concerning censorship in 1970, including one in July, "Why You Haven't Seen *The Battle of Algiers*."[87] Films that had been previously unavailable were then reconsidered, and *The Battle of Algiers* finally played in France (*The Battle of Algiers* was released in the summer of 1970, and screened in a few Parisian theaters in 1971).[88] The delayed and minor release of *The Battle of Algiers* in France was emblematic of the 1970 apparatus; the public more fervently debated censorship and filmmakers struggled to document memories and truths of the previous decade. Still, some remained angry over losing *Algérie-française*; a fire at an empty theater scheduled to run the film was followed by a statement by an organization of repatriated French from North Africa, the ANFANOMA (Association Nationale des Français d'Afrique du Nord, d'Outre-Mer et de leurs Amis).[89] Demonstrating the power of the film as a symbol in and of itself, General Jacques Massu, widely interpreted as Colonel Mathieu (Jean Martin) of *The Battle of Algiers*, entitled his 1971 memoire *La vraie bataille d'Algers* (*The Real Battle of Algiers*), adding publicity by debating the notorious film, and repeating its title. Patricia Caillé writes, "French national culture at large was much more politicized in the early 1970s and the necessity to take a clear stance on decolonization and censorship overrode any real engagement with the political analysis offered by the film [*The Battle of Algiers*]."[90]

The politicized screenings recalled the *cinéma parallèle*, and as such René Vautier and Yves Boisset dared to revisit the conflict now publicly. While both Vautier's *Avoir 20 ans dans les Aurès* (*To Be 20 in the Aurès*, 1972) and Boisset's *R.A.S.* (1973) (*R.A.S.* is a military code for *rien à signaler* or nothing to report) condemned the French military's behavior by including scenes in which French men torture, rape, and kill, Vautier's protagonist radically defects to join the FLN. If Algeria was in a state of relative calm a decade after the Evian Accords, only René Vautier, with his former FLN credentials, accessed Algeria for filming. Boisset on the other hand filmed desert scenes in Tunisia, slightly altering the geographic truth. Both directors, known for their leftist agenda, suffered attacks on their films from right-wing groups, and the French censor proved active when demanding a torture sequence be shortened from Boisset's *R.A.S.* Cinema thus reveals a fractured French identity, confused by the memory of Algeria. Algeria of the present seemed to be of little public interest—even those who once championed Algeria as a model of revolution, now abandoned its cause due to the new state's authoritarian elements.[91] Both films severely critique not only the torture practiced ten years earlier, but also the French torturers whose names and personalities posit a personal judgment absent in the Algerian-Italian production. All three films surface as artifacts of an anti-censor historical gaze; such cinematic opposition to the French military cannot be subtracted from a critique of the United States in Vietnam, and the residual antistate cry of May 1968.

Tahia Ya Didou! and *Décembre*

Commissioned and then rejected by the city of Algiers in 1971, the cinémathèque of Algiers occasionally ran Mohamed Zinet's sole feature film in subsequent years. *Tahia Ya Didou!* (the title means good day in the local dialect of Algiers) combines documentary footage of the city with a loose fictional narrative and experimental touches in sound and editing. The resulting film reconfigures the colonial rapport with acerbic humor; a French tourist couple's racist, ignorant, commentary conflicts with the images of Algiers. Aerial shots and street scenes celebrate a vibrant post-Revolution city, complete with the construction of skyscrapers, a colorful marketplace, and playful children usually in fast motion. However the wounds from the past war remain; the poet Momo (also known as Himoud Brahimi), who directly addresses the viewer in verse throughout the film, sobs on the beach for the lives lost during the Revolution as long shots of cemeteries reveal the death toll in Algiers.

Finally the tension caused by the French couple on vacation in the new nation reaches its climax when Simon (Georges Arnaud) sees a man he had tortured during the war (played by Zinet) at a restaurant. What the camera presents as visual exchange in shot-reverse-shot commences a flashback montage; we then witness the effects of torture without a depiction of the act itself. Shots of near nude men chained to walls with injuries of varying severity concretely relate the aftermath of the abuse, while abstract paintings obscured by dripping blood evoke the extreme pain and humiliation of those tortured. The montage style pays homage to *The Battle of Algiers'* most famous sequence, yet the sound design featuring Algerian Liberation chants and the decision to not include torturing, critique Gillo Pontecorvo's methods. (Evidently, Zinet filmed a torture sequence that he did not include in the final cut.)[92] As Zinet's rhythmic montage continues, it portrays the severity and longevity of France's occupation, framing art depicting the conquest of 1830 with the sound of bombs (this resembles the anticolonial montage of *Fajr al-mu'adhhabin* (*The Dawn of the Damned*, Ahmed Rachedi, 1966) and *La Guerre de Libération* (*The War of Liberation*, Ahmed Fadheli, 1973). The glare of the Algerian he tortured haunts Simon, not unlike the memory of Muriel's stare in the Alain Resnais film. Yet here dramatic irony enhances the post-trauma of torturing with ridicule; after Simon has left the restaurant in fear of a revenge for his war crimes, the Algerian man peacefully guides himself to the exit with a walking stick, a shot that imparts dramatic irony; what the French man understood as a condemning stare, was in actuality blindness.

Made only a decade after independence, Mohammed Lakhdar-Hamina's *Décembre* (1973) represents the sole Algerian-French coproduction to confront torture made in the twentieth century. The script depicts a French general's internal debate of whether or not to torture a suspect, often in monologue format. Both *Décembre* and *Tahia Ya Didou!* place the torture practiced by the French at the center of the revolutionary memory, unifying Algerians through a common pain and oppression so immense that it cannot be fully visualized. As such the two Algerian productions humanize the torturer without invoking sympathy for his character, played in both instances by a French actor. *Décembre* survives as a very unique document of a memory partnership, a vacillating current that we see strengthened by transnational productions in the twenty-first century. In these instances, transnational elements survive in the Algerian cinema governed by the government agencies.

Chronique des années de braise

Cinema *djidid* (young cinema), a 1971–3 movement in which Algerian films aimed to represent the significant concerns and challenges of agriculture, was curtailed due to the ONCIC's return to the Revolution as a central subject. As Chapter 3 demonstrates, Mohammed Lakhdar-Hamina's three-hour epic exemplifies a screen reterritorialization of Algeria; by framing a nomad laborer protagonist and his political awakening in extreme long shots and group montages, the film ultimately portrays the unified plight of the Algerian people. Furthermore, the protagonist's murder by French soldiers near the end of the film conveys martyrdom, bolstering pro-independence, anticolonial fervor. This film, which is the most famous of Algerian state productions, had financial and distribution advantages over all previous depictions of the Algerian Revolution. As mentioned, the director Mohammed Lakhdar-Hamina, already very successful with *moudjahid* cinema and internationally with *The Wind of the Aurès*, presided over the OAA and would later head the ONCIC (1981–4) illustrating the inroads of state promotion and funding, and their reliance on the Revolution as a centerpiece. More than a decade after independence, the global postcolonial economy perceived of the Algerian Revolution with temporal distance; French popular culture welcomed the sweeping epic in the midst of dismissing their own censor. As concepts of Third Worldism and nonalignment linked Algeria to larger movements, this cinematic representation wrought with national uplift found a growing European public curious about colonization.

Chronicle of the Years of Fire does not picture the torture found in the Algerian-Italian *The Battle of Algiers* of 1966, and in the French depictions of the war (*To Be 20 in the Aurès, R.A.S.*). Thus while the spectator witnesses Algerians laboring and suffering from an abusive colonial economy, they are not further demeaned. Although the torture sequence of *The Battle of Algiers* lasts but three minutes, perhaps the absence of any such torture sequence in Lakhdar-Hamina's production increased its marketability in France. Pontecorvo's film won the Venice Film Festival's Lion d'Or prize, but suffered a French resentment at the festivals—Truffaut and the French team left its screening in Venice, and the Cannes Festival rejected it. On the contrary, two Algerian nationalist films, *The Wind of the Aurès* and *Chronicle of the Years of Fire*, which do not feature the French military torturing, won prizes at Cannes—best first work and the Palme d'Or prize, respectively.

La Crabe tamboure and *L'Honneur d'un capitaine*

Although pro-Empire nostalgia largely determines Pierre Schoendoerffer's oeuvre, in his films *La Crabe tamboure* (*The Drummer Crab*, 1977) and *L'Honneur d'un capitaine* (*The Honor of a Captain*, 1982), we specifically locate a response to Algeria's depiction of colonization's evils. Furthermore, both films radically oppose the vision of the French military raping and torturing due to the anxiety of war as found in the French features of the early 1970s. *The Drummer Crab* loosely interprets a biography of Pierre Guillaume, a general imprisoned for eight years for his participation in a failed coup d'état in Algiers, organized by the recently formed OAS in fear and anger over Algeria's imminent independence. The film's eloge to colonialism lionizes the protagonist who joins the OAS to avenge the murder of his brother by *fellaghas* (a derogatory term for Algerian independence soldiers). Scenes of the superior French soldier's exploits in Vietnam and Somalia include locals, soldiers, and prisoners, and yet only an airport and a courtroom devoid of Algerians represent Algeria. Thus, *The Drummer Crab* celebrates the French military and absents Algeria, even when the consequences of Algeria's occupation remain the film's primary subject matter.

Jean-Marie Le Pen, a personal friend of the real Pierre Guillaume, served in Indochina and Algeria as a parachutist and founded the National Front in 1972. While Le Pen supports the use of torture techniques, he continually denies reports that he tortured in Algeria.[93] Clearly, the xenophobic right-wing rhetoric of the National Front gained more widespread popularity in France in the following decades under the leadership of Jean-Marie Le Pen's daughter Marine (who lost in the second round of the 2016 presidential election to Emmanuel Macron). However, Jean-Marie Le Pen's proximity to Schoendoerffer's 1977 success indicates the war's memory as central to the National Front's foundation and appeal, and explicates patriotism as the film's nexus. With less fanfare, a feature film version of Henri Alleg's *La Question* (Laurent Heynemann) also premiered in 1977, illustrating the divisiveness surrounding the memory of the Algerian War in the late 1970s.[94]

The flashback device employed by *The Drummer Crab* even more obviously reassesses and defends the French national memory of the Algerian Revolution in Pierre Schoendoerffer's second feature concerning Algeria *The Honor of a Captain* (1982). Commenting on media's role in the military's defamation, an academic sullies the reputation of a buried general on national television. The general's widow (Patricia Caron played by Nicole Garcia, who had also played Alleg's wife in *La Question*) then seeks to prove that her husband never tortured and in fact contested the procedure. In a mystery formula, interviews with soldiers commence flashbacks, which defend the general. We see him forbidding torture, often helping Algerians, a theme intrinsic to the SCA newsreels—Schoendoerffer himself had begun working for the agency as a photographer during the First Indochina War under Raoul Coutard, who incidentally also shot *The Honor of a Captain*.[95] Through broad strokes Schoendoerffer portrays academics as harbingers of a historical understanding that the narrative then discredits. Schoendoerffer's success proved that the public preferred patriotism to negative portrayals of the French military, which had, in spite of renewed attention, screenings, and press, remained decisively underground.

Regardless of the increase in Algerian immigration to France, Algeria and France grew further apart culturally and economically in the 1970s. President Houari Boumediene guided the country into a more conservative era, gradually increasing the Arabization of schools in a ten-year plan that was completed in 1976.[96] The impetus behind Algerian-French coproductions, *Elise, or Real Life* and *Décembre*, did not rematerialize until the twenty-first century, and French filmmakers did not attempt filming in Algeria. As distribution possibilities for Algerian films diminished, the French cinema began to reflect on the growing multicultural society's economic and geographic divisions—the majority of the Maghrebi population in France dwelled in suburbs or *banlieues* with low wages and unemployment. A lack of Algerian features in these years reveals the state of the economy at the end of Boumediene's presidency (he died in office in 1978) and the chaos that elected Chandli Benjidid a year later.

Le Coup de sirocco

A self-awareness of recent history that had previously been culturally inaccessible first inspired a radical French portrayal of military violence and Algerian *moudjahid* depictions. Yet as the films of Pierre Schoendoerffer demonstrate, such film movements demanded a patriotic French counterpoint. Alex Arcady, a Jewish Algerian actor who had starred in Vautier's *To Be 20 in the Aurès*, directed a dramedy based on the autobiographical novel by Daniel Saint-Hamont. *Le Coup de sirocco* (1979) (sirocco referring to the wind that blows from North Africa across the Mediterranean Sea) addressed an important aspect of the recent history, namely the struggles and discrimination faced by French Algerians and Jews who returned to France. However, the first twenty-five minutes that depict the Narboni family's last years in Algeria (1945–62) envision life during the Revolution with a uniquely European perspective; some Arabic names and dress (the help at home and at their shop) assert the set's authenticity as filmed in Tunisia, while the majority of the production was filmed and set in France. Although not lacking in political content (including a portrayal of the OAS), the film remains in near comic mode by never confronting the violence of the war. At a time when production in Algeria remained difficult, a depiction of the past French-Algerian struggle permitted French *nostalgeria*, and also gave voice to a population previously ignored by cinema.[97] (In fact Benjamin Stora notes that it was the first film treating the Franco-Algerian War to sell over 400,000 tickets in Paris over twenty-one weeks).[98]

Yet this more palatable investigation of the discrimination endured by French-Algerians denies Algerian characters and issues screen time. The most lines of dialogue granted to a non-European non-Jewish Algerian are mumbled with subservience by a luggage porter in a Marseilles train station played by Mohamed Zinet; this two-minute performance of ignorance and guilt shines with irony for those aware of Zinet's own film of eight years earlier, *Tahia Ya Didou!*[99] Like Pierre Schoendoerffer's *The Drummer Crab* and *The Honor of a Captain*, *Le Coup de sirocco* absents Algerians from their own history. However, it is precisely this limited focus that uncovers a forgotten aspect of France's identity struggle post-independence. With varying approaches and reasons, these three productions refute the Algerian epics such as *The Battle of Algiers*, *The Outlaws*, and *Chronicle of the Years of Fire*, which return land to Algerians.

La Nouba des femmes de Mont Chenoua and *La Folles Années du Twist*: Living in France and Directing for the FLN

On many accounts, France failed to economically integrate the influx of Algerians and North Africans. The significant immigration[100] from Algeria to France became a political debate that both blurred and determined the Mediterranean Sea as a fixed border. President Valérie Giscard d'Estaing in 1978 promised to diminish the North African population and its influence by proposing that Algerians willing to return to their birthplace would receive a check of 10,000 francs as incentive.[101] Although such a law never passed Congress, it was nevertheless the subject of Mahmoud Zemmouri's first feature, *Prends 10,000 francs et casse-toi* (*Take 10,000 Francs and Get Out*, 1981) that received both French and Algerian proclaim. Zemmouri's status, like Mehdi Charef, Rachid Bouchareb, and other debuting filmmakers of the early 1980s, defined a movement. Born in Algeria, or to Algerian parents, but yet citizens of France, these artists confused the easy distinctions that the previous patriotic depictions enforced.

Zemmouri's first film, *Take 10,000 Francs and Get Out*, entirely financed in France, severely critiqued the French state's stance on immigration as well as the growing religious conservatism of Algeria (especially surrounding the role of women). Yet the ONCIC did not foresee that Zemmouri's second film would belittle the FLN when they awarded it funding. *La Folles Années du Twist* (*The Crazy Years of the Twist*, Mahmoud Zemmouri, 1986), a wholly original film discussed fully in Chapter 3, relocates a satire current found in the Algerian comedy *Hassan Terro* (Mohammed Lakhdar-Hamina, 1967), a parody of *The Battle of Algiers*. Though one could read *The Crazy Years of the Twist*'s torture sequence as making light of the atrocious criminal behavior permitted and endorsed by the French military, the sequence's indifference ultimately disempowers torture: when his French torturer thrusts his head in a full bucket of water, a thirsty Algerian suspect gulps to relieve his thirst. After several seconds, the French torturer forcefully lifts the victim's head from the bucket and curses in disbelief. The bucket is now empty. If water torture just relieves thirst, then how can it be threatening? The film depicts FLN members as uninspired and opportunistic. Unsurprisingly, *The Crazy Years of the Twist* was banned after its first screening in Algeria, and its success in France was constrained. This bilateral critique that the Algerian government's cinema agency funded and banned illustrates the complications that ensue when Algerians circulate in both countries' film industries and cultures.

While French women gained more liberties during the postwar period and through the 1980s, Algerian women suffered more restrictions following independence (a subject that Zemmouri continually treated, from his first feature until his last film of 2015, *Certifié Halal*). After centuries of suffragist movements, women gained the right to vote in France in 1944 and could at last open bank accounts and work without the permission of their husbands in 1965. More women entered the workplace and in 1983, the Roudy Law was passed to fight against discrimination based on gender in employment and salary. In contrast, while Algeria's 1962 constitution declares the equality of women and men, a growing political and religious conservatism approved the family act of 1982, a law that assigned women a minority status and permitted polygamy (though it continues to be seldom practiced in Algeria). While the experimental films of Assia Djebar, the first North African member of the Académie Française, do not critique the FLN in the straightforward manner of Mahmoud Zemmouri, her exclusive interest in interviewing female participants in the docufiction *La Nouba des femmes de Mont Chenoua* (*The Nouba of the Women of Mont Chenoua*, 1977) comments on women's limited place in both the FLN-curated history and its cinema.[102]

Djebar restores language to the previously denied women of the Revolution while fusing documentary and fiction styles; an actress plays a journalist posing questions in classical Arabic to rural women who recount their experiences in Algerian Arabic and Amazigh.[103] In this way, Djebar counters *The Battle of Algiers* in form and content; she does not employ a documentary style for the semblance of truth, but rather to insert its evidence. Furthermore, the older women's language and traditional clothing in *La Nouba*, contrast sharply with the iconic female bombers of *The Battle of Algiers*, who disguise themselves as French and nearly exclusively speak their few lines in French.[104] Ranjana Khanna finds Djebar's approach indicative of a fourth cinema, as the third cinema movement denied the female experience in the Revolution.[105] The experimental style and the absence of a strong male warrior (the sole male character is the wheel-chair bound husband of the journalist) were probable reasons that the ENTV (Établissement National de Télévision)-produced film played but once on Algerian television.[106] While her first film documents the memory and atrocity of the war of Algerian liberation, the exclusion of men countered the state narrative on film. In this way, *The Nouba of the Women of Mont Chenoua* opposed the family act that would pass five years later, and whose support was already apparent. Likewise, Mahmoud Zemmouri's exposure to both nations (and their films) informed his critique of their binding history. The Algerian government of the period aspired to uniquely disperse an official history of the Revolution as ruled by a unifying, heroic, masculine force. As such the FLN's agencies thrusted their contradicting film matter further into an Algerian periphery.

La Zerda ou les chants de l'oubli and *Combien je vous aime*

The French agreement to pay more for Algerian gas in 1982 suggests diplomacy and continued interdependence.[107] Yet cinema of the same era reflects tensions over memory's ownership. In 1981, France claimed that the entirety of the colonial archives taken from Algeria after the Revolution constituted a *patrimoine commun* that could be visited by Algerians, but not divided between the two countries.[108] The Algerian Minister of Foreign Affairs retorted, "The refusal to return to us our archives amounts to denying Algeria's existence before 1962. They are the material trace of our History."[109] Although French production companies nearly ignored Algeria and the

Revolution throughout the 1980s,[110] Algerian directors subverted a French perspective, a cinematic undertaking that invoked the colonial archive debate. Ahmed Rachedi's *Fajr al-mu'adhhabin* (*Dawn of the Damned*, 1966) had previously incorporated an array of archival footage to make a Third World statement on colonialism. Indicating the influence of government-funded French shorts by new wave directors, such as *Les statues meurent aussi* (*Statues Also Die*, Chris Marker and Alain Resnais, filmed in 1953 and censored until 1964) and *Toute la mémoire du monde* (*All the World's Memories*, Alain Resnais, 1956), *Dawn of the Damned* begins in modern Algerian museums and libraries—these educational settings presage a montage of colonization's evils. *La Guerre de Libération* (*The War of Liberation*, Ahmed Fadheli, 1973) reiterates *Dawn of the Damned*'s montage and rousing voice-over formula, this time isolating the Algerian Revolution.

Although French production companies nearly ignored Algeria and the Revolution throughout the 1980s, Algerian directors subverted a French perspective, a cinematic undertaking that invoked the debate surrounding the colonial archives, and drew from previous nationalist montage endeavors. Assia Djebar's *La Zerda, ou les chants de l'oubli* (*Zerda or the Songs of Forgetfulness*, 1982) and Azzedin Meddour's *Combien je vous aime* (*How Much I Love You*, 1985) represent new access and irony in nonsynchronous sound; with distance from the Revolution, the directors presented found footage as the forgotten truth. Mixing sounds and words in Arabic and Amazigh—incorporating the Amazigh language was a political act in consideration of the Arabization of Algerian schools and the 1980 Berber Spring—Djebar constructed an experimental film poem. The multilingual poetic text (cowritten with Malek Alloula) intertwined silent footage of North Africa from 1912 to 1942 to produce, as the introductory intertitles state, "the voices of the anonymous, gathered or re-imagined, the soul of a unified MAGHREB and of our past."[111] Meddour's *How Much I Love You* chronologically reveals France's domination of Algeria largely through footage mined from the abandoned French television station in Alger.[112] Meddour playfully juxtaposes the hidden truth of images produced for a French-Algerian public with a witty and condemning voice-over, which at times recalls dialogue written for the French characters visiting Algiers in *Tahia Ya Didou!* A hateful and embittered recognition of France's atomic bomb tests in Reggane also defines this unique production that was censored in France.[113] The disjunction between sound and image in both films rearticulates film artifacts, repurposing the oppressor's documentation.

Youssef: la légende du 7e dormant

The end of the 1980s proved to be a highly politicized time in independent Algeria's short history; the unrest caused by a one-party system and a lack of political representation led to widespread protests in October of 1988 (often termed *la semaine sanglante* or the bloody week). In response, President Chanli Benjidid's government agreed to allow other parties' participation in elections in 1989, a decision that resulted in the growing support of FIS (Front Islamic du Salut; Islamic Salvation Front), a party that violently attacked those it deemed to be cultural enemies. As the Benjidid government moved toward chaos, the state funded very few 1980s' films and encouraged directors to find alternative means—the archival montage films previously described represent low-budget alternatives to financing narrative features. Demonstrating the chaotic state of Algeria's cinema affairs, the CAAIC (Centre algérien pour l'art et l'industrie cinématographiques) replaced the ONCIC in 1987, and then held a monopoly over Algerian film until another restructuring and renaming occurred in 1998. Some Algerian directors presented the country's growing conservatism and implied the failures of the Algerian state in their films; Mohamed Chouikh's varied triology—*La Citadelle* (*The Citadel*, 1988), *Youssef: la légende du 7e dormant* (*Youssef: The Legend of the Seventh Sleeper*, 1994), and *L'Arche du desert* (*The Ark of the Desert*,1997)—accompanies Merzak Allouache's *Bab El-Oued City* (1994) to present the turmoil with humor and metaphor. These directors exceptionally filmed during the Black Years, as the civil war halted nearly all film production.[114]

The second of Chouikh's trilogy, *Youssef* recontextualizes the story *Ahl al-Kahf* from Sura 18 of the Quran to question the Revolution's relevance in contemporary Algeria. The film's protagonist Youssef, oblivious of the end of the war in 1962 and the years hence, is humorously locked in the revolutionary past. This schema comments on the FLN-curated history that fails to assess and strategize for Algerian society, and implies that those revolutionary leaders (now in government) disregard Algerians of the present day.[115] *Youssef* additionally critiques film's role in the state ideology: when Youssef hides in a cave, his comrades from the Revolution project *The Battle of Algiers* onto the walls; Youssef at last learns from the film's conclusion that liberation has been won. This overt reference to Plato's *Allegory of the Cave*, speaks not only to the illusion of the spectacle, but to the discord of the victory projected into Algeria's then current climate of murder and unrest. However, the ONCIC perceived this critique of the FLN admissible, for the film more directly exposes the ways in which radical Islamic values (as those of FIS) counter revolutionary ideals. *Youssef*'s humor derives from the severity and sincerity of the protagonist's anticolonialism; the film's irony and pause originate from the portrayal of contemporary Algerians who believe just as fervently in a different liberation. (For example, Youssef's understanding of women as free and equal warriors is at odds with many in Algeria of the 1990s.) A troubling of FLN reverence grounds the film's historic dialectic, and adds to an Algerian tradition of satirizing the Revolution.

Chouikh's film asserts a very unique position, contrasting the memory of the Algerian Revolution and *moudjadists* with the radical Islamic rising of the present. Although Youssef and the new generation are in opposition, their similarly aggressive stance implies the Algerian Revolution's influence on a new generation's mentality. In fact, the film might suggest Luis Martinez's view of a culture of violence in Algeria dictated by *un imaginaire de guerre*.[116] By placing elements and characters of the Algerian Revolution in 1994, *Youssef* replaces the French army with the militant conservativism plaguing the country. After villagers herald Youssef as the embodiment of the Revolution's purity, a sniper assassinates him, an ending that Guy Austin relates to the murder of the politician Mohamed Boudiaf by FIS in 1992.[117] In this manner, Chouikh binds a contemporary national trauma to the previous war and its imagery, and exposes the multidirectional memory of the Algerian Revolution.

Les Roseaux Sauvages

Carrie Tarr illuminates in her now classic *Reframing Difference: Beur and Banlieue Filmmaking in France* the rise of a new French cinema by directors of North African origin during the 1980s and 1990s. Yet the diversity offered by several first- and second-generation Algerian directors in these years usually modifies the present-day *banlieue* and does not extend to Algerian history. The several French films of the 1990s that depict the Franco-Algerian War era are less invested in Algerian characters and due to the civil war could not be filmed in Algeria. Serge Moati directed *Des Feux mal éteints* (*Poorly Extinguished Fires*, 1994) in Tunisia and France with a strong anti-OAS message, and a year later Pierre Delerive filmed *Le Fusil de bois* (*The Wooden Gun*) that narrativizes mental disability in the army, in France and Spain. However, the most successful of the 1990s' French films to address the war was Andre Techiné's *Les Roseaux Sauvages* (*Wild Reeds*, 1994), in which the politics of the era merge with coming of age sexuality.

In a small town in southwestern France, French teens united by desire and split by the war include a young woman (Maïté played by Élodie Bouchez) whose family allies with the French Communist Party; François (Gaël Morel), her best friend; Serge (Stéphane Rideau), who is both interested in Maïté and François and whose brother while serving in the French military was murdered in an OAS attack; and finally Henri (Frédéric Gorny), a new French-Algerian student who eventually sleeps with Maïté, despite their political differences—he supports the OAS as the FLN murdered his brother. Unlike Alain Cavalier's *Le Combat dans l'île* (*The Fight on the Island*, 1964) that employs the friction of a love triangle to ultimately judge and punish the OAS, the 1990s' teen film avoids a strong political statement as the adolescents' sexual interactions transcend their web of grief and allegiances.

The film's discourse absents Algerians; the only Algerian character, the veiled wife of a recently immigrated French-Algerian instructor, has but a few short lines in Algerian Arabic in a momentary screen appearance. Rather than suggesting the rampant xenophobia in France during the epoch as the coproduced *Elise, or Real Life* did a decade earlier, the small town presents the Algerian Revolution as a force that complicates but does not halt teen sexual exploration. This vision of the Algerian Revolution as uniquely inhabited by the French and in France signifies the French impossibility of revisiting 1990s' Algeria. *Wild Reeds* premiered in 1994, four years before PACS (the civil solidarity pact for all couples, including same sex) existed, and in the diminishing midst of Europe's AIDS epidemic and consequential increased homophobia. Although *Wild Reeds* binds homosexuality to the Franco-Algerian War, a nostalgia for a pre-AIDS sexual epoch supersedes an Algerian memory. This and the formerly described *Youssef* illustrate the nations' exclusion of one another in the 1990s; the extreme violence in Algeria divided the memories and distanced the national imaginaries.

Conclusion

A sidelong glance at this broad selection of films reveals how events in one country precipitated a cinematic reaction in the other. We find that autonomous productions not only affected the surrounding nation's future depictions of their shared war, but rippled across the Mediterranean Sea to affect the cinema industry. While both acclaimed new wave auteurs Godard and Resnais addressed the war and torture in their European settings, after a brief reception of an Algerian perspective (via an Italian co-production) in *The Battle of Algiers*, the French industry was mute. The nostalgic French productions that defended the French military by Pierre Schoendoerffer can be read in coalition with an anti-immigrant movement and the beginnings of the National Front, but should also be considered as a response to the success of Lakhdar-Hamina's *Chronicle of the Years of Fire*. As Lakhdar-Hamina's epic denied the development of French characters and the war in France, Schoendoerffer's two films subtracted Algeria and Algerians. The tragedy of Algeria's Black Years destroyed the dwindling film industry, but not before demonstrating Algeria's isolation in Chouikh's *Youssef*. Unable to return to their former departments, the French film industry, diminished Algerians' importance and depicted the war-era less, usually filming in France. While French individuals helped to construct Algeria's film industry, in the decades following independence, the two nations' cinemas alternately reject the other's vision of the past. Finally, at the end of the twentieth century, documentarians building on the foundation laid by historians concerning the past censorship of the October 17, 1961 massacre and the torture committed by the French military paved the path for a joint memory retrieval in coproductions and fiction film.

2

The Algerian Revolution in Three Transnational Documentaries

Algérie Tours/détours (Oriane Brun-Moschetti and Leïla Morouche, 2006), *La Chine est encore loin* (*China Is Still Far*, Malek Bensmaïl, 2008), and *Fidaï* (Damien Ounouri, 2012)

In much of the global north, the Franco-Algerian War (1954–62) has acquired renewed importance since the late 1990s owing to efforts to understand current immigrant malaise and the proliferation of terrorism. The war's significance, however, in present-day Algeria remains an enigma. Although the Revolution, continues to be a fundamental point of political reference, all past presidents have been revolutionary generals of the FLN. In a vast country with a young population (44 percent is under the age of 25),[1] it has become impossible to assess its place in the popular imagination. Réda Bensmaïa cites a study revealing that the Franco-Algerian War has become a primary symbol of decolonization for France's highly variegated immigrant population,[2] but this tells us little about how Algerians in Algeria view the war. The war and not least the French army's practice of torture with which it is widely associated have grown as subjects of historical inquiry in fictional work in France and elsewhere. But evolving understandings of the Revolution and its legacy are exceedingly difficult to trace in contemporary Algeria, where artistic and academic investigations have been rare, apart from officially sanctioned accounts.

However, three documentaries—*Algérie Tours/détours* (Oriane Brun-Moschetti and Leïla Morouche, 2006), *La Chine est encore loin* (*China Is Still Far*, Malek Bensmaïl, 2008), and *Fidaï* (Damien Ounouri, 2012)—provide rare cinematic quests for the Revolution's memory in early twenty-first century Algeria. *Algérie Tours/détours* returns to Algeria with René Vautier, an anticolonial French filmmaker in his eighties, to screen Algerian films from the 1960s and 1970s with contemporary Algerian populations. *China Is Still Far* studies the memory and teaching of the Algerian Revolution in Ghassira, a small village in the Aurès Mountains where the Revolution "officially" began. In *Fidaï*, the director's great uncle confesses and at times reenacts his murderous activities in the name of the FLN, even revisiting the prison in which he was held in France. The adjective transnational—which applies to all three films, because of the involvement of both Algeria and France either financially, in setting, or a combination—serves as a reminder of the countries' interwoven pasts, which a shared cinematic reflection on violence maintains and renews. In their transnationality and in their transhistoric contemplation, the three productions present the rhizome, a term taken from plant life by Gilles Deleuze and Félix Guattari in *Milles Plateaux* (the second volume of *Capitalisme et Schitzophrénie*) to theorize a nonchronological, nonspatial system. The opposite of the *livre-racine* (root-book), which, like a tree, grows in time and space, the rhizome instead "grafts onto it (the tree) and undergoes a flourishing development. This time, natural reality is what aborts the principal root, but the root's unity subsists, as past or yet to come, as possible."[3] A multiplicity of connections that lack order is key to the rhizome; it is the rhizomatic understanding of geography and time that the three documentaries embrace, by exploring a multiplicity of connections without seeking to put them into a recognizable spatial or chronological order. As my short summaries of the films indicate, by reflecting the resonances and vestiges of the Algerian Revolution in the twenty-first century, the productions blur common arborescent readings of history, just as the transnationality of the films problematize the Mediterranean Sea as a continental border.

Nevertheless this particular retrospective anticolonial film movement remains entangled in the very colonial legacy it admonishes.[4] For example, while the three French-Algerian co-productions expose how at least a segment of the Algerian population (which does not include politicians) reads the Algerian Revolution, this exploration (what is the Algerian Revolution according to Algerians?) is largely for the eyes of a French public. As only twenty movie theaters exist within Algeria and most viewership takes place via satellite television and pirated DVDs, even coproductions that the Algerian government helps fund tend to be marketed for European art-house theaters and a festival circuit. The subject, then, requires what Will Higbee and Song Wee Lim call a critical approach to postcolonial transnational film,[5] for the films' content, a search for the memory of the Algerian Revolution in twenty-first-century Algeria, begs questions about influence and audience.

These three experimental documentaries concerning the Algerian Revolution spearhead a diffuse and interactive view of history. An exploration of the relationship between art and production in the three works sheds greater light on the dialectical nature of all twenty-first-century collaborations between former colonies and colonizers. This chapter employs the theory of the rhizome to illuminate the cross-temporal goals and successes of these documentaries. I ask, finally, whether the films' engagement with the colonial past serves to dissipate or consolidate the authors' anticolonial intent.

Algérie Tours/détours

As Chapter 1 explains, the life and oeuvre of René Vautier, an anticolonial filmmaker who came from a modest family in Brittany and died in 2015 at the age of 86, defies easy categorization. In his films and in his personal trajectory, he crossed territorial borders and explored the relationship between transnationality and decolonization. Thus a film that explores René Vautier's life and work intrinsically confuses borders and epochs. As Chapter 1 mentions, in an effort to bring cinema to the Algerian masses, Vautier created *Ciné-pops*, short for *cinéma populaire* and through the program he travelled throughout Algeria, in a truck stolen from the French army, with a screen, projecting political films in villages and monitoring postfilm discussions. Oriane Brun-Moschetti and Leïla Morouche's 2006 debut *Algérie Tours/détours* exposes René Vautier's importance and dialogues with Algeria's cinematic past; the filmmakers return with Vautier to Algeria to recreate *Ciné-pops* for Algerians forty years later, showing now-classic Algerian productions (including Vautier's) that feature the Revolution. Intercut with interviews and postfilm discussions are short nonnarrative super-8 segments that frame the dialogues with an artistic view of Algeria's landscapes. Such footage recalls an earlier era (late 1960s and early 1970s) of filming: René Vautier recorded his early documentaries without sound on 16mm-super-8 film, first marketed in 1965. The Algerian Revolution, though not directly the subject of the film, emerges in nearly every discussion. The octogenarian director reflects on the era when he lived in North Africa, and the majority of the films screened by Brun-Moschetti and Morouche depict the Revolution and/or critique the French Empire.

As the film studies a figure known as the *papa du cinéma algérien*, the first-time directors, Brun-Moschetti and Morouche, were able to supplement their grants from France (Défi jeunes, Villa Médicis, Hors les murs from the French minister of foreign affairs) with Algerian sources (Air Algérie, la Cinémathèque algérienne, CDC [Centre de diffusion du cinéma en Algérie], l'Ambassade d'Algérie en France). While the directors are unable to calculate the modest sum that the film earned, it was featured at many French festivals and screened twice in Algeria with René Vautier in attendance. Despite the film's partial Algerian funding and desired Algerian audience, its message was primarily heard in the directors' native Hexagon, illustrating the complexity of such an international venture. Leïla Morouche has Algerian origins, but like her codirector Oriane Brun-Moschetti, she is French and has only lived in France.[6] The festival circuit and an award at the Pan-African International Festival of Montreal elicited just a few short press mentions in Algeria and France, suggesting that the directors' limited resources and contacts denied the film a larger media presence and subsequent public reach.

The filmmakers together carefully selected the films projected at the twenty-first century *Ciné-pops* screenings, to both question the Revolution's impact on and importance to contemporary Algeria, as well as to reevaluate an Algerian cinematic tradition. In a press release, Brun-Moschetti and Morouche explain their curation:

> If our film permits an emphasis on the implication and the impact of the filmmaker during the war and after Independence, it's above all a chance to revive the mechanism of *Ciné-pops* ... We chose to screen films from the Algerian repertoire because to show these films allowed us to test the resistance, the sense and the impact of images in time, following the regions and the generations and capturing the spectators' sensibility, experience, the interest of the spectators.[7]

Here the filmmakers' objectives can be seen to be rhizomatic, that is, opening lost, nonhierarchical connections and associations between past and present, for both diegetic (within the film) and nondiegetic (exterior to the film) spectators. However, the filmmakers' choices also suggest the desire to recover and perhaps at the same time disturb an Algerian film tradition. Brief shots with subheadings indicate the titles of these films, guiding the spectator through a history of Algeria's early cinema; Vautier presents his already-mentioned anticolonial films *Afrique 50* and *Algérie en flammes* (*Algeria in Flames*, 1958), as well as *J'ai huit ans* (*I Am 8 Years Old*, Olga Baïdar-Poliakoff, René Vautier, and Yann Le Masson, 1961), an experimental documentary short with Algerians orphaned by the war. Other screenings include *Chronique des années de braise* (*Chronicle of the Years of Fire*, Mohammed Lakhdar-Hamina, 1975) and *L'Opium et le baton* (*The Opium and the Stick*, Ahmed Rachedi, 1971), *moudjahid* or freedom-fighter films that were produced by the new FLN government to encourage patriotism by reenacting the revolutionary struggle against the French military. However, the 2006 *Ciné-pops* also screens *Le Charbonnier* (*The Charcoal Maker*) from 1972, a feature from the short-lived *djidid* cinema movement, directed by Mohamed Bouamari who was a student of René Vautier. The *djidid* movement sought to portray Algeria's contemporary labor struggles, and in many instances it also discussed the role of women in Algeria. *The Charcoal Maker*, for example, ends with a woman abandoning the veil. Although the twenty-first-century *Ciné-pops* primarily relates patriotic depictions of the Algerian Revolution, Brun-Moschetti and Morouche also suggest, without fully exploring, a gender tension that is both contemporary and historical. Questions lightly posed about chauvinism extend to the female directors themselves versus their Algerian subjects. One post–*The Charcoal Maker* discussion ends in a lively debate between men (the only attendees); yet, as the directors contend on the film's website, another screening of the same film that was almost entirely attended by women does not.[8] Women are pictured at many but not all of the screenings.

Although such opened connections between the films screened and the film depicting the screening reveal a rhizome—concurrently and paradoxically—we find a power configuration, that is, a nonrhizomatic hierarchical relationship, hovering in the background. The expatriated René Vautier, the original French director at the 1960s' *Ciné-pops* screenings, is joined by two more French directors (despite one's Algerian origins) who have designed the screenings to capture the Algerian audience and their reaction. The very fact of their French nationality resituates the anticolonial furor and Algerian pride embedded in the films within a neocolonial dynamic.

Although technicians in England, France, Germany, and the United States contributed to the movie camera's invention in the 1890s, France historically claims the first public movie screening in 1895.[9] Perhaps partially for this reason, film studies and filmmaking have held a national importance in France—the French government funds many films through the CNC (Centre national de la cinématographie), which also promotes the study of the *septième art* in France's public school curriculum.[10] In consideration of the aspects of nationalism and French history inherent in film study, the 2006 public access to the film invokes the early years of French cinema. As Roy Armes suggests, though the 1895–1905 Lumière brothers' catalogue lists about sixty works filmed in North Africa, it was primarily Europeans that attended their screenings (even within North Africa).¹¹ Lizbeth Malkmus and Roy Armes state plainly that "there is a clear connection between the development of the modern media, such as cinema, in Africa and the Arab world and the existence of the European colonial system."¹² In this instance, like the Lumière brothers' expedition films, *Algérie Tours/ détours* reveals a terrain largely unknown to the Hexagon.¹³ *Algérie Tours/détours* invokes such colonial film heritage by interviewing directors at the association created by and for Algerian filmmakers, the Association Lumières, whose name further claims the Frenchness of the art form. Another setting, the Béjaïa Film Center, a satellite of the Cinémathèque d'Alger,¹⁴ survives only with support from the Alliance Française and the French embassy.

Furthermore, several sequences that depict the three directors posting signs and speaking with citizens to publicize screenings with "the first anticolonial filmmaker" about the "history of Algeria" also indicate a pedagogical aim of the European team. To this extent, the goal of teaching Algerians about their own cinema and history reiterates paternalistic aspects of France's imperial conquest, the *mission civilisatrice*. The word *mission* describes the historically grounded nationalist ideology's similarity to a religious conquest; a view of colonization as the superior French culture's duty to the *barbarie* that simultaneously justified taking the "undeveloped" land. In a book that trained lawyers as well as colonial executives, *Principes de colonisation et de legislation coloniale* (1895), Arthur Girault describes colonization as education. He writes that "to colonise it's ... to educate the indigenous, make them evolve towards the stage of our civilization, ... the primitive barbary will have yielded to civilization."¹⁵ Perhaps this quotation appears ill-matched for a discussion of *Algérie Tours/détours*, a film that never declares French superiority, and consistently demeans the French occupation. Yet the films' altruistic attempt to expose the cultural treasure of film as presented by French experts reveals resonances of a moral duty to share what might be arguably called French values. Other than one screening at a metropolitan university, the postfilm discussions display the Algerian public's ignorance of their national cinema and history. The vestiges of colonialism remain as the French experts declare a canon and educate the Algerian public on the values of the *septième art*.

Finally, as mentioned in Chapter 1, the concept of the *Ciné-pops* itself derives more exactly from a colonial effort of *Le Service de diffusion cinématographique* (SDC) renamed by the French government in 1947, and previously overtly labeled *section de propagande*. In the years following the massacre of Sétif (May 8, 1945), the French government invested in a media platform that would counter future uprisings, the *cinébus*. Lofti Maherzi explains the structure; each deputy commanded a team of trucks and the head of the SDC would organize projection tours in both cities and in the country to address the needs of the specific population. As Paul Muritti, the head of the SDC, notes, "one must tame," the Muslim, "one must gain his confidence ... to oblige him also to benefit from the support that contemporary times offer in areas of sanitation, social, and economique."¹⁶ Such knowledge of the SDC campaign (not disclosed in the 2006 film) more precisely locates the theft reported by Vautier of his *Ciné-pop* materials, and the subsequent effort by Vautier and the FLN to share cinema with rural Algerians afterwards. Both the *Ciné-pops* in the sixties and within the 2006 documentary appropriate a colonial educational/propaganda strategy in order to demonstrate cinema's role in Algerian heritage since independence.

In spite of this resonance with colonial structure, the rhizomatic character of *Algérie Tours/détours* prevails. One shot of René Vautier in the Casbah of Algiers encapsulates most obviously the film's rhizomatic function and success. While Gillo Pontecorvo's Italian nationality is often cited as anchoring *La Battaglia di Algeri* (*The Battle of Algiers*, 1966) in objectivity, the French René Vautier was, in fact, an original co-screenwriter of that film. Pontecorvo discarded his screenplay, as he felt it was too propagandistic and biased in approach.[17] Nevertheless, as Vautier walks up and down the narrow stairs of the still-in-ruins Casbah, his early involvement in the film that for many visually signifies decolonization is poignant. Pontecorvo's images are cross-referenced, as our cinematic memory of the Algiers neighborhood remains in black-and-white. Conversation between Vautier and citizens ensues; he verifies with them the government's false promises of repair, and he points to the hiding spot of the revolutionary martyr Ali

Figure 2.1 *Algérie Tours/détours* (Oriane Brun-Moschetti and Leïla Morouche, 2006)

Figure 2.2 *The Battle of Algiers* (Gillo Pontecorvo, 1966)

Lapointe. In this way, *Algérie Tours/détours* superimposes new images of Algeria and Algerians upon film history, provoking discomfort not through the Casbah of Algiers' radical transformation, but in its eerie sameness amidst a relative calm. René Vautier recalling his life in French at this revolutionary landmark appears not only as a wise witness to the Revolution/post-Revolution period, but as a mediator for the twenty-first century, a figure who bridges perceived historical and national gaps via a cinematic dialogue. While the film distances itself from the past, through the Ali Lapointe plaque and Vautier's memory, the same evidence elides such division.

Thus visual interreferences to Algerian cinema loosen chronology in a contemporary documentary, invoking Deleuze and Guattari's description of short-term memory: "Short-term memory includes forgetting as a process; it merges not with the instant but instead with the nervous, temporal, and collective rhizome."[18] The act of forgetting signifies the lapse between past and present, and it makes revisiting the Casbah of *The Battle of Algiers* uncanny in its familiarity. The disrepair of the Casbah, as well as the cinematic witnessing of today's Algerians convening peacefully with the veteran, French director challenge the border between past and present. Furthermore, Vautier's conversations with people at an Algerian *lieu de mémoire*[19] present a transnational, transhistorical collective. For those who have not witnessed the Algerian Revolution, *Algérie Tours/détours* enunciates a national short-term/rhizomatic memory.

La Chine est encore loin

Like *Algérie Tours/détours*, Malek Bensmaïl's documentary poses questions to history as a discipline. The title "China Is Still Far" ironically references a *hadith* of the Prophet Muhammed, "go as far as China in search of knowledge," and in the Algerian context specifically questions a national history by voicing various political interpretations of the Revolution, as well as the sheer absence of its meaning in Algerian society. In an interview included on the DVD, Malek Bensmaïl explains that he chose this title based of its French translation. "I found the idea of putting the title in French a humoristic way that gave way to understanding that we still have a way to go to reach this knowledge, in any case this China of knowledge."[20] The statement indicates that Bensmaïl sought to appeal to a French public's humor in his product's marketing, perhaps necessitated by the film's French funding—French television stations France 2 and 3 as well as the aforementioned CNC contributed. As such we must consider the audience for which Algeria is being performed, edited, and projected.

In fact, a neocolonial dynamic pervades Bensmaïl's previous catalogue: all films and television shows that the documentarian made before *China Is Still Far* (and several after) were filmed in Algeria and funded exclusively by the French state (CNC) and/or French television channels. The majority of these pictures similarly expose the Revolution's legacy and reveal the hypocrisy of the FLN in Algerian policy—ostensibly for French eyes. For this reason, *China Is Still Far* represents an exceptional moment in Bensmaïl's career, which evokes both the boundaries and gateways of postcolonial, transnational filmmaking surrounding a disputed history. In fact, *China Is Still Far* is the sole film by Bensmaïl to list in its credits ENTV, the Algerian department of culture responsible for the state funding and diffusion of Algerian television and film (and the only one of the three films considered here with Algerian state funding).

Yet Bensmaïl explained in a personal interview that this agreement was purely verbal (no contract was drawn). The state had agreed to a sum—undisclosed by Bensmaïl—half of which was used during filming; however, after viewing a draft of the film, the ENTV revoked the promised remaining sum. Bensmaïl then was forced to return to France, seeking contributions and finishing the film two years later. In this way, *China Is Still Far* signifies an attempt to bring forth a cinematographic dialogue. With state support from both France and Algeria, *China Is Still Far* might contest accusations of colonial traces. Yet when ENTV decided to pull funding and deny the film's diffusion on Algerian TV (according to Bensmaïl because of the documentary's challenges to official state history, and its portrayal of the classrooms as dirty and the students as ignorant), it revealed how impossible it was for the Algerian state to support a rhizomatic film that presented a nonpropagandistic view of contemporary Algeria and exposed the colonial vestiges embedded in its revolutionary history.

Had ENTV stuck with the film and distributed it to a vast Algerian public through its official network, it would have marked a milestone in postcolonial, transnational filmmaking. But this was not to be. In 2016, Bensmaïl conscious of the neocolonial questions raised by his former films' French production, sought funding from nations other than France and Algeria (Germany and Switzerland, for example), and also investigated crowd funding. The ENTV fiasco, therefore, inspired the director to create new forms of international cooperation. Bensmaïl explained that, in order to reach an Algerian audience without state support, he gives DVDs of his films to Algerian piraters. In this way, *China Is Still Far*, filmed in its early stages of development with a portion of Algerian money, perhaps finds, in some measure, an Algerian audience. However, any money earned by *China Is Still Far* derives from France, whether it be through theaters, television, or a commercial DVD release, proving the former empire's still-powerful role in the non-state-sanctioned portrayal of its former colony. If the film had been funded more fully by the Algerian government, Bensmaïl would have had no freedom of subject; French (and now European) production companies provide some of the only opportunities for critical expression by an Algerian documentarian.

Bensmaïl employs the style of *cinéma vérité*, the French documentary style akin to the American-termed *direct cinema* led by the Maysles brothers in the 1950s. It was then pioneered in France by Jean Rouch, the French-born filmmaker who became the *papa du cinéma africain*. *Cinéma vérité* seeks to withdraw attention from the filmmaker.[21] Instead, free of interaction and framed dialogue with the documentarian, subjects live and react spontaneously—or appear to do so, though editing is still crucial. This documentary film aesthetic evokes a well-established *cinéphilic* French view of Africa, and thus in 2010 was unsurprisingly popular with the French press that promotes the art-house and festival circuit. *China Is Still Far* was reviewed very favorably by the *Cahiers du Cinéma*: Joachim Le Pastier writes, "*China Is Still Far* does more than interrogate History. It successfully shows its process of decantation."[22] Dominique Wideman of the left-wing paper *L'Humanité* concurred on the quality of Bensmaïl's filmmaking, "Everything touches and activates the thought at the prism of the œuvre's good intelligence. Framing, lighting, countryside are used beautifully to celebrate the vivacity of human obstinancy."[23] This sampling of reviews demonstrates that Bensmaïl's films are both targeted and viewed by an educated French public that is just as interested in film aesthetics and film history as in Algeria.

Bensmaïl's documentary imparts a portrait of a symbolic and utilitarian geographical location, Ghassira, a northeastern village in a Berber (Chaouia) tribal area where on All Saints' Day in 1954 the FLN murdered a French teacher, his wife, and an Algerian official—this was part of larger coordinated campaign of thirty attacks that began the Revolution and came to be called *Toussaint Rouge*. (Although other scenes and people pictured in *China Is Still Far* intertwine the past and present, the schoolhouse and its interior classroom most particularly applies to my discussion of the rhizome, and the role of history.) Despite the specificity of their place of learning, the children here have little concern for its relevance to Algeria's past. Furthermore, the students who are shown in two courses, classical Arabic and French, find the revolutionary discussion in classical Arabic difficult to grasp linguistically (one student reveals his inability in classical Arabic when he claims that his relative was held in a mosque rather than a prison). This fear of speaking in Arabic is perhaps why the students initially remain silent when their Arabic teacher asks them what occurred on November 1, 1954.[24] The film thus demonstrates how the Arabization of Algeria, an important national campaign of the FLN that the early films in semi-classical Arabic helped promote (as discussed in Chapters 1 and 4), discourages Amazigh-Algerians from participation in the national memory—this inflammatory aspect of Algerian politics will be less legible for the French audience. With further probing, the Algerian Revolution as a

Figure 2.3 *I Am 8 Years Old* (Les Graines de Sable, 1961)

national memory becomes wrought with familial myth; children recount the stories they have been told of their martyred grandparents. The children then realize their imaginative understanding of events outside of language by drawing their vision of a revolution that they never witnessed. The irony is profound; the students invent a crayon revolution at the school where the murder of one of its teachers, according to the official history, "commenced" the war. These children, roughly aged 8 or 9, never witnessed the terror of previous generations, the devastation of the Algerian Revolution, and the dark years of the 1990s. The instructor's insistence on the Revolution represents a national school campaign launched in 2002 to introduce students of 3e to "notions of patriotism, national symbols, and the rudiments of national Algerian history."[25]

This distance from the Revolution, in a scene capturing the children and describing their naïve colorings, directly references a powerful documentary of the Revolution, *J'ai huit ans* (*I Am 8 Years Old*, 1961)—one of the films screened by the 2006 *ciné-pops* in *Algérie Tours/détours*. A ten-minute short by Olga Baïdar-Poliakoff, Yann Masson, and René Vautier, *J'ai huit ans* photographs Algerian orphans under Frantz Fanon's psychological care, whose voices accompany their expressively painted depictions of the violence and destruction that they have survived.[26] For the viewer who recognizes this intertextual reference, the children's age and activity fifty years later demands a comparison. Perhaps to honor the gore and sorrow of *I Am 8 Years Old*, Bensmaïl's camera focuses on the interaction between teacher and student with their oral descriptions, rather than photographing the early twenty-century children's drawings.

The Algerian Revolution in Transnational Documentaries 51

Figure 2.4 *I Am 8 Years Old* (Les Graines de Sable, 1961)

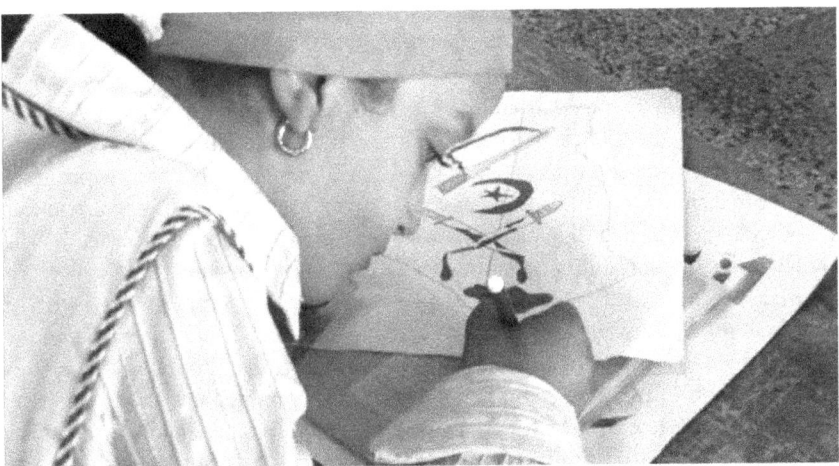

Figure 2.5 *China Is Still Far* (Malek Bensmaïl, 2008)

Nevertheless, the scene concludes with one girl's distinctive rendering—no figures are included, instead bloody knives, a gun, and the Algerian flag's insignia are imposed on the nation, defined by its borders. The map and the signifiers of nation reinforce the film's potent sense of geography—found even in the title with the mention of a far-away China—an especially important element for a film viewed primarily outside of the nation represented. Algeria, floating with no other labeled entities, readily evokes Benedict Anderson's imagined community: belonging to a national group and heritage remains largely conceptual, especially in this fairly isolated Chaouni village. The shot calls to mind Geneviève Mouillaud-Fraisse's description of "mad cartographers," a theory that incorporates elements of the imagined community. She writes, "The crazy cartographer would be the one who attempts to line up exactly, a delimited shape, on a terrestrial map, by a boundary line and a proper name, with his membership in the human community, and if pushed with his own being."[27]

The girl pictured in the midst of a both imitative and creative act represents the convergence of geography, community, and history in Ghassira, a crazy cartography. The young Algerian is active, her self-participation demonstrated by her hands' presence within her very own repetition of nation. Yet, conversely, the drawing illustrates how over time, information becomes increasingly abstract; fifty years after independence, the camera has at last settled on a personless, eventless depiction, with easily transferrable signifiers of violence. Algeria's simple representation in a drawing by an unidentified girl sitting in a historic classroom enhances the camera's consistent, objective distance from characters, a technique that serves to capture diverse understandings and opinions of the Revolution. This distance and abstraction equally apply to the film's transnational status—filmed in Algeria, with some Algerian state money, but otherwise French for a primarily French public. Very far from the *moudjahid* films' efforts to inspire Algerians to identify with their country, Bensmaïl's *cinéma vérité* approach renders the influence of his national identity enigmatic.

The distance from the Algerian Revolution feels less chronological than experiential for children, and yet the filmed testimonies of war participants and the film's anchor—a schoolhouse where Algerian children were educated alongside French-Algerian students—enable the public to see a revolutionary landmark as a nexus of nation, town, and community whose histories intersect. An important elderly character laments the youths' disinterest in the region's past and traditions, but the film itself articulates a new awareness of this disappearance, a notion that is further complicated by the French financial contribution to an otherwise Algerian production. (Is it only when Algerians have French capital that they have the privilege of investigating their past outside of the nation's official history?) Nevertheless, *China Is Still Far* insists on the Franco-Algerian War's symbolic relevance. Furthermore, the film follows characters who fight against the rapid deterioration of the memory of the Revolution and strive, like *China Is Still Far*, to augment the Algerian Revolution's contemporary relevance. The Algerian Revolution's shifting generational interpretations and exchanges render *China Is Still Far* a rhizome, a critical, open-ended form made possible through French support.

Fidaï

Fidaï ("freedom fighter" in Arabic) shares many themes with the two previously discussed documentaries. All three resituate the Algerian Revolution in the twenty-first century, depicting its emotional resonances in the survivor population as well as presenting youth's ignorance of national history amidst contemporary problems of homelessness and poverty. However, by presenting the reflections of an ALN soldier and killer, *Fidaï* engages with the late twentieth-century idea that France had repressed the memory of the Franco-Algerian War. Benjamin Stora first employed the notion of repression in *La Gangrène et l'oubli: La Mémoire de la Guerre d'Algérie* (*The Gangrene and Forgetting: The Memory of the Algerian War*, 1991), and this psychoanalytic interpretation of veterans' post-trauma, which serves as a metaphor for the nation, appeared at roughly the same time in documentaries before entering into fictional film depictions.[28] Preceding the media revelations of the torture policy during the Franco-Algerian War,[29] Bernard Tavernier's *La Guerre sans nom* (*The War without a Name*, 1992) first recorded French veterans' pained description of the trauma that torturing induced. Patrick Rotman directed his own documentary in 2002, *L'Ennemi intime* (*The Intimate Enemy*), which recounts the war and includes the harrowing process of torturing from the ex-torturers'/veterans' perspective.[30]

Fidaï is the first documentary production, however, to investigate the postcombat experience of an Algerian ALN veteran who was both tortured in a French prison and who murdered in the name of a fiercely dogmatic national ideology. The film does not explicitly invite comparisons between the French and the Algerian soldiers and veterans or between their nations; it remains focused on one veteran's unique experience. However, elements of plot and production fuse to reveal the Algerian veteran's pain, where previously the post-trauma of Franco-Algerian War veterans belonged solely to the French. The veteran, the director's great uncle, Mohamed El Hadi Benadouda, or El Hadi, still believes in the necessity of his actions. This tortured FLN assassin's perspective counterbalances the French autobiography of General Paul Aussaresses, in which he described, without any sense of repentance, the French army's policies and acts of torture during the Franco-Algerian War. In addition, El Hadi's lack of remorse contrasts with the sincere confusion and regret of French veterans in turn of the twenty-first century documentaries. Nevertheless, by the end of the film, El Hadi's great-nephew director has captured an important change in the man's emotional state: the intensity of recalling the trauma of killing others and of being tortured has shaped El Hadi's perspective of his experience.

The Algerian-French heritage of director Damien Ounouri, his upbringing in France, and current residence in Algeria generate this cross-Mediterranean perspective. Laura U. Marks's term *intercultural cinema*, which describes films and videos that depict the "experience of living between two or more cultural regimes of knowledge," comes to mind.[31] Ounouri studied at the Sorbonne under Chinese *auteur* Jia Zhangke and made his film thesis, *Xiao Jia rentre à la maison* (*Xiao Jia Going Home*, 2007), with and about him in China. This experience gave his Franco-Algerian feature a tricontinental internationalism: several Chinese crew members are credited for both films, and the eminent Jia Zhangke became one of *Fidaï*'s producers. *Fidaï* also credits additional grants from Kuwait and Germany, a combination that destabilizes a neocolonial Franco-Algerian economic binary. By attaching his first feature-length film to internationalism and a famous director's name, Ounouri received more publicity; *Fidaï* was shown at several international film festivals (including the Toronto Film

Festival, as well as *Films from the Arab World festival* in New York). *Fidaï* received positive reviews from mainstream American publications, such as *Variety* magazine and the *New York Times*.[32]

Ounouri's poetic and cinematic references to Italian poet, essayist, and director Pier Paolo Pasolini further blur nation and time, as well as add to his film's lingual associations. Pasolini, who addressed homosexuality and state corruption and whose 1975 assassination remains shrouded in mystery, evokes communist ideology and controversial filmmaking. His 1963 cinematic essay *La Rabbia (Anger)* pairs archival news footage of oppression and revolution with a rousing poetic text, and it supports Algeria's anticolonial movement and new nation. However, when *Fidaï* opens to a blank screen accompanied by a woman's voice reading a line of poetry in Arabic, the new context dissimulates Pasolini's authorship. This introductory line ("Even if I don't want to remember, war is a terror that does not want to end in the soul, in the world") describes the involuntary role of memory on a veteran. A bird's-eye view of El Hadi cocking a gun in an alley follows as the film's first shot. His voice-over replaces the woman's to say, "Any *fidaï* or soldier must die," before he declares in synchronous sound to the camera in a medium shot, "it's better to die as a *fidaï* than a man of the people who could be shot without reason. It's better to die with sword in hand."

Through translation and sound editing, the Italian poetry of Pasolini, which could be used to describe any postwar reflection, instead grounds El Hadi's statement, specific to FLN ideology, in escapable memory and terror. Likewise, El Hadi's words recontextualize the poetry of Pasolini to describe the particular case of an Algerian independence fighter fifty years later. Increasing the emotional intensity, the faceless female voice (who is none other than Meriem Attoui, the translator of the lines and subtitles) recites Pasolini's poetry in Algerian Arabic or darija at key moments throughout the film, complicating time, language, and viewpoint. The film does not credit Pasolini in a subtitle, and the female voice does not acknowledge its author (though he is listed in the closing credits). Pasolini's poetry, presented in Arabic and modifying a specific Algerian soldier's past, thereby appears as an authentic source of the Algerian Revolution. Simultaneously, the verse broadens the significance of the film as a statement that pertains to all warriors. In fact, the director describes his action as stealing the poetry of Pasolini and reappropriating it for a new cinematic function, largely through its Italian-to-Arabic translation.[33]

Furthermore, by posing questions uniquely in French to his great uncle, who responds almost entirely in Algerian Arabic, Ounouri audibly infuses his filmic text with multiculturalism. Through sound, the spectator of *Fidaï* remains conscious that, in spite of the director's familial alliances, a French perspective guides the reframing. The mixture of languages, generations, and cultures that the two men represent when conversing converge even further as the film begins in Algeria and then moves to France to retread the path of El Hadi's ALN duties. The mise-en-scène thus reiterates the international dimension of production, proffering a dialogue between continents, resulting in an essential aspect of the rhizome ideal. In fact, Deleuze and Guattari use the concept of languages to illustrate the rhizome's principles of connection and heterogeneity, which applies to the use of French and Arabic in all three of the films that I have discussed in depth: "There is no mother tongue, only a power takeover by a dominant language within a political multiplicity ... A method of the rhizome type, on the contrary, can analyze language only by decentering it onto other dimensions and other registers."[34] Both the dialogue and the poetry of *Fidaï* decenter the Mediterranean languages of Arabic, French, and Italian. Although the director speaks only French on camera and thus reminds the viewer of the film's governing language, the dominant screen presence of Algerian Arabic, and its interchange with French, results in a questioning of order and a depiction of multiplicity.

While the film's opening line ("Even if I don't want to remember, war is a terror that does not want to end in the soul, in the world") describes the power of involuntary memories on a war survivor, the film itself documents a forceful and successful attempt at retrieving such suppressed thoughts. Ounouri guides his uncle to geographic locations that are important to his biography in chronological order, recording his memories and directing his reenactments (at the police station, at the jail). Such an approach resembles a traditional psychoanalytic treatment of trauma victims as first pioneered by Pierre Janet (1859–1947), who concluded that only segments of the traumatic event are remembered because the overwhelmed memory fragments the experience, often resulting in amnesia. By contrast, the more flexible narrative memory places the painful moment into a storyline, allowing one to regain an order of events. Thus, the goal of post-traumatic rehabilitation is largely to give a traumatic memory a narrative. If El Hadi does not demonstrate the effects of trauma in the film's introduction, his family members allude to a repression of the war period when confessing their ignorance of this time in his life, which he has scarcely mentioned. Ounouri's film then imposes a chronology on these memories—perhaps scattered, and seldom if ever shared—triggering their retrieval via geographical associations. Interestingly, the chronological investigation of memory actually worsens El Hadi's emotional state in the short time period of the filming, demonstrating that the vicissitudes of the Revolutionary War permeate the present and cannot be framed in the past.

Although *Fidaï*'s attention to the chronology of El Hadi's indoctrination and imprisonment does not allow for a traditional "flashback" of the 1960s era, a montage of war documentary footage functions to much the same effect. Maureen Turim explains how the word *flashback* was coined to describe the narrative film device, and was later used to describe the memory image of soldiers after combat in World War I.[35] It is precisely this dual significance that the newsreel montage depicts; it validates El Hadi's description of the cruelty and omnipresence of the French military, while invoking the post-traumatic compulsion to repeat events. After El Hadi recounts his childhood reaction to the murders and the display of corpses, silence accompanies a carefully selected one-minute newsreel in which the spectator views shootings, a bombing, barbed wire, beatings, and arrests. This silence and the black-and-white film contrast starkly with the contemporary interview footage of El Hadi in color. Moving directly from a close-up shot of El Hadi speaking of his childhood anxiety to the black-and-white footage of a French soldier shooting an Algerian, the newsreel takes an up-close incident that could have been witnessed by the child El Hadi as its point of departure.

The film verifies El Hadi's particular memory, but places it in a larger historical context through the use of news footage, all taken from a French documentary, *La Guerre d'Algérie* (Yves Courrière and Philippe Monnier, 1972). The narrative function

Figures 2.6 and 2.7 *Fidaï* (Damien Ounouri, 2012)

and post-trauma of the "flashback" sequence depend on an archival presence. Jacques Derrida develops a theory of archive fever (or *mal d'archive*) in studying Sigmund Freud's writing that applies to the function of the montage sequence from *La Guerre d'Algérie*. Derrida describes the archive as containing both the repetition compulsion and death drive:

we must also remember that repetition itself, the logic of repetition, indeed the repetition compulsion, remains, according to Freud, indissociable from the death drive. And thus from destruction. Consequence: right on that which permits and conditions archivization, we will never find anything other than that which exposes to destruction, and in truth menaces the destruction, introducing *a priori,* forgetfulness and the archiviolithic into the heart of the monument ... The archive always works, and *a priori,* against itself.[36]

The horrific montage represents truth for the spectator, and in the context of the film, the experience of El Hadi. However, the montage of clips from *La Guerre d'Algérie* also illustrates an urgent need to replay the archived truth for those who did not witness such atrocities, a desperate effort to save this remembered truth from destruction.[37] The director's comments agree with this interpretation; Ounouri explains his decision, "One loses, and it's normal, the reality of the epoch. And language reaches its evocative limits for people who haven't lived through this period."[38] The archive fever thus entails hopes for the future. Derrida writes, "It is a question of the future, the question of the future itself, the question of a response, of a promise and of a responsibility for tomorrow."[39] Such a statement applies to the camera's attention to Algerian youth, and the interviews with El Hadi's granddaughter, who says, "I know nothing of my country's revolution." As such the archive as representative of reality attaches to the film's larger pedagogical motive, which like the film's production and distribution carries elements of *la mission civilisatrice* as found in *Algérie Tours/détours.* However, if Derrida admonishes the archive for excluding many divergent realities, the archive footage here aims not to limit the individual's account but to empower him with the officially guarded memory.

El Hadi's final words in the film metonymize the play between trauma and the *mal d'archive* driving the entire production: "Those who have never known colonialism wouldn't believe it. It is unbelievable." By recording and replaying El Hadi's memories, by verifying the atrocity of colonialism in archives (even while implying that it is beyond representation), *Fidaï* guards the past as a vital element of the present. In both *lieux de mémoire,* Algeria and France, the spectator witnesses the cohabitation of past and present, revealing the rhizome in both the production process and the resulting documentary. Ounouri may use cinema as a vehicle to be what Derrida labels an archonte, an authority who guards and determines what will be the official history.[40] Yet the director's familial alliance and the film's larger international production trouble the still-present French paternalism. Ultimately *Fidaï* finds the Franco-Algerian War drifting toward the present, the ropes to nation and history loosening.

Conclusion

Each of these films explores a specific moment for Algeria and France with many intersecting points: a generation that witnessed the Revolution reaching the end of their lives; and a new generation confused by, and curious about, the war's symbolism and consequences. Elements of dialogue and setting, of cinematic and poetic references, blur epochs and borders. The three documentaries are bound together both stylistically and thematically, for they all reveal a cross-Mediterranean ambiguity concerning chronology. More precisely, this small grouping displays a creative attempt to revisit the Algerian Revolution, to map many possible entrances and exits to the war's memory, as well as their connectivity: the grandchild to the ALN soldier, the French prison to the Algerian school, the present farm to the past torture chamber, and so on.

Once again the concept of cartography is a helpful tool in discovering the implications of the groupings' multilayered relationship to France and Algeria. However, unlike the mad cartography of Mouillaud-Fraisse, who suggests a postcolonial artist's inflection of self in the tracing and naming of an independent nation, mapping for Deleuze and Guattari is the opposite of a repetition. Their concept is hence especially applicable to the documentaries' reliance on and destruction of geographical borders. Their text reads thus:

> The map does not reproduce an unconscious closed in upon itself; it constructs the unconscious. It fosters connections between fields, the removal of blockages on bodies without organs, the maximum opening of bodies without organs onto a plane of consistency ... The map is open and connectable in all of its dimensions; it is detachable, reversible, susceptible to constant modification. ... Perhaps one of the most important characteristics of the rhizome is that it always has multiple entryways.[41]

Whether it be the children drawing their version of the Revolution, or the veteran and his nephew reenacting a murder attempt on a Parisian street, the films record contemporary Algerians modifying the Revolution as a memory, an archive, and a question. Deleuze and Guattari's concept of the unconscious as a rhizome relates to the films' open form, which, like a flashback, denotes both individual and national post-trauma and post-memory. The films reverse, detach, and endlessly connect the Franco-Algerian War to the present as well as to both sides of the Mediterranean Sea.

As I have suggested, however, the French involvement in these projects (whether in funding, production, or direction), which are filmed for the most part in Algeria, contradicts the rhizome by inscribing a neocolonial paradigm into the films. All three documentaries have a pedagogical perspective that bears the traces of the *mission civilisatrice*. The films seek to educate a population ignorant of the Revolution through cinema and archives, and at moments they also seek to expose and frame this Algerian ignorance for a (primarily) French audience, inadvertently evoking a colonial downward gaze at the Other. These neocolonial presences do not illustrate the map of the subconscious, with varied openings, that lacks subjects or objects, because neocolonialism itself does not decenter power relations, but rather reinforces or again traces them on a vertical axis. To be clear, the directors did not produce these films with the explicit intention of perpetuating a neocolonial relationship between Europe and North Africa. Given each of these films' rhizomatic structure concerning generations and events, we can assume that the directors sought to promote a horizontal, egalitarian, noncolonial approach to traversing time and space. Nevertheless, the very existence of films about Algeria that are screened for Europeans reinscribes aspects of economically determined notions of European superiority and African ignorance that may inhibit the promotion of new understandings of the two nations' complicated relationship.

Ultimately, in viewing the films as a discourse, we find the inherent contradiction does not overpower the rhizomatic and post-traumatic elision of space and time. Although Deleuze and Guattari would consider such colonial resonances as ruptures (and, more metaphorically, "ants," in keeping with their biological imagery), such ruptures are intrinsic to any attempt at renovating the rigid and the seen with a multitude of possibilities. The ants' presence constantly threatens the rhizome, just as here the contradictions of imperialist thought nibble at the projects' idealistic aims. The theorists write, "You can never get rid of ants because they form an animal rhizome that can rebound time and again after most of it has been destroyed."[42] Colonial Orientalism is always encroaching and can never be fully eliminated from Franco-Algerian discourse. In fact, its mysterious animal form (for Deleuze and Guattari non-identifiable) makes its destruction even more difficult to address. At the same time, although ants or colonial resonances are always present, the very existence of the rhizome threatens their destruction as well. The rhizome can grow. Still, for the filmmakers to reproach colonialism in Algeria critically, they must at least financially depend on backers who remain to some degree in the thrall of a French discourse of domination. Therefore, while *Algérie Tours/détours*, *China Is Still Far*, and *Fidaï* seek to map the residues of French oppression, a degree of visual colonization continues. The very innovative and elucidatory qualities of these documentaries derive from a struggle against the colonial paradigm that cannot be wholly redacted from the process; these films' reach across time and space complicates a binary that has yet to be dissolved.

3

The Specter of Torture and Atomic Bombs

L'Ennemi intime (*The Intimate Enemy*, Florent-Emilio Siri, 2007) and *Djinns* (*Stranded*, Hughes and Sandra Martin, 2010)

Introduction

In the twenty-first century, the Franco-Algerian War (1954–62) is inseparably linked to torture, now proven to have been a systematic practice of the French armed forces, and an element of the military's larger aim of psychological warfare. While it is difficult to give an accurate count of the Algerians who suffered and died from torture conducted by the French military, military documents, the confessions of French veterans and the excruciating accounts of the victims[1] together demonstrate both torture's brutal and consistent use during the war, and as well as a twenty-first-century historical gaze on the scarred past. (Even more shrouded in mystery is the number of French prisoners of the ALN, whose circumstances have never been publicly acknowledged in spite of some historians' efforts.[2])While the French military legitimized torture as a way to retrieve information, those who recount their participation and/or victimization reveal torture as often arbitrary, sexualized, deadly, and unrestricted. The inherent cruelty of torture helped inspire a movement against French-Algeria during the conflict, not only among Algerians who experienced the viciousness and/or heard the tortured's testimony firsthand, but also in France where the policy was read about clandestinely and where returning soldiers' spoke about their service. The controversy surrounding torture in France and its French state-approval have with time secured the Algerian Revolution's place as a primary symbol of decolonization.[3]

Film is in no small part responsible for the Algerian Revolution's association with torture; the torture montage of *La Battaglia di Algeri* (*The Battle of Algiers*, Gillo Pontecorvo, 1966) propels a powerful component of an anticolonial, pro-Algerian independence message. Yet in this most memorable sequence, the torturers' reasons and emotions remain unexplored—in fact the French soldiers, in identical uniforms, in medium and long shots, often smoking, appear as unpersonalized units of a torturing whole. Furthermore, the torture that opens *The Battle of Algiers* is an efficient means of procuring the address of Ali La Pointe's hide-out. The Prix Goncourt–winning novel of 2011 by Alexis Jenni, *L'Art français de la guerre* (*The French Art of War*), also admonishes the film's representation, "It was a lot more sordid than the film dares to show ... the parachutists electrocuted guys stuck in their shit ... it seemed weird to me, this simple film."[4] Demonstrating the new understanding of the soldiers' relationship to torture and a need for its cinematic expression, other twenty-first-century French films about the Franco-Algerian War depict torture as heinous: films such as *La Trahison* (*The Betrayal*, Philippe Faucon, 2006), *Mon Colonel* (*The Colonel*, Laurent Herbiet, 2006), *L'Ennemi intime* (*The Intimate Enemy*, Florent-Emilio Siri, 2007) and *Djinns* (Hughes and Sandra Martin, 2010) position the French military as caught in an ambiguous, paradoxical, conflicted web, in which they are themselves essentially victims of the torture they practice. However, as Chapter 1 acknowledges, some films had already portrayed the psychological turmoil of the French torturer; most obviously *Muriel ou le temps d'un retour* (*Muriel or the Time of Return*, Alain Resnais, 1963) approaches the post-trauma of torturing and the psychological damage caused by the acts; *Décembre* (Mohammed Lakhdar-Hamina, 1973, a rare Franco-Algerian production that studies in nearly monologue format the pain and anxiety of a French general who orders torture; and René Vautier's *Avoir 20 ans dans les Aurès* (*To Be 20 in the Aurès*, 1972) and *R.A.S.* (*Nothing to Report*, 1973) that depict torturing due to the harrowing loss and fatigue of war.

While these twentieth-century films focus on the soldiers' loss, cinema of the early twenty-first century addresses the repression endemic to the trauma of torturing, resonating with a broader cultural current that confronts guilt. *The Intimate Enemy* investigates this phenomenon thoroughly with a study of a soldier's transformation through three scenes of torture, and provides a soldier cum veteran's reflection on the war in the past tense as the final scene. *Djinns* employs a subgenre, military-horror, to evoke the atrocity of the violent French soldiers' emotional chaos, and through a MacGuffin (which here is a suitcase holding the atomic bomb codes), cinema demonstrates the guilt surrounding the little studied French atomic test explosions, four of which took place before Algerian independence in 1961. While *Djinns* features less torture, the film more violently evokes a French troop's internal violence due to guilt, rage, and confusion in desert warfare. In a horror fantasy spectacle, *Djinns* envisions the atomic bomb tests (the first known by its code name *Gerboise Bleue*, a blue jerboa or desert rodent) as part and parcel of the same physical affront to Algeria, and thus compounds with the guilt of murder and torture. A pairing of these two features filmed in Morocco for a *grand public*, locates the Franco-Algerian War's advance from the art-house to the mainstream action film, and its acceptability and admonishment in the B-series horror genre. The productions completed in the same three years recognize the past military's criminal behavior in the midst of a larger ambivalence shared by the public at the French box office.

This chapter will first study the three torture sequences of *The Intimate Enemy* in narrative order, thereby presenting the evolution of a French character's conscientiousness and contradictory actions in Algeria. *The Intimate Enemy* continuously compromises between the newly elucidated facts of the war and a loyalty to French citizens and historical narratives. Twenty-first century-film's reconsideration of the French torturer in *The Intimate Enemy* prepares us for the national guilt of torture, murder, and atomic bomb testing found in *Djinns*.[5] An exploration of the sub-genre, military-horror, illustrates the Algerian Revolution's current state in the French imagination. I will then demonstrate how the film reduces collective guilt into Orientalist signs of Islam, here *djinns* or ghosts. Jacques Derrida's specter, the invisible-visible that haunts the future, describes not only the actors, the Algerian dead, and their superimposed ghost-like form, but the bomb's fearsome apocalyptic presence. I conclude the chapter by revisiting questions of history's cinematic form and the time-deferment implicit in such historical reflections.

L'Ennemi intime

L'Ennemi intime (*The Intimate Enemy*) reveals the most direct representation of a French torturer in Algeria, with both millennial remorse and retrospective acceptance of the military's dark past. In fact, considered together, the three scenes set in the torture chamber evoke a paradigm shift in the understanding of French military torture in Algeria, an essential component of the early twenty-first-century *épistèmè*. My discussion draws largely from Marnia Lazreg's book on imperial identity and the torturer's management of consciousness, *Torture and the Twilight of Empire*[6] and transfers Raya Morag's defense of Israeli perpetrator's post-trauma in film (*Waltzing with Bashir: Perpetrator Trauma and Cinema*[7]) to contemporary French cinema's portrayal of a more distant war. The arguments of Morag and Lazreg illustrate the complexity of *The Intimate Enemy*, a film that portrays the horror of torturing and its psychological ramifications, but that also reenacts the discrimination and bias at the root of colonialism.

Torture Sequence 1: Liberating the Victim

The protagonist of *The Intimate Enemy*, Lieutenant Terrien, arrives in Algeria as an idealistic love-torn soldier, a motif found in other contemporary films about the Franco-Algerian War such as *Mon Colonel* and *Djinns*, as well as the influential Vietnam-War film *Platoon* (Oliver Stone, 1986), which *The Intimate Enemy* highly resembles in production style and theme. Terrien's evolution from an overseer with moral superiority into a torturer, who is then victimized by warfare, constitutes the film's central theme. Terrien's innocent and well-intentioned beginnings provide an access point for a contemporary *grand public*, whose limited knowledge of the events and military procedure derives from an antitorture stance. In fact, in 2007, four years after leaked photos from Abu Ghraib exposed the US military's criminal torture practices, an anti-torture sentiment in France was more prevalent, bringing the subject of the Franco-Algerian War into a new shameful context. *L'Ennemi intime*'s introductory torture sequence illustrates both the severity of the French military's practice, as well as one soldier's firm antitorture stance, and in this way, equalizes the horror of the images and the historic acts with contemporary knowledge and reason. To this extent the sequence mirrors and builds the public's presumed antitorture position, admonishing the military's ferocity.

Written by the director Florent-Emilio Siri with historian Patrick Rotman, the fiction film is largely a narrativization of Rotman's 2002 documentary series by the same name, in which he interviewed elderly veterans on their experience during the war.[8] These interviews then advanced a view of the French military as a group of individually challenged young men. Consequently, by sympathizing cinematographically and narratively with Terrien, our protagonist who ultimately tortures, the scene sways the audience's view of his future actions. In fact, throughout the sequence, as Terrien walks past the soldiers in the canteen, the camera alternates between facing him in a steady medium close shot, and in a travelling shot depicting his sober gaze over the drunken soldiers. When he at last comes to the source of the deep moaning, heard with increasing intensity, Terrien opens the torture chamber door. Yet rather than a shot of the torture taking place (which will be the following shot), we see a close-up of Terrien in anger and disgust, proving again our shared values and cementing our identification.

In the following shot, low-key lighting displays a presumed Algerian man in a circular wooden tub, grey-bearded and shirtless, being subjected to pain caused by attached electrodes. Two soldiers stand around him, and a third, a *harki*, sits turning a hand motor to power the electricity. The protagonist then steps into the long shot of the three to dismantle the electrodes (at the victim's ears), which results in a very brief close-up of the tortured, also from the protagonist's perspective. In this way, the camera emphasizes not the pain of torture, but rather the valor and ethics of the French man who stops the session. Furthermore, the camera movement and blocking also demonstrate Terrien's sovereignty over the platoon; his domination of the frame (he is in nearly every shot) evokes his power over the fate of the tortured as well as the torture squadron, and even the soldiers' carousal—when he exits he knocks over a table and turns off the music to which they are listening.

Figure 3.1 *The Intimate Enemy* (Florent-Emilio Siri, 2007)

This wins the public's trust and allows his vision and image to guide the rest of the film. Terrien's reaction to witnessing torture and his dismissal of the session evoke Marnia Lazreg's description of the rare soldier's interior protest, *une crise de conscience*—historically there were many men who struggled with their acts such as Général Jacques Pâris de Bolladrière who spoke directly to the public.[9] Yet Terrien's *crise de conscience* happens early in the film, and his exposure to Algeria and warfare complicate his humanitarian notions with the identity of empire, the nexus of the French military's torture policy in Algeria. In fact earlier, the film similarly emphasizes Terrien's humanitarianism when he finds and saves Amar, an Algerian boy hiding in a well from the ALN who have massacred his village. These two altruistic actions combine when Amar further idolizes Terrien for stopping the torture session. The next day, while Terrien takes notes on a map of Algeria, illustrating imperial territory and claim, Amar brings him a cup of coffee. Terrien then assigns the child the daily task of coffee service and comforts him by saying, "On s'occupe de toi maintenant" (From now on we will take care of you). In this way, the scene augments a metaphor present since Terrien's rescue of Amar: the boy represents the Algeria many colonists and French imperialists envisioned, a helpless and ignorant child, while Terrien, symbolic of France's *mission civilisatrice*, offers the aid and protection that Amar (Algeria) needs to survive. Terrien's *crise de conscience* destructs the torture session, and adds a sympathetic foundation to the layered experience of warfare. However, "conscience appears to be extremely malleable."[10]

Torture Sequence 2: Torturing to Death

Protagonist Avatar

As the camera work of the first torture scene suggests, the early twenty-first century aim of *The Intimate Enemy* is complex; while all of the scenes in the chamber visually account for the cruelty practiced, also embedded in the narrative is an explanation of the young French men's inculcation. In this way, the fictional cinematic investigation attempts to solve a national, and for many familial, mystery of the Franco-Algerian War. Although Marnia Lazreg does not treat any film productions, in *Torture and the Twilight of Empire,* she interprets veteran accounts that expose the military philosophy and training as denials of culpability. She notes that in fact, "the realization that one was manipulated in the army ... was used as an exculpatory argument in several trials."[11]) Indeed, the second torture sequence of *The Intimate Enemy* similarly investigates ethics, for the scene tampers its depiction of torture's viciousness with a sympathetic portrait of how such torturing takes root. Furthermore, the protagonist's previous acts of goodwill and the camera's former sobriety, lessen the magnitude of the protagonist's most shameful scene.

When we return to the torture chamber, Terrien, drunk and in mourning, desires revenge for the in-combat murder of a French captain (a captain that argued for torturing with phrases such as "la guerre psychologique" and who had predicted that Terrien would torture, "Vous allez changer comme nous avons tous" [You will change like we all have]). As Terrien walks through the canteen to the chamber, the camera

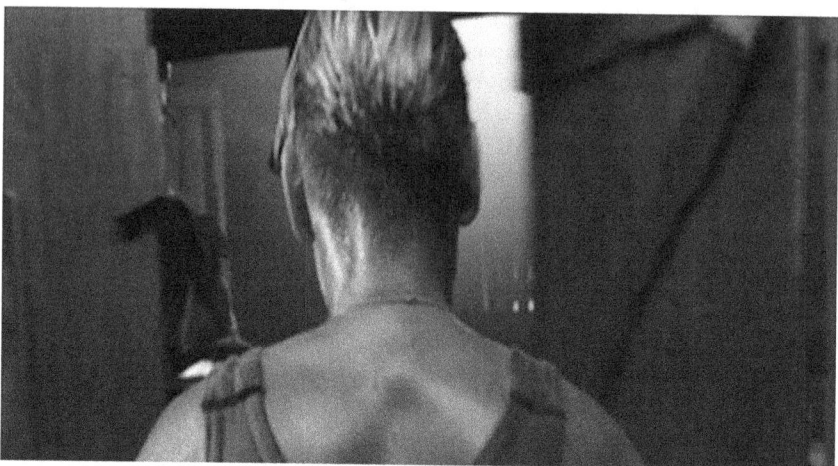

Figure 3.2 *The Intimate Enemy* (Florent-Emilio Siri, 2007)

sways from side-to-side to portray and sympathize with his loss and altered state. As in Terrien's first walk through the drunk soldiers and their revelry, he remains centered to emphasize his importance; yet this time we view his back (rather than his front as in the sober first torture sequence). This posterior view then combines with the swaying to demonstrate that Terrien is no longer in control of his actions. Reminiscent of the video game *Splinter Cell* (2002),[12] based on a Tom Clancy novel, which Florent Emil Siri also directed, Terrien appears as an avatar with another person or force dictating his movements; he is central and dominant, but yet guided by outside forces.

Sexual Torture

The torture montage of Pontecorvo's *The Battle of Algiers* in 1965 likewise depicted the degrading nudity, or near-nudity, of Algerian torture victims. However, more than forty years later, the torture sequences of *The Intimate Enemy* proffer a very different vision that belies the French soldiers' emotional state, and suggests sex abuse and entertainment as aspects of this specific torture phenomenon. Increased nudity proves both the diegetic military's and the film's escalation in torture; upon Terrien's return to the torture chamber, he passes a naked man being whipped, and in the chamber's centerpiece, the tub, the victim has nude limbs, unlike in the previous sequence in which the victim wore pants. The Algerian prisoners' insinuated nudity illustrates Lazreg's extensive research, "The prisoner must strip, and strip fast as the *séance* must begin immediately to prevent any symbolic equality of exchange from taking place between prisoner and torturer."[13] It is a part of the film's compromise that we as a public do not witness the victims stripping. Furthermore, the men's nudity is implied, if never verified—shots and water prevent full exposure. In this way, the sexually laden torture command of stripping, which has taken place before we enter the scene, does not further harm a vision of the protagonist and his platoon. As in Lazreg's words, the transposition of the strip club to the torture chamber exists in many accounts,[14] and *The Intimate Enemy* here attempts a delicate cinematic rendering for a French public. There are perhaps ten men visually and audibly present in the sequence; several pairs of feet dangle from a loft (in the first sequence, there were only two bystanders), and at least four other men contribute to the act of torturing. As three or four sit in the loft to watch without touching, we find a theatric element that contributed to the victims' humiliation. As this male diegetic torture public chants "Speak, speak" (Parle, parle) without participating, the film tropes representations of strip clubs and gang rape. Yet the film only lightly treads on what Lazreg argues is the sexuality inherent in torturing.

When a soldier yells "Dans les couilles!," crudely ordering the electrocution of the suspect's testicles, the film does refer to the sexual abuse in the many torture testimonies while protecting a protagonist who symbolizes the French Republic. The language here connotes the documented practice, the sex organs were a primary target in the French military's torture; the sensitivity of these areas would cause pain, and the psychological degradation was central. Furthermore, verbal clues evoke imagery, a prop; the scissors held by another soldier who suggests that they cut the suspect's testes connote castration to the viewer—at times the French military ripped the Algerian's masculinity and destroyed his ability to have children, exerting a colonizer's biopolitical control. In this way, *The Intimate Enemy* in dialogue (or rather chanting) and in setting (realistic and yet shaped for an interior public) suggests the sexualized, entertainment value of torture found in the Franco-Algerian War documents.

Nevertheless, specific steps must be made to place the protagonist, with whom we have previously identified as an antitorture and child-saving humanitarian, in this violent sphere, namely inebriation (turned to out of sorrow) and revenge (a consequence of loss). Yet the sexual dimension of torture, perhaps augmented by its homosexual nature, or perhaps lessened for a mainstream public by its all-male cast, could destroy the audience's belief and empathy for our protagonist. *The Intimate Enemy* thus measures the new-found verity of the military's sex crimes and the destined public carefully, lightly suggesting and implying, but never stating. For example, when Terrien comes forth to torture, he places the electrodes on the victim's chest, without a close-up of the hands and nipples that might enhance the sexual association of the technique. Furthermore, Terrien our protagonist, not speaking, neither suggests the victim's sexual organs nor complies with such requests. Although these techniques are uttered, and the scissors are held in an accomplice's hand, the victim conveniently dies before any such acts can be committed. By beginning to torture in media res when the victim is already weakened and about to die, but before any directly sexual acts can be committed, Terrien's inclusion and responsibility for the victim's death cinematically carry an air of ambiguity that is only further enhanced by his inebriation. After torturing a man to death, Terrien calmly exits the building to smoke—continuing the sexual metaphor.

Perpetrator's Visual Domination

As my description of the second torture sequence demonstrates, while *The Intimate Enemy* strives to show the atrocity of torture and its immorality, the consistent focus and center is the torturer rather than the pain he induces. In *Waltzing with Bashir: Perpetrator Trauma and Cinema*, Raya Morag summarizes the history of trauma studies, and its insistence on the victim as a distinctive aspect of the psychoanalytic movement of the 1990s that theorized the aftereffects of the Holocaust on survivors. She then argues for a societal need to equally uncover the *perpetrators'* trauma and thus the exigency of complex perpetrator depictions. Although Morag focuses on Israeli films concerning the Intifadas (two periods of intensified Israeli-Palenstinian violence that by most accounts occurred during 1991–5, and 2000–2005), her argument pertains to cinematic treatments of the Algerian Revolution. In fact, *The Intimate Enemy*, as many of the documentaries Morag analyzes, is made in the first decade of the twenty-first century, in the wake of trauma studies, and also seeks to find (as the third torture sequence we will study most readily evokes) the pain of perpetrator trauma. The Algerian victim tortured to death but accessorizes the degradation of a hero turned (briefly) torturer. Nevertheless the ambiguous position of the French soldier innovatively evokes the futility of the *pacification* (as the French government officially called the Algerian War of Independence).

Half-submerged in the circular tub, the camera slants upwards at 30 degrees, capturing the viewpoint of the tortured looking up from below. However, the victim's point of view shot does not enhance the audience's understanding of the victim, but rather reduces his importance and detaches the audience's empathy. Ultimately these point-of-view shots are but a device to keep the torturer dominant in the camera's center. When we do have flashes of the victim in four intercut shots, the tortured man's face is not centered; upside down at a three-fourth turn, his head leans back, conveying weakness and pain, but also disfiguring and diminishing his cinematic value. In this manner, the camera further dehumanizes the nameless torture victim as his individual traits become irrelevant and arbitrary, a point Marnia Lazreg illustrates succinctly with the metaphor of the werewolf: the Algerian "tortured to a virtual animal state of tamed quiescence."[15] Demonstrating that the Algerian victim's death is more important to

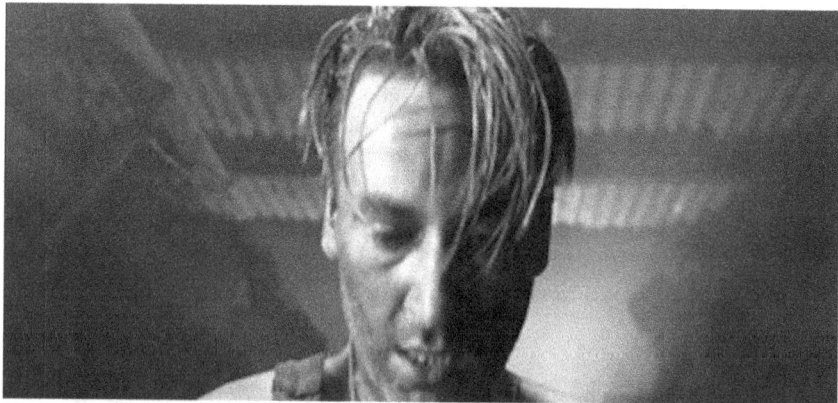

Figure 3.3 *The Intimate Enemy* (Florent-Emilio Siri, 2007)

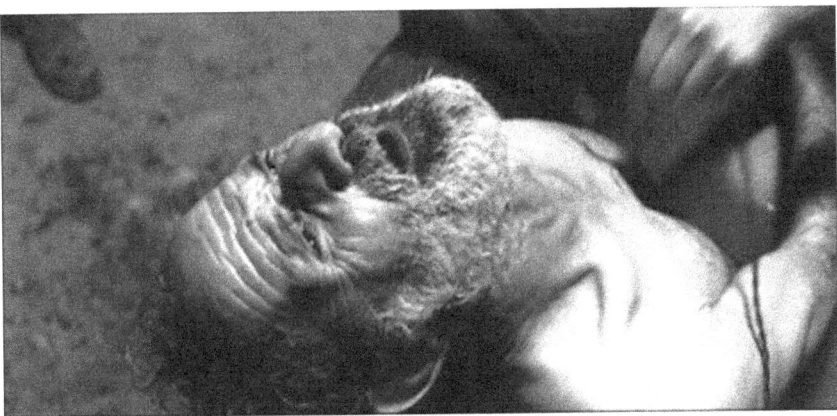

Figure 3.4 *The Intimate Enemy* (Florent-Emilio Siri, 2007)

the film than his life, his face is given the most screen time (three seconds) after he has died.

Although one may read the camerawork of *The Intimate Enemy* as a reiteration of the act of torture that keeps the nameless victim an anonymous Other, it is this insistence on the protagonist, his drunkenness, sadness, anger and group involvement, that the film seeks to expose. Could one film narrative allow an equally developed portrait of the tortured to compete with the perpetrator's experience? It should be noted that while the camera sympathizes with the French protagonist-turned-torturer, the plot punishes him. Amar, the boy that Terrien rescued early in the film proving his altruism, is distraught that the man who rescued him and who once stopped a torture session now in fact tortures an Algerian to death. Therefore, at the end of the film, Amar takes revenge and shoots his former colonel. In this way, *The Intimate Enemy*'s camera work and plot mix to clothe the military in ambivalence; the twenty-first-century film does provide a moral consequence for the defended protagonist, which can be retrospectively deemed productive in the fight for independence.

Torture Sequence 3: The Post-Trauma of Torturing

If the first torture sequence exposes the practice and presents the protagonist as a humanitarian, and the second evokes how the situation of the Franco-Algerian War turned many young men into accomplices, it is of course that the third portrays the mental scars caused by witnessing, ordering, and committing torture. In this way, this post-trauma torture scene propels *The Intimate Enemy* into the late twentieth-century- and early twenty-first-century episteme, one largely informed by trauma studies as well as by France's revelation and acceptance of torture's ubiquity in the Franco-Algerian War. While the first two sequences marginalized the pain of the Algerian victims in positions of anguish, sorrow, and death, the third completely erases the Algerian Liberation fighters. In fact, the third scene in the torture chamber focuses solely on French soldiers as both instruments and victims of their own war machine—here one soldier (Sergeant Dougnac played by Albert Dupontel) orders his own electric shocks. In this way, the film pedagogically guides the audience through the process of a soldier's self-destruction during Algeria's war of decolonization; idealism, entrapment, and self-reprimand. However, while this cinematic exposure to the effect of the Franco-Algerian War and the torture policy on the French soldiers reveals an evolution in approach and understanding, it nevertheless reiterates Algerian torture victims and survivors as secondary and/or forgotten.

In *Three Essays on the Theory of Sexuality*, Freud argues that inflicting pain on others is primary to masochism, which "is nothing more than an extension of sadism turned round upon the subject's own self."[16] Especially in consideration of the underlying sexual connotations, *The Intimate Enemy*'s torture sequences hold a similar logic; for in the first and second torture sequences, we witness the sadism embedded in military procedure, so that the reversal of activity to passivity in the third sequence appears as a reflexive extension. In tandem, the French soldier's agency counters his self-degradation; it is evident to the audience that Dougnac has chosen to take off his shirt (though not his military green pants—a material signifier of his status), sit in the tub of water, and place electrodes on his chest, before ordering, under the threat of his gun, a *harki* to manipulate the wheel that will power the shocks. If applying Freud's early thesis, the *harki* inflicts pain as an active subject: "An extraneous person is once more sought as object; this person, in consequence of the alteration which has taken place in the instinctual aim, has to take over the role of the subject."[17] Nevertheless, it is the French Dougnac who controls the scenario, for despite his passive, masochistic position, he holds the firearm—the phallus. Again, the film protects Dougnac from overtly erotic imagery; there is no nudity, and it is not clear where the electrodes are attached to his body, for we only see the cords wrapped around his shoulders and waist. In this manner, the sexual nature of masochism in Dougnac's self-torture, though present, remains unexplored, just as the film alludes to but never depicts the torture on sex organs that many suffered in the Franco-Algerian War, and that Lazreg convincingly argues is an inherent aspect of torture.

The Intimate Enemy's last torture sequence counters and evokes the most famous self-torturer of the Algerian Revolution, General Jacques Massu, an advocate of the interrogation procedure who proved his objectivity by assigning only those torture techniques that he had first tried on himself. Evidently, Massu found electric shocks tolerable, for he wrote "the condition *sine qua non* of our action in Algeria requires us to admit these methods, as they are necessary and morally valuable in our souls and in our conscience."[18] By planning his own electrocution, Dougnac demonstrates his familiarity with torture techniques, and proves that he has witnessed and/or committed such acts. Yet, unlike Massu, Dougnac's self-torture does not attempt objectivity—he appears drunk, and by turning his own gun briefly toward himself, is on the cusp of suicide. In this way, *The Intimate Enemy* presents a soldier not testing the torture practice, or arguing its worthiness per Massu, but one who, already assessing the procedure as excruciating, relies on the instruments as the means of self-punishment. Massu's description of torture as "morally valuable in our souls and in our conscience" has a dual meaning of self-condemnation if attached to a soldier suffering from post-trauma, such as Dougnac in this scene. Yet Dougnac, never speaks about torture, and we do not see him in the torture chamber during Terrien's previous visits. Therefore, just as the plot minimizes Terrien's torture with instances of humanitarianism, our lack of visual evidence against Dougnac guards his character from a harsher judgment.

Furthermore, despite a very important discrepancy in torture subjects, the scene maintains the film's racialized hierarchy, which was a military reality. In fact, this film has in all three torture sequences placed *harkis* at the wheel, where they act as mere physical components of torture—*harkis* were often used for translation and communication with fellow Algerians (the majority of the French military did not attempt to learn Arabic or Amazigh languages). In the torture chamber of *The Intimate Enemy*, the *harkis* are but thoughtless, wordless, physical power. In fact, here the sole close-up of the *harki* in all of the three scenes displays his grief and tears over energizing the torture of a French man—a sorrow that the camera does not extend to scenes of torturing Algerians. This depicts a reality of torture and its racism; anti-semitic language was an aspect of the torture of the Jewish journalist Henri Alleg chronicled in *La Question*,[19] and anti-Arab racism generally played a crucial role that conspired with other elements to manage the consciousness of the French military. As a veteran account that Lazreg labels "Aldop" notes, racism "was the principal reason for torture on a grand scale ... and for the ease with which torturers were recruited."[20] Ultimately, Saïd (the *harki* played by Lounès Tazairt), like the other Algerian characters tortured, accessorizes and permits the actions and deeper realizations of primary French characters, and here, in his hesitancy and sorrow of torturing a French man, reflects the racism and discrimination by which the army attempted to maintain order.

Therefore, as exemplified by this lone tearful close-up in the torture chamber of the participating *harki*, the scene's cinematography evokes a bias that exceeds the difference between an active and passive or reflexive act. As I have already demonstrated, shots of the nameless Algerian tortured to death in the second sequence are rapid expressions at disfiguring angles meant to invoke the torturer's point of view. In contrast, when the French Sergeant situates himself as a torture victim (as he is bare-chested and throws his head back in agony), the camera centers him in an upright position. Once, the camera does exceptionally capture Dougnac jutting his chest and pelvis upward in pain from a bird's eye view, but the French self-torturer is nonetheless centered, healthy and young, displaying his muscularity in contrast to the seldom pictured bodies of the scrawny, aged, Algerian torture victims. Thus, the apparatus views a French soldier's self-torture with a respect and interest withheld from Algerians. Lighting follows a similar tendency; while the eerie blue tint of night lights are seen in the previous two torture sequences, in the third, orange and yellow hues warm the chamber. This medium-key lighting design enhances the friendship and sobriety of the scene, for it is our protagonist Terrien who enters the chamber and halts the self-torture of his fellow officer by retrieving his gun.

In addition, the rising tension of the group in the second torture sequence is absent in the third, as there are only two men in the chamber with a French victim and they speak rather than chant. This exchange of dialogue and glances between the three men thus allows for egalitarian shot-reverse-shot close-ups, which are absent from the other torture scenes. *Harkis* do have dialogue in other scenes of *The Intimate Enemy*. Nonetheless, the lack of dialogue given to an Algerian torture victim (like his

Figure 3.5 *The Intimate Enemy* (Florent-Emilio Siri, 2007)

lack of name) not only represents the racism of the 1950s and 1960s, but reinforces it. Lighting and camera angles enhance the dominance of the French military and diminish the power of the Algerian liberation movement, even when implying its imminent victory. Ultimately, the message of the sequence speaks to multiple levels of the soldier's experience: Dougnac demonstrates how torturing others extends to self-punishment, while the sovereign Terrien controls situations dangerous to other French men—another way in which the narrative absolves his character even after torturing an Algerian to death. Although the film, and the third torture sequence in particular, posit an analogy between the pain endured by the French perpetrators and the suffering of their Algerian victims, it is the little-represented trauma of the perpetrator that the film considers more valuable and tragic, especially in consideration of the depicted military's lofty beginnings.

In conclusion of my analysis of these three scenes that evoke a larger national reckoning, I return to Raya Morag who ventures that "the core of perpetrator trauma lies in the profound moral contradictions challenging the perpetrators."[21] By creating a narrative with three views of torture and one consistent character whose position shifts, *The Intimate Enemy* represents the confounding paradox at the root of many veteran confessions, bringing the reality of the French military policy in Algeria into a new historical and psychological frame of reference. Morag believes that depicting the complexity of a perpetrator experience has healing capabilities for a society with perpetrator veterans and collective perpetrator guilt, and that this reckoning will eventually bring the society as a whole to commiserate and identify with the pain of the tortured Other. She writes, "I suggest untangling the current hidden connections between the victim and the perpetrator and exposing this discarded ghost as a new way of deepening our responsibility towards the (usually ethnic) other's truth and healing the rift in the fabric of the social order."[22] Morag's thesis, which is centered on the Israeli documentaries concerning the Intifadas, expresses an optimism that we can extrapolate to refer to *The Intimate Enemy*; we do find in Dougnac's self-torture a spatial and experiential connection between the victim and perpetrator (complicit, implied, or indirect) that also seeks repentance for the former national crimes in its early twenty-first century transhistorical space.

Yet do such historical torture representations "deepen our responsibility towards the (usually ethnic) other's truth"? Does this cinematic investigation of the French military's shame and criminal behavior evoke more than sympathy, a need to readdress the Algerians unfairly tortured and killed by the French military in a subsequent French feature? In this respect, Marnia Lazreg is unyielding; she agrees to no apologies for the French military's torture practice in Algeria. To age and inculcation she responds, "Explanations of the systematization of torture and the wanton disregard for life evinced by French troops have often focused on the young age of the soldiers," yet, she argues, "torturers' backgrounds varied greatly, and do not appear to be determining factors in their behavior."[23] *The Intimate Enemy*'s portrayal of torture, the torturer, and the post-trauma of the French military does not fully excuse or permit the behavior of the protagonist who tortures and kills an Algerian suspect. Yet ultimately cinematography that encourages viewer identification with the protagonist, complete with actions of humanitarianism, and/or the influence of peer pressure and alcohol, lighten the torturer's culpability. Furthermore, by concluding the representation of torture with a Franco-French man who guards another from self-harm, *The Intimate Enemy* places patriotic fraternity before the "ethnic other." Notwithstanding, in 2007, these retrospective explorations do demand that French viewers forgive and accept their veterans and a tainted military past. In this respect, *The Intimate Enemy* promotes a distinctly early twenty-first-century French patriotism that negotiates the historical truth of French-Algeria with a forgiving bias.

Spectator Guilt Management

A cultural artifact for its contemporary public, primarily because of its torture sequences, *The Intimate Enemy* demonstrates a larger paradigm shift in the understanding and interpretation of the Franco-Algerian War. The production of the film, at 9,780,00 euros and its mediocre box office receipts (at 409,912 tickets in the first month, the film's earnings did not exceed its budget) do not illustrate any obvious effect on the French national imagination. Yet, the feature negotiates early twenty-first century information and a discussion of torture's immorality with French nationalism, exhibiting and contributing to the place of the Algerian Revolution in France in 2007—the same year President Nicolas Sarkozy declared in Algeria that "the Algerian Revolution made innumerable victims on both sides ... And today I want to honor all of the victims."[24] The very specific French national dialectic present in *The Intimate Enemy* obliges me in conclusion to consider the targeted French public, and the ways in which their viewing of *The Intimate Enemy* provides a media negotiation with historical accounts.

Diegetically, nearly all of the characters in *The Intimate Enemy* witness torture. In fact, such torture viewing is fundamental to its activation, not only through the group element (those who participate with words and machinery, without touching the tortured) but in the visual awakening to torture before committing it. Furthermore, it should also be noted that witnessing torture propels one Algerian boy into fighting for liberation and killing the torturer, the polarizing consequences of watching such inhumane behavior. *The Intimate Enemy* then provides a sensation of viewing torture transhistorically, sharing the experience and perspective of the French military during their Franco-Algerian War service. This pertains specifically to a French audience as the film had but a very minor distribution in the UK, Sweden, and the United States—through fiction film one at last sees what their government censored and what the free market deemed unacceptable. Due to a mutual identification with the French language and nation,[25] or even family members—in consideration of Marianne Hirsch's theory of post-memory,[26] *The Intimate Enemy* provides a catharsis, a repetition of actions at the root of collective guilt, while the camera and narrative depict the military men themselves as the primary victims of war pressures.

The meaning of guilt as described in *The Language of Psycho-Analysis* by J. Laplanche and J.B. Pontalis suggests this shared experience, particularly between the screen self-torturer and the French viewing public. They write, that guilt "is characterized in particular by self-accusations, self-denigration and a tendency towards self-punishment that can end in suicide."[27] When Sergeant Dougnac craves punishment because he feels guilty for witnessing and/or participating in a torture *séance*, a similar need for self-reprimand likely invades the film's intended French audience. Moreover, not unlike the guilt that drives Dougnac to torture himself/order his own torture, the consummation of the film, specifically the scenes of French abuse, represents self-castigation. Sympathetic camera angles, the effect of alcohol, a systemization of torture policy, the loss of a captain, and post-trauma all mitigate the military's torture in various contexts, for the narrative portrays the men as idealistic individuals in highly compromised situations. Marnia Lazreg's term "management of consciousness"[28] describes how many of the French who tortured and were complicit reasoned their participation and situation; the forgiving plot and cinematography permit the spectator to continue viewing, just as elements of a dream prolong one's sleep.

Nevertheless, cinema in its forgiveness only partially erases what remains a highly disturbing vision of torture—the sex-crime element present yet unexplored, as well as the underlying cruelty, and racism. To this extent, French spectators, ashamed of their military's past policy, but compelled to continue watching the film, unconsciously commit guilt-induced self-harm. As a twenty-first-century French production, *The Intimate Enemy* originally exposes the notorious Franco-Algerian War torture from a sympathetic if still critical perspective, an outlier in French cinema, but one that participates in a larger national sentiment. Thus, the film artfully directs collective guilt, cinematically constructing a way for French spectators to punish themselves for their national past. Furthermore, the film suggests that one survives the witnessing and/or complicity of torture through self-punishment—for it is the soldier who sits in the tub who lives, and as his concluding voice-over informs us, eventually reenters French society. In this way, *The Intimate Enemy* models itself on the self-torture that allowed one to endure the actuality of torturing and warfare, and through this same mechanism, the viewer abides the discomfort of the French presence in Algeria, dually confronting the sensation of the military policy in an audio visual experience and rendering its atrocity ambiguous via various threads of self-victimhood.

Extending the soldier's *crise de conscience* to discover a larger national discourse present in *The Intimate Enemy*, we locate a management of guilt both through film and in its national spectatorship. Thomas Elsaesser's term management of guilt,[29] coined to describe similar early twenty-first century tendencies in German film, resonates with *The Intimate Enemy* as part and parcel of a current that finds France revisiting the Franco-Algerian War trauma with a veteran's subjectivity and regret. By borrowing Elsaesser's terminology, and in consideration of the theories proposed by Raya Morag concerning a twenty-first-century-film interest in the perpetrator trauma of Israeli Intifada veterans, we find that France's management of guilt shares stylistic tendencies and patriotic motivations with other national cinemas seeking to expose and forgive their perpetrator past. As Christian Metz declares that moving images reveal the author's and public's wish fulfillment,[30] *The Intimate Enemy*'s existence as a cultural artifact, surrounded by other nations' ambiguous confrontations with perpetrator guilt, indicates a desperate desire to reinvestigate and replay the military's abuse of the Other, in an attempt to legitimize past acts of torture. To conclude with such an international remark is neither to ignore *The Intimate Enemy*'s very specific historical reference made to the Franco-Algerian War nor to erase the complex but powerful transhistorical current that the Algerian Revolution exercises over contemporary France. *The Intimate Enemy* deserves our study and interest because it represents a struggle with France's very specific collapse of empire that torture both illustrates and embodies. However, the historic truths and the consequential negotiations put forth by *The Intimate Enemy* can be extrapolated to describe a larger sphere, connoting cinema's power to clothe revelations and post-trauma in acceptability.

Djinns (2010)

The Title

Any film title warrants our close attention, and, in this instance, *djinns*' etymology reveals the so-named 2010 film's motivation, theme, plot, and style. In fact, the title choice relates a twenty-first century Orientalism that pervades the entire production, as *Djinns* opposes two cultures while gazing upon an exoticized population. Noëlle Roussel-Cubberly writes plainly in her semiotic study that the language of a film title instigates a series of images, all excited by the expectation of viewing:

> If a film title naturally belongs to the linguistic domain, it designates a work of pictorial character, however it seems that the linguistic literary play, useful as it is, does not permit our comprehension of the phenomenon in its entirety: a few words send the reader back to a complex ensemble of millions of images, themselves commented on verbally—simultaneously on screen and off screen.[31]

In this instance, a word from Arabic (djinn a French spelling, jinn the English term) immediately entices with the mystery of another religion as well as its Middle Eastern geography. In a Franco-French context, this allusion to Otherness combines with the fear implicit in the word's meaning as the Larousse dictionary defines *djinn* as follows, "In Muslim beliefs, genie or demon, generally hostile to man. (Jinns play a big role in folklore.)"[32] As such the word *djinn*, merging and inspiring associated images, generates concepts of Muslim beings in opposition to man, and within a realm of superstition and magic. (*Azur et Asmar* [2006] animated by Michel Ocelot reimagines jinns as small mouse-like creatures that fly in colorful clothing). Although the concept of jinns derives from early Arabian spirituality, Islam subsumed many aspects of this tradition, perhaps excusing both the French dictionary's and French film's loose definition. Demonstrating jinns' importance to Islam, the Qur'an devotes the entire 72nd chapter, *Sūrat al-Jinn*, to the so-named entities. This chapter describes jinns as imperceptible to the human eye and, as such, jinns represent an invisible dual universe that can negatively affect humans who do not believe in them.

The French film title simplifies Islamic vocabulary to simultaneously signify horror while the Sahara region recalls Edward Saïd's critic of other such historic synecdoche: "Islam, or a seventh-century ideal of it constituted by the Orientalist, is assumed to possess the unity that eludes the more recent and important influences of colonialism, imperialism, and even ordinary politics."[33] However, *Djinns* remains more enigmatic as it streamlines Islam in order to critique colonialism (even with strains of ambivalence). In fact, the film *Djinns* most specifically invokes an imagined folk-Islam as the wrath of the Algerian soil and its people on French soldiers in the dawn of the atomic bomb testings—tests that fatally affected some French military and Algerians in the Sahara in 1960, when the war's end was imminent. Thus the vaguely religious concept of jinn thematically modifies the very specific historic information hidden by the respective governments. The word's root derives from the Arabic verb *janner*, meaning to conceal, and as such aptly describes the creatures' invisibility to most humans. The directors interpret this as invisible to those who are haunted and manipulated, but not to the spectator and the two characters who are mystically enlightened. The unseen matters of Algeria and the disguised atrocity of the atomic tests mirror the jinn's inconsistency—while the Qur'an does not describe the jinns with visual details, it mentions several times that jinns derive from smokeless fire.[34] Perhaps the mention of smoke inspired the directors to portray the jinns as smoky outlines, but the jinns' transparency, which fades in and out, dually relates the war's previous censored status that attempted to guard the war from popular knowledge. Thus, as the events that haunted young soldiers remained largely unnoticed by many in the metropole, the ghostly jinns are invisible to those French in Algeria who have behaved heinously by disrespecting the lives and territory of Algerians.

In addition, French veterans with post-trauma lived in a society that seldom mentioned the past horrors in which they had participated and/or witnessed. In a cowritten chapter, Nicolas Bancel and Pascal Blanchard describe the stages of France's collective memory with specific dates and references that envelop film culture: "Simultaneously, colonization returned through the remnants of the memory of the Algerian War—and more particularly of torture—holding the bases of a national debate on the colonial question at the end of the 1990s."[35] They then chart the developments of this French awakening: "The invisible (1962–1992), the past became tangible (1992–2002), then completely visible and recurrent in the bosom

Figure 3.6 *Djinns* (Hughes and Sandra Martin, 2010)

of French society (2002–2008).''[36] While such categorizations (to which I will return in Chapter 5) appear facile and do not immediately relate the complexity of the works produced before the late-twentieth-century reassessment (as my first chapter suggests), the ghost-like figures in *Djinns* represent the ways in which the completely visible years interpret the past decades, those years in which the trauma of the French soldiers was ignored, and the acts of torture and bomb testing on Algerians remained unacknowledged. The ghost-like figures' climbing motion, up walls, and on the ground, but always identical in motion and form that fades in and out, conveys such cycles of remembering and forgetting—the national phenomenon described first by Benjamin Stora in *La Gangrène et l'oubli: La Mémoire de la Guerre d'Algérie* (*Gangrene and Forgetting: The Memory of the Algerian War*).[37] As the dictionary entry reveals, the title *Djinns* in French cinema holds an immediate association with demons and demon-imagery. However, the film subversively applies this Franco-French interpretation of Islamic symbolism and language not only to critique the war and colonization, but the Franco-Algerian War's past media life. It is precisely in the "completely visible" twenty-first-century present that the once "invisible" crimes of the past reemerge as a haunting. While such an understanding of the Franco-Algerian War doubtlessly depicts the once ignored post-trauma of soldiers, the film's supreme originality lies in its address of the 1960 atomic bomb tests, which the jinns equally convey as air-forms that mortally infect their surroundings.

In this way, Jacques Derrida's understanding of the moving-image as a perpetuator of ghosts applies literally to the jinns of *Djinns*. In the film *Ghost Dance* (Ken Mcmullen, 2006), Derrida first speaks about the ghosts inherent in photography/film, one that joins Roland Barthes's work in *Caméra Lucida* concerning *l'effet du réel* (the effect of reality) and the photographic referent—Barthes finds that the photograph declares a true fact, that the person or object photographed once existed in such a precise configuration (an argument that contemporary technology challenges).[38] In the film, Derrida ends a near monologue by saying, "Modern technology, contrary to appearances, although it is scientific, increases tenfold the power of ghosts. The future belongs to ghosts." The statement suggests that technology gives birth to its natural opposition, the afterlife, paganism, and souls. Later, in *Echographies of Television: Filmed Interviews*, Derrida speaks with Bernard Stiegler of this past statement, and goes further to investigate the etymology of ghost's synonym, specter, that shares its root with spectacle, aligning the ghost presence further with screens.[39] Derrida's description of the spectacular specter precisely adheres to our film's limited interpretation of jinn and its visual depiction in the horror film (including all historical and metaphorical insinuations): "a specter is both visible and invisible, both phenomenal and nonphenomenal: a trace that marks the present with its absence in advance."[40] The jinns of *Djinns* enact Derrida's argument, for they continually dissolve and reappear, and are only visible for moments. The smokeless creatures both exist and yet do not. As alternate spheres of fiction and reality that encompass both the invisible past and visible present, the jinns symbolize an undeclared war and nefarious atomic tests whose damage was never fully recognized.

Gerboise Bleue

When reading both the jinns of *Djinns*, as well as the film itself as Derrida's specters, a spectographic history emerges. As *Djinns* presents the truth of the *Gerboises* tests with suspense, elements of mystery slowly reveal the facts of their occurrence—it is nearly the final sequence which frames a confidential letter signed by Charles De Gaulle with the determined date of *Gerboise Bleue*, this shot dissolves into a simulation of the first 1960 explosion. The revelatory, spectacular manner in which *Djinns* informs the public of the truth of the atomic bomb tests in the Algerian Sahara modifies the secrecy of their deployment, and lightly suggests, without directly addressing, the cover-up of those wounded and killed. As all military defense strategies, secrecy surrounded the operations. Although the French government did not reveal its nuclear bomb laboratory until the first tests had taken place in 1960, the decision to use the Algerian Sahara as testing grounds was nearly simultaneous with *Toussaint Rouge* (the onset of FLN attacks that were later declared the beginning of the war on November 1, 1954). Far from mainland France and scarcely populated, Reggane, in the southern Algerian Sahara, was chosen by scientists and politicians together as the location for bomb tests. The first test, coded as *Gerboise Bleue*, took place fifteen years after the cataclysmic American bombs in Hiroshima, yet the French bomb quadrupled its American predecessor in weight and power.[41] The bombs were most often ignited from a tower of approximately 100 meters high each weighing up to 70 kilotons—the surrounding populations were not consulted or considered.[42] The initial tests spelled out the French flag with blue, white, and red. However, officials rushed to explode *Gerboise Verte* (*vert* meaning green) after the putsch of 1961, in order to guard the information from those OAS members seeking to take Algerian territory. This test aimed to examine the possible effects of a hypothetical battle by placing 195 French soldiers (who had been serving in Germany) in the bomb's vicinity for three hours.[43] Luckily, due to a technical mistake, the bomb released ten times less the atomic power than intended, which is not to say that the medical effects on the men were not profound. Upon studying press contemporary to the tests, one finds very few French reports other than the president's laudatory comments, but a considerable negative press initiative from East Germany. One documentary Karl Gass's *Allons les enfants ... pour l'Algérie* (*Let's Go Children ... for Algeria*,1962) interviews a German legionnaire who witnessed 150 Algerian prisoners serving as guinea pigs.[44] In consideration of the war censor, such a lack of French reporting was also the result of the state labeling such information *confidentiel défense*. The atomic tests validated France as an international superpower and utilized the embattled colonial territory for proof of its global relevance, even while the harm on French soldiers and Algerian civilians remained unchecked for decades.

Initially, the French twenty-first-century fascination with the Algerian Revolution, which included at last declaring it a war 37 years after the fact, did not transfer to a shared interest in the *Gerboises* tests—in fact, Stora's *Gangrene and Forgetting* fails to mention their occurrence. Yet the geographic and temporal simultaneity of the war and the bomb tests prove their interconnectivity as related aspects of an empire's exercise of power and territory. The national investigation of the Franco-Algerian War that demanded a reevaluation of post-trauma, censorship, and torture preceded and motivated a release of information concerning the atomic tests in Algeria. In 2001, a veteran group called AVEN (Association des vétérans des essais nucléaires) formed to confront what was responsible for their current health problems, that is their military participation in the Sahara and exposure to nuclear bombs.[45] Finally, in 2008, France agreed to pay compensation to the soldiers who were exposed to the atomic air and suffered from resulting medical difficulties, such as cancer and infertility, a fight that many veterans had waged for decades.[46] Then in 2010, *Le Parisien* accessed a key document, edited in 1998 and sent anonymously (though presumably by Pierre Billaud who had worked for the atomic laboratory), titled "la Genèse de l'organisation et les expérimentations au Sahara."[47] The *Nouvel Observateur* and *Libération* also exposed the tragedy of French soldiers used as atomic guinea pigs. Questions remain, as the corpses of 150 Algerian prisoners being used as guinea pigs were found at the site of *Gerboise Blanche*.[48] The test explosions of 1960-2 (*Gerboise Bleue, Gerboise Rouge, Gerboise Blanche*, and *Gerboise Verte*) coincide with a growing anxiety over Algeria gaining independence, and reclaiming the nuclear bomb testing grounds. Charles de Gaulle's government strategically attached French rights to testing in the Sahara for four more years to the independence agreement, demonstrating a less obvious value of Algeria to France.[49]

Nevertheless, the French press exposure of the secret documents and its effects on veterans encouraged an international discussion concerning the *Gerboises*. After Algerian pressure on the International Atomic Energy Association in 1995, new tests were done to measure the radioactivity at the past testing sites in 1999, the results of which were published in 2005. While the report found little residue, the report includes a section labeled "Late Effects," which explains the scientific links to cancer even decades after exposure to atomic gases, and the possibility of hereditary effects.[50] Several Algerian documentaries followed the tests, the first of which *Vent de sable: Le Sahara des essais nucléaires* (*Wind of Sand: The Nuclear Tests of the Sahara*, Larbi Benchiha, 2008) returns to Algerian communities near the test sites that suffer residual effects. A year later, another documentary, *Gerboise bleue* by Djamel Ouahab, premiered at festivals in France and on the French/German network Arte. In addition to meeting with villagers in Reggane, Ouahab's documentary paints an empathetic portrait of two retired French military officers, Lucien Parfait et Gaston Morizot, who lost many physical functions due to exposure, but received no financial compensation. In consideration of these documentaries, we find that *Djinns* contributes to a larger transnational *épistèmé* that includes new scientific and historical interest (even if limited) in the Gerboise cycle.

As this monograph generally argues, in conjunction with a mainstream of international scholars, the twenty-first century witnessed the renewed historical importance of the Algerian colonial conquest and its demise. In addition, the breadth of this interest includes the French atomic bomb tests at the margins of a wider excavation. As former military members confessed of their war years at the end of the twentieth century, and as new tests in the Algerian Sahara brought attention to the continued traces of the nuclear bombs, Algerian and French media brought the historic events into the present day. The films' production dates indicate that the writers of *Djinns* most probably did not see the documentaries before conceiving their horror picture. Nonetheless, their releases in consecutive years indicate a larger historical reflection in motion, one that reframes the atrocity in the Algerian sphere, as well as its boomerang effect on the French military. The new comprehension of the *Gerboises* as the government's final desperate clasp on colonial domination had now resurfaced. In this way, the B-horror flick locates a popular need to mitigate the antitorture, anticolonial sentiment with a defense of the individual, ignorant, French men, painted as mentally unsound due to the circumstances of war. While *The Intimate Enemy* and *Djinns* both expose such circumstances in order to destabilize a villainous stereotype of the French military in Algeria, it is *Djinns* that further clothes guilt in a generalized fear of and fascination with Islam. This simplified understanding of a foreign religion then proffers the atomic bomb tests as the dystopic mysticism of war.

Soldiers chase the jinns, and/or threaten other soldiers due to confusion caused by the jinns—in fact only Daouïa, the wise Algerian woman played by Raouia, who refers to herself as the village's spiritual guardian, and Michel, the soldier she intuits as their future spiritual leader, perceive of the jinns objectively with calm. In this way, the effect of the jinns' presence replicates a mental disorder in which those suffering hallucinate images that repeat their trauma (in one instance, a jinn appearing as a murdered woman, encourages her assassin to kill his fellow soldiers). Therefore, *Djinns* applies an external visual signifier of a mental and thereby concealed disorder, through the use of superimposed direct animation. Fantasy and related special effects portray the damaged human mind as a flowing existence in space. However, the concept of filmic jinns or ghosts, an externalization of an internal disorder, never diminishes their power. Furthermore, film form establishes all of the participants' mortality (a sensation Derrida feels when watching a scene from *Ghost Dance* in which he shares a dialogue with costar Pascale Ogier, shortly after her death). The film itself testifies to the subjects' mortality, the evidence of both the actors' lives presumes their eventual death. On a historical, diegetic level that pertains to the jinns' space in a contemporary B-horror film, the lives of Algerians lost in the mediatized Revolution are invoked as readily as the aura of their eventual deaths. The jinns of *Djinns* reiterate a past absence and importance while struggling for longevity in the present tense.

The jinns' lack of eyes, a detail that simplifies their shape, denies engagement and entry into their consciousness. As Derrida notes, spatially we exist within the screen image's line of vision, but we cannot return the film subjects' regard of us, even when staring directly at their image. Derrida speaks of the disparity of exchange with the actor on screen, "I can't meet the gaze of the Other but I am in his sight."[51] This places the specter/screen image for Derrida in a realm of superiority and judgment that dominates the viewer. As Derrida explains, "The specter enjoys the right of absolute inspection ... I am who am because of him, owing to him obedience, incapable of exchanging with him (not even a glance)."[52] Others correctly identify a spectral gaze that haunts Bernard in *Muriel*—the tortured woman's stare obsesses him after her death.[53] Similarly, we can extrapolate this concept of visual media to the jinns of *Djinns* who represent the Algerian wrath, specters of atomic bombs. Despite shot counter shot, the soldiers cannot establish eye contact with the smoke forms, and without the possibility of an exchange, the French soldiers cannot amend their past judgment.

Furthermore, the specter of Saharan tragedy extends to the viewing public—in fact, Derrida's words more intentionally describe the spectator's relationship to film and filmed subjects. In terms of the Algerian Revolution setting, our literal absence from the history of the Algerian Revolution replicates the fictionalized film narratives; we are incapable of meeting a photographed person's eyes. While McMahon locates the specter of colonial history in *Muriel* primarily through the discombobulation of sound and image, forty-seven years later *Djinns*' spectators are further distanced from the quest for justice and verity during the war—in fact fifty years exactly separate *Djinns*' premiere from the *Gerboise Bleue* test. The eyeless jinns that embody an imagined vengeful Algeria cannot perceive our stares, and the French soldiers depicted cannot interact with the twenty-first century, an exchange that might theoretically curtail the military's viciousness or the narrative's looming atomic bomb test.

The device of a super-8 camera additionally joins *Djinns* to *Muriel*. The prop records the experiences of both films' protagonists (Bernard of *Muriel* and Michel of *Djinns*) and stylistically imposes variation by interweaving their films. In a study of the many personal films made by French soldiers in Algeria, Jean-Pierre Bertin-Maghit demonstrates how such cameras, usually the 8 mm Bauer 88 or Reinette super HL 9.5 mm (all of which did not record synchronous sound) served to paint an idealized portrait of the time abroad for family and friends in the metropole. The cameras and their young directors did not seek to make documentaries, and to this extent the gruesome scenes of corpses and torture were avoided in favor of footage of playful young men, many times helping children in the Algerian countryside.[54] The climax of *Muriel* evokes the stark contrast between the soldiers' filmed testament and the cruelty to which they contributed—Bernard, the protagonist scarred from his past service and returned to France, plays his personal films (which take the full screen) of men in uniform, who smile and joke in the countryside. Yet his accompanying voice recounts the torture, rape, and murder of an Algerian woman in which he ambiguously assisted; such an unsettling paradox between sound and vision, memory and public evidence, critiques the censor.[55] As proposed in 1975, *Muriel* represents the paradox between the vision of the *événements* put before the French people by their government, in which the visual evidence of the torture of Algerians was eliminated, and the conflicting sounds of veterans' oral testimonies.[56]

Muriel's powerful statement frames all discussions of cinema's portrayal of the French soldier's post-trauma, and the ways in which filmmaking further implicates the protagonist in constructing the memory. Thus, the several short takes of Michel's films in *Djinns* differentiated in the narrative by black and white film, ressemble the montage in *Muriel*, faithful to the true combatants' films. Just as *Muriel*'s Bernard provides no film evidence for the atrocious actions of which he speaks, *Djinns*' Michel, who sometimes films the Algerian villagers but more often his fellow soldiers, neither captures the war's criminality nor the ghost-like forms that instigate the soldiers' increasingly ruinous outbreaks. Thus the absences in the super-8 films of *Djinns* echo a past critique within a transhistorical commentary and judgment, for diegetic scenes of torture and murder in Algeria surround the soldier's *lettres filmées*. Furthermore by 2010, the interior absence now reveals a ghostly form—just visible enough to draw attention to its lingering past, reemerging and retreating. While the soldier's camera never frames the murder and torture of Algerians by French hands, the spectator does witness these acts, as well as their posthumous haunting. Thus the space that exists between the interior film and its feature mirrors that between the year of the film's setting (1960) and subsequently its year of production (2009). This temporal dialectic incorporates the horror genre, revisiting the specter of the Franco-Algerian War.

The Military-Horror Genre

By employing the horror genre to expose the Franco-Algerian War and the atomic bomb tests, *Djinns*' attempts to reach a niche market and as such represents an evolution of the war's symbolism in the popular imaginary. Indeed, we are very far from the intellectualism of *auteur* films by new wave directors such as Jean-Luc Godard's *The Little Soldier* and Alain Resnais's *Muriel* (both released in 1963), or even the art-house features produced but a few years prior such as Michael Haneke's *Caché* (*Hidden*) in 2005 and Philippe Faucon's *The Betrayal* in 2006. Chapter 5, concerning the biopic gangster diptych of 1970s' criminal Jacques Mesrine, demonstrates fully the ways in which the twenty-first century's inclusion of the Algerian Revolution in genre films evokes an acceptance if ambivalence toward history. However, the lack of time devoted to the still controversial war setting, and the more subtle interest in its overarching symbolism, permitted the Mesrine films' superior box office success. Furthermore, the gangster genre in which a powerful antihero typically governs, rather than the horror-genre film primarily signified by mise-en-scène and sound design, exposes the Franco-Algerian War's enduring symbolism in a more covert fashion.

This is not to say that the horror genre does not internally represent a battle of revelatory and repressive currents. In a study of 1970s horror films, Robin Wood offers a perceptive generalization, "The true subject of the horror genre is the struggle for recognition of all that our civilization represses or oppresses, its re-emergence dramatized, as in our nightmares, as an object of horror, a matter for terror and the happy ending (when it exists) typically signifying the restoration of repression."[57]

As Woods notes, mortality and sexual violence become primary themes as these arguably voice the primary subject of humans' unspoken fears and anxieties—or, on a more morbid note, desires. However, one can equally apply Wood's comments to a French historical sphere, illustrating the suppression, oppression, and reemergence of the facts of war cruelty. To this extent we find cinema exposing and encouraging these changes in Algeria's symbolism and in the French national consciousness. As already demonstrated, the jinns evoke the invisible years (1962–92) when little evidence of the Franco-Algerian War was found in mainstream French currents, while the war's presence in horror cinema reiterates the third, when after 2002, the majority of French society realized the importance of the Franco-Algerian War, which at last rendered a critique possible. Regardless of the fact that the unique horror film about the Franco-Algerian War achieved neither critical nor box office attention in 2010 (*Djinns* premiered at twenty-seven French theaters and was in eighteenth place during its release week), the production validates an examination of the atomic bomb tests in Algeria—a subject never completely investigated as the military files have not all been revealed to the public. Fifty years later, the realm of fantastic horror declares the reemerging historical evidence of the atomic tests and insists on the spatiotemporal relationship of the atomic tests to the Franco-Algerian War.

For this reason, our study must consider genre, as it combines the military historical film with horror motifs and thus bridges the ramifications of the military's psychological trauma with the mystery surrounding the veritable causes. In "The Military Horror Film: Speculations on a Hybrid Genre," Steffen Hantke identifies the basic plot structure of a cluster of early twenty-first century pictures, their style, and their thematic aims.[58] Hantke first locates the phenomenon within a larger cinematic tradition that includes the work of George Romero. He then closely studies three British productions, *The Bunker* (Rob Green, 2001), *Dog Soldiers* (Neil Marshall, 2002), and *Deathwatch* (Michael J. Bassett, 2002) in order to construct a more succinct definition. Despite its geographic difference, the French production *Djinns* neatly fits into Hantke's categorization, for like other military-horror pictures, *Djinns* portrays a platoon's traumatized soldiers violently turning against one another in an abandoned location, until there remains but two surviving members. Hantke writes that unlike the traditional war film "in the military-horror film, however, only one route seems available: as soon as the external threat begins to manifest itself, the social body begins to disintegrate."[59] In *Djinns*' case, it is not the past murders and torture per se (though we do see a murder of an Algerian woman and the light torture of Algerian prisoners), but rather their haunting that poses an external threat to the lost platoon, as the jinns' supernatural presence fractures the soldiers' already fragile mental state. However, the murderous soldiers' actions unknowingly work in tandem with the government's larger atomic testing network to wreak havoc on the people unified with the land; the film ultimately reveals a cosmic geographic attack of fantastic proportions and consequences. Contrary to Hantke's finding that the historicism of the war depicted in military-horror films is by and large rather arbitrary, *Djinns* insists on the very specific time period, 1960 (given in both intertitles and in diegetic documents), and the southern Algerian Sahara where seventeen atomic bombs from 1960 to 1966 were detonated. Thus, *Djinns* draws the viewers into a year and place to expose a historic horror; the visual grandeur of the tests relates the inevitable spiritual forces that the platoon, ignorant of their planning, cannot undermine.

Several framing shots, which commence and conclude the film, build suspense around the possibility of this future explosion and the mystery that still surrounds *Gerboise Bleue*, though dramatic irony ensues for the viewer aware of the atomic tests. The first sequence finds a man in torn clothing, with a scarf covering his face, and bloody wounds on his arms, struggling to walk down a desert road, while holding a dinted metal suitcase. This flash-forward in the opening credit sequence contains the film's Macguffin—although the soldiers do not know of the locked suitcase's contents, they are magnetically drawn to the object, and in one instance fight till death for its possession. At the film's conclusion, we see the footage again, now in context; a barely surviving soldier delivers the suitcase to a base and the viewer at last witnesses its opening—a letter from Charles de Gaulle with the atomic codes. This revelation at the film's conclusion neither directly explicates the soldiers' abhorrent actions nor the jinns' force on their behavior. Instead, *Djinns* arms such horrific phenomena with historicity, propelling the viewer to investigate their veracity.

A dream sequence early in the film also builds mystery and suspense around the bomb tests. In Michel's dream, an Algerian child—a child also a horror trope—finds Michel's super-8 camera on the ground and attempts to run away with it. However, when Michel follows him, he holds out his left hand to be held in friendship and protection. In a long shot, we see the outlines of Michel and the boy watching a bomb's explosion in high contrasts from a distance. This dream sequence, which appears in the film's first quarter-hour, frames the rest of the action, for the film concludes with a bomb detonation; a graphic match to the dream explosion, Michel departs from the Algerian tribe he now leads to watch, accompanied by the Algerian boy who holds the super-8 camera. The spectacular sequence of special effects thus

Figure 3.7 *Djinns* (Hughes and Sandra Martin, 2010)

attaches to the suitcase coda already described, as it affirms that the explosion was in fact *Gerboise Bleue*. The camera remains a symbol of power and witnessing, exterior to the banality of the films shown. After the initial explosion, the camera changes direction and provides a close-up of the boy recording the event, the camera against his face. We thereby intuit that Michel having abandoned his previous life's European qualities bequeaths his prize possession to a youth, emblematic of a new Algerian generation. In this way, *Djinns* refreshes historical recollection with the optimism of fiction and the film medium; the French soldier's camera retrospectively empowers the disenfranchised with proof, but does not disavow a contradictory display of paternalism.

Likewise, the film's conclusion, in which a divined French man leads Algerians and pauses to view the bomb explosion from a mountain, complicates a portrait of French guilt and Algerian revenge. In fact, Michel's character ultimately transforms a hybrid of already established male and female, Algerian and French identities. The marabout Daouïa explains to the French soldier Michel that he will carry the community's spiritual legacy after her death, an inevitability that she foresees as part of the soldiers' mutiny. She, in her late fifties or early sixties, in white flowing gowns, a headscarf, and elaborate facial tattooing—a common symbol of marriage for Algerian women during the war-era—is the only Algerian villager who speaks French. She thus represents the only communication link to the people of the Sahara and their spiritual landscape for both the French army and the Francophone public. Michel, tall, fair, and blond, starkly contrasts with her typical Maghrebi features to symbolize the visual union of North Africa and France. This union becomes literal when Fatima finally dies and Michel acquires her facial tattoos through supernatural transference; a cut from the dark room where she is dying from a gunshot wound to a two shot of her face (eyes closed evoking death) and Michel's (now covered by her tattoos) outside in the sunlight, depicts the otherworldly force responsible for his Algerian transformation. The blond soldier who captured Algerians at gunpoint, in seconds becomes an Algerian tribal leader, and the ethnic markings that represent a historical female Other for a Francophone public magically disarm his Frenchness without eradicating it. In this way, a spectacular vision of imagined Algerian spirituality isolates and forgives a French soldier, providing the audience with an exception to relieve what might have been a damnation of the French military. The skin signifiers leave Michel less military, less French, and more tied to the mystical order that condemns the atrocities. When Michel at last leads the Algerian villagers, he has additionally acquired a white turban that visually defines his new spiritual and cultural belonging.

Though the soldiers' criminal actions of murder and torture fully deserve blame and morally warrant the haunting of the jinns, the atomic bomb test exerts a strength beyond their human control and due to secrecy, beyond their knowledge. The enormous mushroom cloud in purple and grey illustrates, like the jinns, the transient nature of air, its dangerous and transparent qualities, that surreptitiously affect the health of the surrounding beings. This dream of a bomb early in the narrative grounds the soldiers' mental injuries and cruelty in the supernatural; an airborne current translates their fate, and breathes the horror of bombs into the already-present psychological doom of PTSD. However, while the super-8 camera imparts the specter of the censor in Michel's films, in the Algerian boy's hands it signifies witnessing and control over history's formation, a feat that the film *Djinns* itself equally undertakes.⁶⁰

The Specter of History

Just as the personage/ghost on screen evokes a past and the inevitability of a future absence, *Djinns'* jinns reveal the Algerian Revolution's estranged pertinence to both temporalities, as well as demonstrating the impossibility of the viewer's direct communication with the war era. In this way, the jinns represent hybrids of military post-trauma, national reckoning, guilt, and an imagined Islamic reprimand, all in the guise of atomic smoke. Just as the phantoms/jinns haunt the diegetic French soldiers by confusing their present with their past misdeeds, moving images grant the exterior spectator access to a painful national past (painted in fantastical action sequences) as part and parcel of their own perceived present spectatorship. History itself, written, recorded, and reenacted, always carries such burdens of time deferment. Derrida writes, "But the recording of an event, from the moment that there is a technical interposition, is always deferred, that is to say this '*différance*' is inscribed in the very heart of supposed synchrony, and the living present."⁶¹ *Différance*, a term that Derrida coined to speak of words' dependence on surrounding words of contrast and modification and how they together create meaning, in this instance relates to recorded media that with the smallest delay allows the past to interfere with the present. In this way, just as moving images create a multitude of ghosts, history through a camera's lens becomes itself doubly phantomantic, already recorded in the time period with *différance*, and then revisited to place the phantoms of the Franco-Algerian War and the atomic tests in relief with a rapidly passing 2010 present. The jinns depicted as ghosts or specters thus dually infer the regret and ignorance of all the French soldiers stationed in Algeria, while haunting the current spectator with the revelation of this abominable past.

Conclusion

Both *The Intimate Enemy* (2007) and *Djinns* (2010) awaken the viewer to French military behavior during the Franco-Algerian War, as well as to many soldiers' conflicted emotions of humanitarianism and revenge. Such narrative themes modify the French productions' larger ambivalence to the French military presence; while *The Intimate Enemy* and *Djinns* both expose torture and unjustified murder by French soldiers, they proffer a detailed description of extenuating circumstances that might surround such behavior. Furthermore, the films attach an early twenty-first-century perspective of post-trauma to this national memory; the self-inflicted torture endured by Sergeant Dougnac in *The Intimate Enemy* helps relieve the military of the audience's blame, for the torturer already suffers mentally and physically for his crimes. *Djinns* similarly depicts the French military hurting themselves (both stabbing and shooting one another, and in one instance an accidental suicide) as the jinns confuse and frighten soldiers with the memories of their criminal violence against Algerians.

To this extent, the twenty-first century produces plots that both punish and absolve the French military from a once hidden past. The military-horror film set during the Franco-Algerian War demonstrates an acceptance of the setting and its evolution. No longer weighed by verisimilitude, the ghosts interweave post-traumatic memories with the residue of atomic air, and thereby haunt the ephemeral screen-present.

4

Reclaiming the Screen Algerian Revolution

Cartouches Gauloises (*Summer of '62*, Mehdi Charef, 2006), *Hors-la-loi* (*Outside the Law*, Rachid Bouchareb, 2010), and *Les Folles Années du Twist* (*The Crazy Years of the Twist*, Mahmoud Zemmouri, 1986)

Introduction

Moudjahid cinema describes fiction films funded by the Algerian government in the 1960s and 1970s that sought to reiterate the pain of the Revolution (1954–62) and inspire anticolonial, nationalist unity. The best-known works of Mohammed Lakhdar-Hamina, the most celebrated Algerian director of his generation, *Le Vent des Aurès* (*The Wind of the Aurès*, 1967) and *Chronique des années de braise* (*Chronicle of the Years of Fire*, 1975), are in fact *moudjahid* features; both won awards at European festivals and garnered global acclaim. In these two features, Lakhdar-Hamina focuses on the desperation of Algerians dislocated by colonialism and war, both end in anticolonial fervor. Unsurprisingly, a different generation of transnational Algerian-French films and filmmakers dialogue with the *moudjahid* film legacy and most pointedly reveal the influence of Lakhdar-Hamina. In fact, while Rachid Bouchareb's big budget *Hors-la-loi* (*Outside the Law*, 2010) may initially draw comparisons with the *moudjahid* Western *Les Hors-la-loi* (*The Outlaws*, Tewfik Farès, 1969), from which it takes its name, Lakhdar-Hamina's stylistic influence in fact proves more dominant in this epic concerning three Algerian brothers who eventually work for the FLN in France. We also find Lakhdar-Hamina's *moudjahid* films' influence in another transnational vision of the Revolution from the 2000s, *Cartouches Gauloises* (*Summer of '62*, Mehdi Charef, 2006), in which an Algerian boy wandering through Oran on foot witnesses a series of horrific events in the days before independence is declared. Both twenty-first-century depictions reveal how the most celebrated *moudjahid* films by Lakhdar-Hamina remain important signifiers of the screen Algerian Revolution. Will Higbee correctly identifies *Summer of '62* and *Outside the Law*'s relationship to French cinema, by labeling them counter-heritage films.[1] Yet a broader investigation uncovers the extent to which an Algerian film legacy also anchors the films. As Hamid Naficy argues,

"Little sustained and systematic attention has been paid to theorizing the expatriot or exile genre. Recent shifts in the global configuration of capital, power, and media, however, have made such an attempt necessary ... Transnational filmmakers have ... enriched the cinemas of their home and adopted lands."[2] By locating the Algerian strains in these coproductions, and the ways in which an Algerian film legacy touches, merges, and sometimes contradicts French and American influences, we expose an evolution in the international imaginary of the eight-year war. The directors' education and professional experience, the films' financing, and audiences form a complex web that defines postcolonial cinema.

After locating *moudjahid* characteristics of nationalistic uplift in Bouchareb's and Charef's twenty-first-century interpretation of the Algerian Revolution, we will consider *Les Folles Années du Twist* (*The Crazy Years of the Twist*) from the 1980s by a fellow transvergent director Mahmoud Zemmouri. A comedic outlier, *The Crazy Years of the Twist* satirizes Lakhdar-Hamina's classics to force a new interpretation of the war on film. If the twenty-first-century features *Outside the Law* and *Summer of '62* paid homage to the *moudjahid* epics of Lakhdar-Hamina, how could an 1980s' film (with exclusive Algerian government funding) mock the patriotic vision of the decolonization movement? The chapter's conclusion considers the episteme that permitted Zemmouri's sardonic production of the war and the reasons why a comedic feature concerning the Algerian Revolution remains an impossibility in the early twenty-first century. Deleuze and Guattari's terminology surrounding the *terrain*, as borrowed by Réda Bensmaïa in *Experimental Nations* to discuss North African authors and directors, will provide a useful lens through which to view the Algerian Revolution filmed by dislocated Algerian directors; I will therefore define deterritorialization and reterritorialization with examples from *The Wind of the Aurès* and *Chronicle of the Years of Fire*.

Algeria's Cinematic Reterritorialization: *Moudjahid* Films

Reterritorialization, creating a founding mythology that attaches a people to a *terrain*, was a natural, necessary step after decolonization—a way to reinvoke a people's purpose and right to land that had been confiscated. Réda Bensmaïa employs the term when describing the decolonized national mood:

> There was, in other words, a concrete effort to build from scratch but without improvising: to build upon the debris of a social and cultural community that had barely escaped disaster and total upheaval ... For to create or to re-create a terrain, to define something like a national trait, is an act of reterritorialization.[3]

Cinema was a vital part of this intensive "self-fictioning," and served a government function. To summarize Guy Austin's opening explanation of *Algerian National Cinema*, in a vast country with a multilingual, multicultural, and highly illiterate population (by most accounts 80–90 percent in 1962), cinema appeared to the new government as an obvious and powerful distributor of propaganda nationally and internationally.[4]

In the official review *Novembre*, Casbah Film—Yacef Saâdi's agency that produced *The Battle of Algiers*—declares the need to "raise the political conscience and breathe new life into the revolutionary spirit" and recommends that Algerian filmmakers "initially, put the slogans in images."[5] Algerian cinema, a tool of the government, thus depicted the battle against colonization as a cathartic, pedagogical force. In this way, the deterritorialization on screen depicted a political truth for many, and also served the government's larger goal of enforcing a historical vision with national uplift, thus reterritorializing Algeria. Lotfi Maherzi's writes that "the Algerian Revolution took flight and developed in the countryside, in a rural milieu … In this way, we are returned (by cinema) to the concept of patriotism, which will make the land problem, a chief component of Algerian nationalism."[6]

The Algerian writer and political figure Mostefa Lacheraf's most negative interpretation of *moudjahid* cinema from 1976 reads, "A pseudo-patriotic exploitation of war heroism, generating a futile head of steam which diverted the people from the new realties."[7] Such a critique correctly asserts that Algeria's first films did not address the nation's post-Revolution strife (e.g., a coup d'état ousted the first president Ahmed Ben Bella on June 19, 1965), but instead dwelled on a repetition of the revolutionary struggle, aiming to seize the people's spirits through traumatic recapitulation. Yet Lacheraf's simplistic characterization does not account for the artistry of Lakhdar-Hamina's award-winning depictions, nor the slippery question of *The Battle of Algiers* (is this transnational film part of the *moudjahid* tradition?) Ultimately the *moudjahid* film's political style often recalls early Soviet cinema. In fact, Lakhdar-Hamina's epic revolutionary dramas *The Wind of the Aurès* and *Chronicle of the Years of Fire* demonstrate his study in Czechoslovakia. Guy Austin remarks that imported styles whether they be Soviet or the American-Western—as found in *The Outlaws* (Tewfik Farès, 1969) and *L'Opium et le baton* (*The Opium and the Stick*, Ahmed Rachedi, 1971)—prolong the development of an Algerian cinema aesthetic.[8] However, in spite of foreign influences, Algeria's first films uniquely claim Algeria's landscape in their settings. To be clear, Algerian cinema does depart from *moudjahid* films, most notably the agrarian films (*cinéma djidid*) that address the farming crises in the 1970s[9] and as this chapter will later discuss, a simultaneous comedic tradition. However in this chapter, I disentangle the unacknowledged kinship between these twenty-first-century coproductions by transvergent directors and the *moudjahid* features as exemplified by Mohammed Lakhdar-Hamina's *The Wind of the Aurès* and *Chronicle of the Years of Fire*, as all use similar techniques to depict the Algerian Revolution with nationalistic fervor.[10]

In studying Lakhdar-Hamina's key texts, several "national traits" emerge. One of which is Lakhdar-Hamina's tendency to pan Algerians in groups and to present these groups outdoors, demonstrating not only the people's peasant status and their related class solidarity, but visually reinforcing their tie to nature, and their right to their land, a literal reterritorialization. Medium panning shots of groups are consistent, as well as a montage that stops for a second or two to identify a face before cutting to the next, justly allotting the spectator the seconds necessary to comprehend the pain and to connect the sorrow of each into a victimized group. In *The Wind of the Aurès*, this ensemble montage, and panning of people outdoors is a motif; both in shots of the

Figure 4.1 *Chronicle of the Years of Fire* (Mohammed Lakhdar-Hamina, 1975)

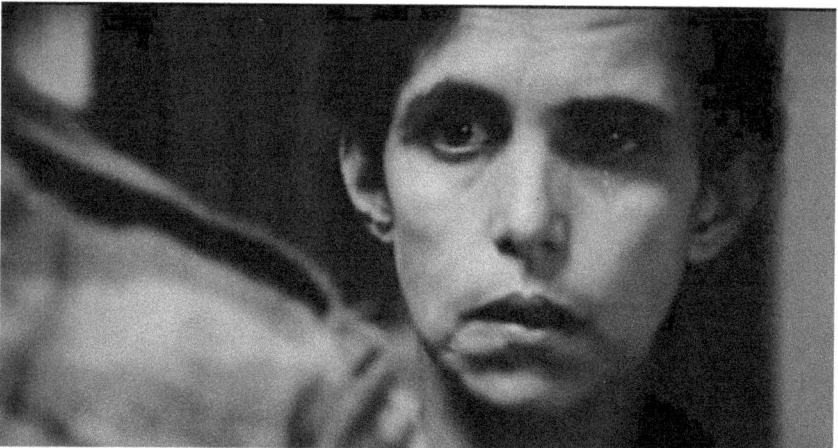

Figure 4.2 *The Battle of Algiers* (Gillo Pontecorvo, 1966)

work camps, and in shots that picture those waiting outside the camps and prisons for their family members. The torture sequence from *The Battle of Algiers* includes perhaps the most memorable ensemble montage that depicts the Algerian Revolution. Close-ups evoke an individual's sorrow, but only for a second, so that the tortured lack personalization and serve as a member of a collective. With cigarettes and in identical uniforms, the *moudjahid* films diminish the French soldiers' humanity, while emphasizing the common pain of Algerians. We find this technique equally in both *The Wind of the Aurès* and *Chronicle of the Years of Fire*; while the films' framing varies, both share pans of groups of people as well as montages that depict unnamed peasants' facial expressions.

In Lakhdar-Hamina's *The Wind of the Aurès*, among these pans and ensemble montages, a mother proceeds as the symbol of nation embodying this connection to land as she travels by foot to work camps in search of her imprisoned son. When she at last finds her son's dwelling, she guards and encircles it, even after his implied death. Finally, soldiers shoot her outside in the winter snow, her body strewn across the wire fence that has separated her from her offspring. A nomad like all *moudjahid* screen Algerians, her home has been demolished, her family dead and scattered, and her existence depends on the hope of finding her son alive. Thus, she subsists outside of state boundaries and rules; surrounding the prison camp is clearly against their policy, and the faceless yells in French by soldiers imply as much. Yet, not only does this performance of deterritorialization affect the intended audience's sympathy, but does so because of the Algerian spectators self-identification. The Revolution had scattered Algerians in camps throughout the country; most men had either left their homes to fight in the Revolution and/or die in the process (many more immigrated to work in factories in France, a topic largely absent in the Algerian cinema of the era). In this way, while *moudjahid* cinema simplifies the Algerian landscape and Algerian-French relations, it reflects the historical reality of a displaced population, and their enforced nomad state. (A similar nomad state is central to *Chronicle of the Years of Fire* in which a father wanders for both work and to find his family; he finally lives in hiding as a guerilla warrior.) Therefore, the depiction of Algerians as deterritorialized nomads in *The Wind of the Aurès* and *Chronicle of the Years of Fire* was accurate and resonant, and consequently a vital component of the FLN-funded films. Or conversely, reterritorialization through cinema meant portraying Algerian characters as common victims of deterritorialization; nomads who would persevere and reclaim Algeria.

Although Gilles Deleuze and Félix Guattari very specifically target psychoanalysis in *L' Anti-Oedipe*, volume I of *Capitalisme et Schitzophrénie*, these comments concerning the Oedipus complex can be extracted to generally understand the interdependence of deterritorialization and reterritorialization in early Algerian cinema:

> What acts as an objective and public element—the Earth, the Despot— is now taken up again, but as the expression of a subjective and private reterritorialization: Oedipus is the fallen despot—banished, deterritorialized—but a reterritorialization is engineered, using the Oedipus complex.[11]

By placing the Earth and the Despot in competition and yet confusing their sameness through punctuation, the theorists declare that the utterance of land or *terrain* inherently evokes its ruler. Oedipus is comparable to the Algerians who rule in the people's name, have suffered trauma, both physical and psychological, as well as cultural and physical displacement, in addition to death ("a million and half martyrs" is the FLN's key phrase that quickly evokes the extreme loss). As the previous examples illustrate, film was a vital element of a reterritorialization, engineered by the FLN, and whose impact could be debated, but whose intent cannot. Deleuze and Guattari suggest that the Oedipal complex, in its structural arrangement, and far-reaching intentions, provides an avenue for the deterritorialized's reterritorialization. The concept also applies to the nation-building *moudjahid* films' representational and metaphorical power, which rules the terrain by reinvoking the memory of tragic displacement. As with *The Wind of the Aurès*, the many panning shots portray the mother's point of view and her shared pain with all Algerians, further represented by her travels across the country through the seasons, which together assert a historical claim of the Algerian landscape.

Language geography: *Summer of '62* and *Outside the Law*

Although a fair number of French films produced during the Franco-Algerian War allude to the warfare and the post-trauma suffered by French soldiers, and although the *cinéma parallèle* primarily screened shorts and documentaries in the margins, *moudjahid* cinema provided the first fictional portrayals, or reenactments, of the war, and the first cinematic Algerian account of the trauma endured. Both Mehdi Charef (born in Maghnia, French-Algeria, in 1952) and Rachid Bouchareb (born to Algerian parents in Paris in 1959) built their reputation by exploring the friction between French and Algerian cultures. In fact, both directors' debuting films, Bouchareb's *Bâton Rouge* (1985) and Charef's *Le Thé au Harem d'Archimède* (*Tea in the Harem*, 1986), depict the displaced Maghrebi-French subject in the 1980s. In this way, the directors' complicated national identity inflects their films concerning the Revolution, and very obviously resituates the action. *The Battle of Algiers*, which is doubly complicated by the director's Italian nationality, presents an example of a geographically precise city with distinct locations. However, Lakhdar-Hamina's two epic productions of the Revolution find Algerians wandering through vast nameless towns, desert regions, and mountains. If the Aurès Mountains reiterates Algerian geography in the title (another act of reclaiming Algerian terrain), the film deletes any other specific verbal references. Forty years later in a historic portrait, the depictions of the Revolution by Charef and Bouchareb relay the traces of their first films with an insistence on the merging of Algerian and French cultures, a complicated union that also connotes the nature of their productions that are both Algerian and French. Both transnational productions employ French and Algerian-Arabic or darija to accurately depict the era. However, funding and film references also influence what may first appear as a geolinguistic association.

Cartouches Gauloises

While a film concerning the Algerian Revolution obviously dictates a smaller viewership in France, a consideration of *La Môme* (*La Vie en Rose*) by Olivier Dahan, also released in 2007 provides an interesting comparison; the story of French icon Edith Piaf sold 2,870,592 tickets in the two weeks and ran for twenty weeks, while *Summer of '62* sold but 62,240 tickets in the two weeks before it was pulled. However, the reaction of the press is also part of the equation; *Cahiers du cinéma* did not review *Summer of '62*, and the other left press publications were critical of Charef's style, as well as the pacing of violence—the progressive *Les Inrockuptibles* was an exception reviewing the film very favorably. Although research suggests that contemporary French cinema and television have revitalized the Algerian Revolution as a popular subject, the public proves less enthusiastic than the filmmakers. In fact, after the financial failures of both *Mon Colonel* (*The Colonel,* Laurent Herbiet, 2006) and *Summer of '62*, the films' coproducer (now director) Mohamed Salem Brahimi told me he would never again make a film about the Franco-Algerian War because "les Français ne veulent pas le voir" (the French do not want to see it).

One frequently feels the influence of the *nouvelle vague* in Mehdi Charef's cinematic oeuvre, and *Summer of '62* recalls the French new wave's freedom of filming on city streets, a technological advancement of the mid-1950s with portable cameras that paired well with an aleatory plot. Generally, new wave movies filmed in Paris during the *événements* did not strive to be historical accounts of war or war trauma. Consequently, the new wave's reputation for supporting French-Algeria has consistently been under debate. Still Charef's references to new wave films and techniques can be noted, and Sonia Lee even argues that Charef thus demonstrates his integration as an immigrant in France.[12] In *Summer of '62*, the wanderings (grocery delivery, paper delivery) of the quiet child protagonist (Ali played by Mohamed Faouzi Ali Charif) infuse the plot with an element of improvisation, denied by Lakhdar-Hamina's *moudjahid* epics, films that in no way demonstrate the influence of the contemporary once–new wave directors across the Mediterranean. In *Summer of '62*, the bustling city of Oran (though it was in fact filmed in Tlemcen) relates the intricacies of Ali's quotidian trauma, as the plot remains character determined, dictated neither by a desperate need (as in *The Wind of the Aurès* and *Chronicle of the Years of Fire*) nor by an omniscient narration (such as related by the subtitles of faux-news in *The Battle of Algiers*). In this way, the outstanding number of atrocities that Ali witnesses (bombing, murders etc.) represent chance, increasing the absurdity of death. Equally present is Ali's freedom expressed in child's play and games that confuse and contradict the surrounding war, joys absent in *moudjahid* cinema, in which no characters seek diversion.

This detailed if chaotic mapping of Oran, a coastal city, does not include a shot or reference to the ocean, implying an autobiographical current (the director was born hours from the coast in Maghnia) as well as perhaps a pragmatic function (filming locations were limited to Tlemcen, which is not coastal, and the south of France). Cinematically, the expanse of earth that Ali treads in residential neighborhoods, commercial districts, and in nature better situates the film within a *moudjahid* tradition, which also generally retreated from the coast and its possibilities. The cartography of *Summer of '62* does include an apartment where Ali lives with his mother, a dwelling that only slightly disturbs the visual reverberations of an Algerian nomad-status, a necessary ingredient of deterritorialization/reterritorialization found in all *moudjahid* films. Ali travels throughout the city for work (as well as for play), and carries the financial responsibility of his one-parent family household; we only glimpse the shadow of his absent guerrilla warrior father. As Charef's reimagining of the Algerian-Revolutionary protagonist transgresses a traditional, commercial narrative, we find what Gilles Deleuze describes as the time-image rather than that of the action-image.[13] To this extent Ali exemplifies the nomad from the *Anti-Oedipus*:

> The nomad has a territory; he follows customary paths; he goes from one point to another; he is not ignorant of points (water points, dwelling points, assembly points, etc.). But the question is what in nomad life is a principle and what is only a consequence. To begin with, although the points determine paths, they are strictly subordinated to the paths they determine, the reverse happens with the sedentary. The water point is reached only in order to be left behind; every point is a relay and exists only as a relay. A path is always between two points, but the in-between has taken on all the consistency and enjoys both an autonomy and a direction of its own. The life of the nomad is the intermezzo.[14]

Here the territory of the nomad/protagonist is the city of Oran. The discussion of the sedentary paths versus those of the nomad can also be used to understand the *moudjahid*'s narrative style, an art-form constructed for nation-building purposes (sedentary) and Charef's vision, which finds a youth charged solely with the goal of survival and in constant movement, witnessing in the process, but never determining the actions of others.

Although *Summer of '62* reiterates the Algerians' relationship to the earth as found in *moudjahid* cinema (Mehdi is barefoot, and his work as well as his play keep him in constant contact with the city's geography), the film simultaneously evokes the trauma of a varied collection of departing European friends, a notion foreign to the Algerian Revolution as portrayed in other Algerian features.[15] In fact, we see soldiers who medically examine Ali and other Algerian children with care. Ali delivers goods to an elderly French-Algerian couple who invite him to dine with them, and all of his friends from school are French-Algerian. He even discovers the bloody aftermath of a French-Algerian family murdered in their home. Furthermore, unlike *moudjahid* cinema's portrayal of Algerian-French relations, in which the French language is solely used by the French military to command Algerians, *Summer of '62* employs French as a language of exchange between Ali and a community that includes the French military, as well as children, and families.[16] French is economic, as many of the child's conversations with the French-Algerian population in French concern money, but French equally imparts friendship, sadness, and understanding. The Arabization of Algeria (Article 76 of the 1963 Constitution that Boudmédienne implemented with a ten-year plan in 1965)[17] was a powerful and primary element of the FLN government's reterritorialization that in moving pictures mythologized Algerians as a unified people. In fact, the *moudjahid* features present Algerians as speaking only Arabic (with a few examples of French being spoken to the French for conning purposes such as the women carrying bombs in *The Battle of Algiers*, and the prisoners planning their escape in *The Outlaws*). Thus a monocultural myth could emerge in cinema; for example, despite the Amazigh-speaking population known to inhabit the Aurès mountains, the Algerians of *The Wind of the Aurès* communicate exclusively in semiclassical Arabic. As Ali the nomad of *Summer of '62* walks a line between cultures, identities, and their intrinsic languages, his pathways extend to convey a city map of in-betweenness that contradicts the nationalist reterritorialization of early Algerian cinema.

To this extent, *Summer of '62*'s map of Oran emblematizes the nomad's intermezzo, revealing a social network that frequently extends sympathies toward Europeans,

Figures 4.3 and 4.4 *Summer of '62* (Mehdi Charef, 2007)

as well as Algerians. Until the contradicting conclusion of *Summer of '62* in which an Algerian flag waves, the film depicts Oran of 1962 not as a *terrain* belonging to France or to Algeria, but as a land of instability and fluctuation that the protagonist similarly embodies in his own varied interactions and bilingualism. In this way, the 2006 coproduction affords Algerian cinema a compromise, not possible in the years of nation-building. As Bensmaïa posits, the struggle of Algerian writers (and I will add filmmakers) to the puzzle of the postcolonial nation was whether to write in the language of the colonizer (French) with guilt, in the language of the government (Arabic), or the language of the people (which might include any combination of languages including Amazigh). He writes of the Algerian artist's postrevolutionary lingual turmoil, "How can we live within several languages and write in only one?"[18] *Summer of '62* suggests that such limits imposed on early Algerian cinema by the government and/or through the necessity of nation-building have largely evaporated, bequeathing a neorealist portrait of a boy as the cultural, lingual, and historical compromise of dual grieving.

Hors-la-loi

Hors-la-loi (*Outside the Law*) is a true transnational production; while primarily private and public French companies financed the endeavor, the credits also list the AARC (Agence Algérienne pour le Rayonnement Culturel), the ENTV, and the Minister of Algerian culture. Therefore, the film could compete at at the Academy Awards as an Algerian feature. Although *Summer of '62* and *Outside the Law* are both coproductions that treat the Franco-Algerian War, they are in some ways stylistically opposed: the former influenced by the new wave and neorealist traditions; the latter entrenched in Hollywood aesthetics. Furthermore, the two films share little in their mapping of the Revolution. In fact, *Outside the Law*'s biggest challenge to nearly all previous films concerning the Algerian Revolution is to depict the war's violence in France. One should not forget Okacha Touita's *Les Sacrifiées* (*The Sacrificed*, 1982), a film that similarly depicts the independence group fratricide within the Algerian shantytowns of France. Yet *The Sacrificed*'s subtle realism neither represents the early twenty-first century awakening nor the transnational partnership that *Outside the Law* signifies.[19] Rachid Bouchareb's decision to return to this little known history broke conventions by combining *moudjahid* cinema with Hollywood style and conventions, attempting if not succeeding to attract a mainstream public. Marketing may have played a role in Rachid Bouchareb's subject and setting, as for *Outside the Law* he raised 20.5 million euros, more than any previous production by a North African director.[20] How did a director of Algerian heritage making a film about the Algerian Revolution that incidentally does not portray France favorably raise this much money? Perhaps the biggest factor was the unprecedented success of Rachid Bouchareb's previous film *Indigènes* (*Days of Glory*, 2006), which had visible political impact for Maghrebi World War II veterans and starred the same three box-office drawing Maghrebi actors (Sami Bouajila, Roschedy Zem, and coproducer Jamel Debouze).[21] However, the investors' hopes proved incorrect. The films' box office receipts were grossly different: in its first month, *Days of Glory* sold 2, 276,360 tickets, while *Outside the Law* sold only 381,106. Although many other factors contributed, the public's preference for a World War II setting is obvious. Jean-Michel Frodon writes of the two films at the box office, "The abyss between his two films is a shining example of our relationship to history."[22] In spite of the results, depicting the Algerian Revolution in France, an often-ignored historical reality, was an intelligent marketing decision;[23] France interests the European box office more than Algeria. Nevertheless, Bouchareb's decision remains radical because it claims the geographic territory of France as Algerian, rather than the prevalent contradictory narrative.

Not unlike Lakhdar-Hamina's *Chronicle of the Years of Fire*, Rachid Bouchareb depicts a broad historical period in order to demonstrate the motivation and reasoning of revolutionary fighters, and in particular to explain, if not justify, the FLN's violent strain. Before the plot leads the characters to France, an Algerian sun brightly lights two scenes. The opening sequence set in 1925 (noted in intertitles) narrativizes the confiscation of ancestral land by the French and thus depicts the widespread deterritorialization in the homeland. Such appropriation was more commonly a practice in the nineteenth century, but the film's historical inaccuracy, while noted by others, contributes to the film's intended emotional tour de force and pedagogical aim.[24] Several documentaries made in the years before *Outside the Law* (*Pacification en Algérie* [André Gazut] in 2002, *Mémoires du 8 mai 1945* [*Memories of May 8, 1945*, Mariem Hamidat] and *L'Autre 8 mai 1945 aux origines de la Guerre d'Algérie* [*The Other May 8, 1945: The Origins of the Algerian War*, Yasmina Adi] both from 2008[25]) prepared fiction cinema for the first detailed reenactment of the Sétif Massacre,[26] and a presentation of the tragedy as central to the Revolution's beginnings.[27] Despite these preceding documentaries' opinions and disclosures, the full-scale war sequence provoked a scandal at the 2010 Cannes Film Festival.[28] Narratively the scene provides the three brothers with motivation to fight for Algerian independence as their father is murdered. However, *Outside the Law*'s style more obviously pays tribute to Hollywood, most notably the *Godfather* series (all by Francis Ford Coppola, 1972, 1974, and 1992) and *Once Upon a Time in America* (Sergio Leone, 1984)—films that *Outside the Law* further resembles as the immigrant brothers resort to gangster-like behavior, extorting money and killing in the name of the FLN. Although *Outside the Law*'s characters invoke the deterritorialized nomads of *moudjahid* cinema, they alternatively subsist in France.

As such, *Outside the Law* reterritorializes French cinema's most common city as an Algerian independence setting. The climax takes place on October 17, 1961, the day on which the FLN organized a march in Paris against the curfew enforced against Algerians; the pacific march of between 20,000 and 30,000 Algerians turned quickly into a massacre, with thousands arrested and many (the number is still debated) killed by police force. Although the government censure helped to hide the grim reality, the Algerian Revolution's twenty-first-century reemergence included a confrontation with the day and its dissimulation.[29] In fact, *Outside the Law*'s inclusion of the October 17, 1961 massacre followed a documentary wave[30] that had already made significant fiction inroads: *Vivre au Paradis* (Bourlem Guerdjou) of 1999; *Caché* (*Hidden*, Michael Haneke) and *La Nuit Noire: 17 octobre, 1961* (*Black Night: October 17, 1961*) of 2005. The closing scene of *Outside the Law* occurs in the Porte des Lilas *métro* station evoking what are now well-known photographs of the horror of massacre—protestors attempt to escape by descending into the station, but then suffer more police brutality.[31] The setting of the *métro*, a sign of Parisian modernity, highlighted by the station name Porte des Lilas on the wall, transgresses early Algerian cinema's reterritorialization where warriors and martyrs struggled and battled in the homeland. Furthermore, the scene counters France's censor that largely masked the truth of the massacre. Thus the *métro* scene signifies the culmination of an early twenty-first century Algerian reterritorialization. The public's witnessing of the dislocated brothers, whose lives around Paris consist largely of a struggle against state violence, now progresses into the ultimate reimagining of oppression in France. The most intelligent brother, who is consequently the most invested in the independence cause, Abdelkader (Sami Bouajila), dies from the police beatings—this sequence is accompanied by swelling music while other anonymous bludgeoned Algerians surround him. In consideration of the family's deaths at the hands of the French state, and most notably the film's conclusion, we find that Guy Austin's short definition of the *moudjahid* cinema defines *Outside the Law*, "the filmic reflection of this glowing official martyrdom."[32] As such the film tradition associated temporally and geographically with the early years of Algeria can be extracted to describe a coproduction between Algeria and its former colonizer in 2010. In using this vocabulary, we assess a cultural need to claim this deadly massacre attributed to the Paris police force as an inspirational Algerian moment. For the generations of immigrants living in today's France, the police versus immigrant dynamic recalls more recent suppressions of riots in the *banlieues*, and the tension resulting from the terrorist attacks of 2015. The Paris *métro* and the Paris Massacre of 1961 become sites of immigrant memory that survive as a recognition of injustice and a call to political action.

Language both enhances and signifies the cinematic landscape confiscated and claimed in such portrayals. More specifically, language in *Outside the Law* both troubles and further asserts a vision of Paris as an Algerian site of memory. *Outside the Law*'s reterritorialization of the metropole by the colonized denies French characters' dialogue or development. In fact, there are but two French characters, Hélène (Sabrina Seyvecou), an attractive blond woman who with but a few lines and a kiss proves Abdelkader's heterosexuality, and the xenophobic police chief who connotes Maurice Papon and, with very sparse dialogue, conveys revenge and spite. In this way, a film that takes place for the most part in Paris is almost exclusively inhabited by Algerian characters and their voices; the Algerian brothers live in an Algerian shantytown directly outside of Paris in Nanterre where they meet with one another and with other FLN Algerians.[33] In addition, they extort money from Algerians in the community and murder members of the rival Algerian independence group the MNA. Despite or because of the independence cause, the main characters have very few verbal interactions with the French, and there is but one short sequence in which French police officers speak among themselves.

However, this twenty-first-century French coproduction that largely takes place in the French capital does not depict Algerians as monolingual Algerian-Arabic speakers. Drawing on Bensmaïa's categorization of languages, French in *Outside the Law* remains "the language of urban economic and political powers,"[34] a *vehicular* language. While we hear no French in the beginning Algerian scenes, we hear French over speakers in Indochina where one brother, Messaoud (Rochedy Zem) serves in the French army—the radio discourse aims to convince the Vietnamese to support France. French then slowly inserts itself into the brothers' darija through economic exchange: when Saïd trades his watch for a shack in Nanterre, the other immigrant responds with "c'est bon, ça marche" (that's good that works) and when Saïd first ventures into the pimp marketplace, he speaks in French with the Algerian teaching him the ropes as well as with his Algerian prostitute.

Thus, we witness the immigrants learning or incorporating French in labor and capital and then, paradoxically, borrowing the colonizer's language to demonstrate authority in the revolutionary cause. For example, the brothers purchase guns and a bus in Germany to hide their activity, yet make the transaction in French. Furthermore, they mix French with a few darija expressions to publicize the FLN to immigrant laborers at a car plant, and when they teach Algerian immigrants how to shoot. To this extent we witness the vehicular language killing the vernacular—in fact, at a top-level FLN meeting organizing the pacific march against the curfew that became the 1961 Paris Massacre, the suited Algerian immigrants speak largely in French, though still including some Algerian-Arabic phrases. Obviously, the film's marketing might also have influenced the decision to increasingly include French dialogue, as French, like France, sells more tickets than Arabic or darija—another aspect of the vehicular language's destructive economic power. Nevertheless, a consistent lingual flow of darija prevails in the film's familial interactions: the mother speaks exclusively darija and in each of the brother's deaths this language rings as the language of martyrdom. *Outside the Law* like *Summer of '62* thus represents a screen compromise between the languages and their previous screen depictions, perhaps striking closer to the reality of an Algerian community that drew on several dialects and languages in a vernacular. Nevertheless, as the Arabic *moudjahid* cinema demonstrates, this depiction is but interpretive. *Outside the Law*, a film that brings the screen Algerian Revolution to France, allows many immigrants to reterritorialize French as a language of Algerian independence, a precedent set in Francophone Algerian literature by authors too numerous to name.

Les Folles Années du twist

Mahmoud Zemmouri's *Les Folles Années du twist* (*The Crazy Years of the Twist*), made twenty years before *Summer of '62* and *Outside the Law*, questions rather than pays homage to *moudjahid* cinema and a national myth, with specific references to the works of Lakhdar-Hamina. Rather than resituating the *moudjahid* cinema's nation-building sentiment in France as *Outside the Law*, or negotiating the displacement of the Algerians with that of their French-Algerian community, *The Crazy Years of the Twist* instead depicts an Algeria with neither identity nor community, and in effect sympathizes with no one—French-Algerian, Algerian, military, or FLN. As such, Bensmaïa's understanding of the third stage of independent Algerian literature can be extracted to talk about this unique comedic feature:

> We begin to see not simply the denunciation of national myth as a "transition from an allegorical reality to an allegory become reality" but as its interruption. And this is where the third and final period begins. With the writers of this period, the myth of the nation was interrupted, and its very interruption gives voice to and exposes an unfinished community.[35]

The Crazy Years of the Twist is neither fashioned after nor resembles the evocative optimistic prose of Nabile Farès, the primary writer of Bensmaïa's grouping whose novels *L'état perdu* (*The Lost State*, 1982) and *L'exil au féminin: poème d'Orient et d'Occident* (*Exile to the Feminine: Poem of the Orient and of the Occident*, 1987) were published also in the 1980s. Nevertheless, we do find similar currents of dismissing a national mythology that has come to incorrectly represent Algeria's reality, and an exposition of Algeria's multiplicity. As such *The Crazy Years of the Twist* interrupts the early Algerian cinematic vision of the war. In fact, the unempathetic portrayal of nearly every character and group represented negates what was once the nation's reterritorialization.

Before detailing the ways in which the 1986 film repudiates the *moudjahid* tradition, one should note that the exclusive Algerian state funding of a film that was very critical of the FLN (as well as of the French military) did not go unnoticed. Although Algeria's ONCIC (Office national pour le commerce et l'industrie cinématographique) uniquely produced *The Crazy Years of the Twist*, a government committee refused its distribution after viewing it. Three years later, Zemmouri won the right to its French distribution, but despite positive reviews his second feature left French theaters after only two weeks.[36] The signing of a petition to fire the ONCIC's director, none other than Mohammed Lakhdar-Hamina (the Palme d'Or–winning director discussed throughout this chapter), appears simultaneously.[37] Lakhdar-Hamina's government approval of *The Crazy Years of the Twist* might have been reasonable, for the film follows an Algerian comedy tradition begun by comedian Rouïched, whose first production *Hassan Terro* (1967) remains one of the highest grossing films in Algerian history, which then spawned popular sequels: *L'évasion de Hassan Terro* (1976), *Hassan Terro au maquis* (1978), *Hassan Taxi* (1978).[38] Originally *Hassan Terro* was a play, penned by Rouïched, concerning a politically indifferent bourgeois man who becomes a terrorist suspect during the Algerian Revolution. However, it is the film's direction by Mohammed Lakhdar-Hamina in 1967 that subverts the *moudjahid* tradition (which Lakhdar-Hamina in part created!), specifically *The Battle of Algiers*, complete with militaristic theme music, pans, and ensemble montages, and even direct references to Ali La Pointe, whom Rouïched falsely identifies. If *moudjahid* cinema demonstrates a repetition compulsion indicative of a national post-trauma, and more directly an engineered nation-building film culture, *Hassan Terro*'s popularity reflects a simultaneous desire to laugh at the dramatic Algerian depictions of the Revolution. The bourgeois status of the protagonist sharply contrasts with the nomadic laborer/revolutionary of *moudjahid* cinema, and as such reposits PTSD as humor—Rouïched even dreams of his imprisonment and being guillotined, which becomes a joke when he wakes up happy to find his neck. To this extent, the *Hassan Terro* series illustrates a counterpoint to the *moudjahid* cinema, underpinning Algeria's reterritorialization and Revolution with the role reversal of the carnivalesque. *The Crazy Years of the Twist* thus followed a successful model, addressing the national post-trauma of the Algerian Revolution with satire.

The two young men central to *The Crazy Years of the Twist*'s plot are the complete opposite of the suffering, *moudjahid* hero. Instead, the unmotivated, lazy, pair live off of their parents, while committing petty crimes of convenience for fun. In their political indifference to the war and their cowardice, they resemble the comic antihero, *Hassan Terro*'s Hassan, yet contrast sharply in their location. Rather than in Algiers, they dwell in a small village, and rather than bourgeois, they come from what in revolutionary Algeria could be labeled struggling, but petty-bourgeois families (shopkeepers who can buy washing machines if they skip their FLN tax). This casting further affronts the *moudjahid* tradition: one of the main characters is played by

Fawzi B. Saichi, whose unusually short height and posture indicate a genetic defect while Malik Lakhdar-Hamina, the handsome son of Mohammed Lakhdar-Hamina, plays his best friend.

In 1983, Lakhdar-Hamina was the most powerful name in Algerian cinema; the head of the ONCIC largely controlled state funding, and one can hypothesize the reasons why he allotted funding to a comedic rendering of the Algerian Revolution starring his son. Perhaps it was because he was optimistic after *Hassan Terro*'s proven success with the Revolution in a comedy, or perhaps he sought a vehicle for his son's acting career. If the latter, one acknowledges that Malik's casting as a lazy outgrown adolescent juxtaposes his most famous previous screen appearance in *Chronicle of the Years of Fire*. In his father's epic filmed seven years earlier, Malik represented the traumatized but resilient new nation. As a survivor of the Algerian Revolution after the deaths of his father and godfather/seer of sorts Miloud (played by his real father, the director Mohamed Lakhdar-Hamina), the 12-year old boy searches and sobs for his dead friend. We find him running through the mountains in the final shot of the three-hour epic, accompanied by soaring music, which in context intends to draw the public into an emotional and political fury against colonialism. Malik Lakhdar-Hamina's previous role of epic importance and family heritage inject his second role of indifference with a bitter irony, his casting enhances the script's pregnant questions about the ways in which national myth denies its citizens. *The Crazy Years of the Twist* equally references Lakhdar-Hamina's *moudjahid* films and forces a comedic comparison by mocking the six chapter titles of *Chronicle of the Years of Fire* (*The Years of Ashes, The Years of the Cart*, etc.). In this way, the fire images of the Revolution are replaced by a European dance, indicative of nonchalance and apathy. A study of the film's opening preface provides clues concerning the film's mapping of the Revolution and its accompanying linguistic framework, our touchstone to the early twenty-first productions already discussed. In a written preface—the film's first frame—Zemmouri addresses education and history in French, inserting a pedagogical goal in the spectator's consciousness.

The first words denounce the French education system and reflect both a French citizen's knowledge and an Algerian's outrage: "La guerre d'Algérie, comme d'autres moments 'peu glorieux' de l'histoire française, n'a pas encore l'honneur de figurer à tous les programmes scolaires." [The Algerian War, like other 'not very glorious' moments in French history, does not yet have the honor of being part of the school syllabi.] Here Zemmouri writes from the perspective of a French citizen (the adjective *tous* and the definite article *les* represent a belonging and association with French schools), enforcing his own immigrant/exiled/transvergent status onto his narrative and public. Yet, this preface exclusively criticizes teaching in *French* schools, and fails to mention the national memory in Algeria. While the preface may initially flirt with Algerian patriotism by criticizing a French history curriculum, and by stating that its true subject is "the people," the Algerian people's portrait quickly descends into the negation of *moudjahid* cinema with terms, such as cowardice, opportunism, and indifference. The result might dually be read as a subversive criticism of Algerian history courses that present all Algerians as unified against the French and that deny Algerians' cultural differences.[39] In this manner, Zemmouri's text with its changing viewpoint clothed under an omniscient narration resembles the *discours semi-direct*, principally associated with the nineteenth century novelist Gustave Flaubert, as it reflects several viewpoints and criticizes two alternate systems in several sentences. The preface begins by insulting colonizers—while taking their position—and likewise introduces what will become a thorough negation of the Algerian national history as expounded by Lakhdar-Hamina's *moudjahid* productions.

To continue our discussion of the geography and linguistic representation of the Algerian Revolution, the anti-*moudjahid* men of *The Crazy Years of the Twist* are in fact counter-nomads, whose static village existence arrests their development. An incessant dialogue of whether to go to the *maquis* (as the underground FLN army's area was called in reference to the French resistance of World War II) and join out of boredom more than anything else appears absurdist, a remote possibility that laziness and parental dependence will never drive to fruition. In this way, *The Crazy Years of the Twist* abandons Algeria's previous cinematic reterritorialization; the camera addresses neither the landscape nor the people's attachment to it. Although, once the friends steal oranges from a French-Algerian's farm, the film style lacks any romantic view of nature. In fact, the incident connotes the grander disharmony of the Algerian people; the two Algerian men who work for the French-Algerian turn the duo in to the police and ironically claim allegiance to the FLN. Though the young men want to leave, their laziness bars the walking found in the *moudjahid* films; once they do try and steal a motorbike and fail, but such automated transportation remains a financial impossibility. In this sphere of lethargy, the FLN and the French military, *l'Algérie française* and *l'Algérie indépendente*, appear equal.

The Crazy Years of the Twist continues with the theme of youth culture and alienation found in Zemmouri's first feature, *Prends 10,000 francs et casse-toi!* (*Take 10,000 Francs and Get Out!*, 1981) in which an Algerian family in Paris returns to live in the *bled* with their teenagers. The influence of European popular culture on the adolescents' imaginations evokes a similar notion of in-betweenness, augmented by a rural location. Being lodged somewhere between a romanticization of European values and mores (rock 'n' roll as indicated in the title and what the young men envision as their attached accessories, namely cigarettes, alcohol, and ripped jeans) incites a rebellion against the enforced FLN values, which hypocritically deny citizens such vices—in the film, the FLN stop the young men and confiscate their wine only to drink it themselves. In fact, filming twenty years after Algerian independence, Zemmouri cast men with their noses cut off (a common FLN punishment for smoking during the Revolution) as extras, and the two friends reference the interdiction while they secretly smoke— the illegality increasing the thrill and enhancing their small pleasure. The two men who neither seek the approval of their parents nor that of the police, and who rebel in small ways against FLN mandates and the French military with indifference, represent a motif of Zemmouri's work—alienated, advantageous Algerian youth.

In Lakhdar-Hamina's *moudjahid* films, only the French military speak the French language in a command form, and as noted in *The Battle of Algiers* and Farès's *The Outlaws*, French is spoken by Algerian characters in efforts to thwart the French. As follows, French in early Algerian film represents but the vehicular language. As previously mentioned, the fact that *Outside the Law* was set in France and coproduced by France indicates the increasing French influence in the Algerian immigrant vernacular, while *Summer of '62,* also a French coproduction, compromises to allow an Algerian to express and understand emotions in two languages. Yet, what Zemmouri's film depicts is linguistically outside of such categorization, for not only is French the vehicular language (spoken officially in FLN meetings and with the military), but for the young homosocial couple, French evokes an ideal. Although the two speak Algerian-Arabic with their families, when talking to each another they frequently use French to tell one another of their desires and dreams and to add hipness to their swagger. Obviously, the friends' aesthetics do not manipulate the audience. Yet this negation of Arabization and this comic depiction of the idolization of the French language in the midst of war portray a bilingual Algeria with varying linguistic associations, some of which are romantic. This view of the Algerian Revolution as a rural inescapable inertia, and French as part and parcel of the dreams that it denies, flattens the dramatic, historical remembrance essential to nation-building that returns as a potent ingredient in twenty-first century coproductions.[40]

Conclusion: Flags

The visual utterance of nation and flags reiterates themes of unity and *terrain* present in a nation's mythological founding. Therefore, when both millennial Algerian-French productions that depict the Revolution, *Summer of '62* and *Outside the Law,* conclude with a waving Algerian flag, the film's political bias affirms a national allegiance, in short, a reterritorialization. Interestingly, a statement on the powerful subliminal effects of flags taken from a psychological study concerning Israel and Palestine applies.

> The national flag of any country is one of the most pervasive cultural and ideological images, and as such it has the potential of exerting significant influence over our behavior. Symbols of this sort are known to have two functions. First, they communicate certain ideas, beliefs, and goals. Second, they bring about thoughts and behaviors that are concomitant with these ideas. Hence, given that flags are often used to express unity and patriotism, they are likely to be able to bring about unity. Given the vast research on nonconscious processes succinctly described above, we argue that this effect of national flags may occur outside of conscious awareness.[41]

The concluding Algerian flag is a call for Algerian unity, one that strengthens an official Algerian slogan with which to remember the Revolution, "one sole hero, the people." However, this becomes a complicated visual appeal in consideration of the transnational viewing public. Furthermore, the propagandistic nature of the flag reiterates the Algerian state's partial funding. Yet the flag doubly signifies an Algerian victory for a French public—with the passage of time, the Maghrebi population of France has only grown, and as this book and the films it studies indicate, subsequent generations seek information about their families' past.[42] The Algerian flag as featured in twenty-first-century French-Algerian productions unifies not only Algerians, but

Algerian immigrants of multiple generations, which also might identify, like the films' directors, as French, thus signifying transnational reterritorialization.

In *Summer of '62*, the film's compromise between depicting French and Algerian grief, in Algerian-Arabic and French, leans toward Algeria with the inclusion of the Algerian flag. As the new nation's flag waves on a soccer goal, the protagonist Ali yells "papa" in Arabic and runs toward a joyous crowd's chanting. Patriotic projections of the word "papa, father/nation/god" indicate the reterritorialization of the Algerian Revolution's memory, one that silences the film's previous message of friendship and shared trauma in French-Algeria. This carefully chosen moment, wrought with nationalist fervor, invokes the emotion of victory. By combining the flag and the presence of a crowd, *Summer of '62* recalls the Algerian unity found within *moudjahid* films. The boy protagonist's previous ties to French-Algerians and French, his previous language of both economy and friendship, dissipate suddenly and naturally, Ali's big eyes and wide smile blend into the surrounding excitement. Yet this decision to conclude in a glorious, majestic sequence locks the protagonist and his city in an extremely brief historic moment. In fact, such a denial of the bloodshed that followed the Revolution recalls the mythologizing gestures of early Algerian independent cinema. Though figures vary, on the day that Algerian independence was announced, July 5, 1962, and for several days after, a mob of Algerians massacred as many as 3,000 Europeans (those who had not departed for France), the majority in Oran.[43] Throughout *Summer of '62*, the setting of Oran is precise and consistent; the camera narratively maps specific city details through Ali's walking. Thus the film's insistence on the horrific quotidian violence in the last month of the war follows its protagonist's patterned relationship to the city. Although such traumatic realism does expose the aftermath of one French-Algerian family's murder, this appears unique, and not part of the larger massacre that occurred with the announcement of independence. Like the severed friendships with French-Algerians, *Summer of '62* abandons the true violence and chaos for the march toward the Algerian flag and the allegorical father's imminent return, an ending that suggests the film's possible compromise with the Algerian state for shooting privileges and funding.

The overt symbolism and the reterritorialization of France in *Outside the Law* also lends itself to flag iconography. An Algerian flag in Sétif in 1945 plays a vital role in *Outside the Law*'s controversy—the massacre began when a young man holding the Algerian flag was shot by a French-Algerian—here standing very close to one of our protagonists, Abdelkader. In this manner, *Outside the Law* introduces the viewer to the Algerian flag as a symbol of martyrdom, a visually arresting display of patriotism when bloodied. Martyrdom strengthens the flag's symbolism once again when, after the gruesome closing metro scene, a celebratory credit sequence magically transports the audience back to Algeria (this change resembles the ending's skip to victory in *The Battle of Algiers* after the loss of the battle, with very similar footage of a celebration). Enhanced by slow motion and a sorrowful score, we see Algerians waving Algerian flags triumphantly. Again the transnational funding and viewership compound the on-screen dilemma: What does the displaced Algerian population's historical migration to France in the revolutionary era suggest for the contemporary French of Algerian or Maghrebi descent? Why does the film abandon the plot in the

Figure 4.5 *Outside the Law* (Rachid Bouchareb, 2010)

credit sequence so as to return to Algeria with melancholic nostalgia? The film's swift transfer from the immigrant plight to the homeland concretely rejects France, while embracing its immigrants. Still *Outside the Law* reclaims the Algerian immigrant experience in France as vital to the Algerian Revolution, and the interchange between Algeria and France renders the Revolution intercontinental. Despite the support of French companies, and despite the director's French citizenship and celebrity status, *Outside the Law*'s credit sequence brands an already self-critical French feature as Algerian. Similar to *Summer of '62*, *Outside the Law* critiques the FLN (specifically by portraying the FLN's extortion from the immigrant community and the independence movement's inner murders); yet a flag finale illustrates pride in the Algerian victory, one that also suggests the Algerian state's contribution to a French partnered epic. Natalya Vince's 2015 study of women freedom fighters' role in the national Algerian memory thus applies; the official slogans and memory of the Revolution continue to be invoked, even when speakers (or filmmakers) suspect such recapitulations and/or proffer significant changes.[44]

In comparison, the most subversive depiction of the Algerian Revolution was in fact thirty-some years earlier in the film *The Crazy Years of the Twist*, a production funded exclusively by the Algerian state. Rather than evoking the flag as a symbol of martyrdom or celebration, Zemmouri emphasizes the flag's function in a new Algerian economy. Now that independence has been declared, Boualam's father, taking advantage of the opportunity, has shut his deli, and sits at his storefront among a collection of Algerian flags for sale that his wife has recently sewn. Unfortunately, unaware of the official new symbol's details, the flags he sells have red stars with four points instead of five. Thus a character earlier identified as an FLN officer notices the mistake and threatens the shopkeeper with a gun. In this way, Zemmouri criticizes not only the new government, but also the Algerian citizens and their immediate investment in symbols that the entire film projects as empty. We next see a parade of girls all holding such identical flags—albeit with five-pointed stars. This vision, critical of Algerian patriotism and symbolism that negates the systematic reterritorialization of *moudjahid* cinema, reflects the 1980s era in which the memory of independence propaganda was fresh, and the new state was failing economically; in fact by the late 1980s there were

Figure 4.6 *The Crazy Years of the Twist* (Mahmoud Zemmouri, 1986)

widespread protests against a one-party system and a burgeoning Islamist sentiment. Eventually, this led to the formation of FIS and the party's participation in elections—inciting a series of events that led to a decade long Algerian civil war. Therefore, an examination of Algerian solidarity and the ways in which the state took power was in order. *The Crazy Years of the Twist* with well-known French comedians (Richard Bohringer, Jacques Villeret),[45] eventual French distribution, and French and Algerian-Arabic dialogue evokes a brief period when Algerian productions sought international viewership. In this manner, *The Crazy Years of the Twist* exposes a crack in the state's film programming, a mistake that ridiculed its funding—as well as everyone else.

An anomaly, *The Crazy Years of the Twist* demasks and confronts *moudjahid* cinema's nationalistic gestures, a paradox in consideration of the twenty-first century films that show the influence of and pay homage to Lakhdar-Hamina's patriotic epics. Ultimately, the twenty-first-century significance of the Algerian Revolution in transnational dialogue inscribes new pain via historical reflection. With distance, the satire of apathy seems an impossibility in the 2000s. *The Crazy Years of the Twist* once satirized the absence of the teaching of the Algerian Revolution in French schools, and implied a critique of the state mythology disseminated by Algerian institutions. However, the early twenty-first century coproductions evoke a pedagogical purpose intrinsic to the Algerian Revolution in France—specifically the February 2005 law and its controversy concerning the teaching of the positive elements of French colonization "especially in North Africa." If *Summer of '62* and *Outside the Law* stylistically invoke the French new wave and Hollywood respectively, *moudjahid* cinema's influence emblematizes the Algerian quotient of the films' transnationality and compromise, further indicated in credits by Algerian state approval and funding. Of course, the films' "northern" modes in part conflict with the patriotism found in Lakhdar-Hamina's work, and the films' lack of financial success indicates that such allegiances derailed a French public.

Indeed, the *moudjahid* cinema style relies on national uplift more than historical fact, and the waving flags of the films transcend their transnationality. Although tempered by French cooperation and support, *Summer of '62* and *Outside the Law* represent an Algerian reterritorialization of twenty-first century film.

5

A Scission in the Memory of the Franco-Algerian War

Mesrine Part I: L'Instinct de Mort (Killer Instinct), Part II: L'Ennemi Public No. 1 (Public Enemy No. 1) (Jean-Paul Richet, 2008)

Introduction

The life and legend of the most famous French criminal of the twentieth century, Jacques Mesrine (1936–79), was at last ripe for a commercially and critically successful film in 2008—and the public's new awareness of the Franco-Algerian War contributed to the icon's twenty-first-century significance. Mesrine's criminal exploits included numerous bank robberies, holding a judge hostage in the courtroom where he was being tried, and escaping prison twice (to this date there is no evidence of the thirty murders Mesrine claimed to have committed). The media, including a 1984 film *Mesrine!* (André Génovèse, 1984), typically forgot Mesrine's mandatory military service in Algeria in 1959, and his evolving relationship to the OAS. However, in 2008 these involvements became salient, for the production followed a greater revelation of France's torture policy during the Franco-Algerian War and the censorship of the Paris Massacre of October 17, 1961.

When considering *Mesrine Part I: L'Instinct de mort (Killer Instinct)* and *Part II: L'Ennemi Public No. 1 (Public Enemy No. 1)* together, the contradictions concerning the Franco-Algerian War and its legacy evoke what Nicolas Bancel and Isabelle Veyrat-Masson label the war of memories (in their similarly titled edited volume), a multicultural contemporary society grappling with differing views of French colonialism.[1] The same categorization "The invisible (1962–1992), the past became tangible (1992–2002), then completely visible and recurrent in the bosom of French society (2002–2008)" which I employed in Chapter 3 to locate *L'Ennemi intime* (*The Intimate Enemy*, Florent-Emilio Siri, 2007) and *Djinns* (*Stranded*, Hughes and Sandra Martin, 2010) within France's changing relationship to the Franco-Algerian War, also informs our reading of the 2008 Mesrine dyptich.[2] For while the two films were released in 2008, as period-pictures they together expose the era in which the war was dismissed and forgotten, before commenting on its changing status in French society from the twenty-first century present. The Mesrine diptych thus in fact exposes and refutes the memory of a government and mainstream public censor.

For this reason, the film's paradoxes, both unified and divided by the diptych format, recall Jacques Derrida's theory of the scission—the distance between the two films demands the viewer's consideration of the Franco-Algerian War's symbolism in contemporary France. Derrida writes, "The present can only represent itself as such by relating back to itself; it can only aver itself by severing itself."[3] Certainly, Jacques Mesrine's relationship to Algeria (as well as his on-screen relationship) changed; while we witness Mesrine killing an Algerian prisoner on command in the opening scene, in the second film, *Part II: Public Enemy No. 1*, the antihero tortures a racist anti-Algerian independence journalist. As such, cinema depicts the present's judgmental view of the French military during the Franco-Algerian War, but repeats this past in order to disagree, or rather the films reiterate a former interpretation in order to dismiss it. Our introduction to Mesrine as a soldier in the torture/death chamber as well as his transformation and the subversion of the torture subject in spectacular fashion, reflect a newly found guilt. This guilt nourishes revenge—one that renews Jacques Mesrine's cultural capitol in the twenty-first century. Such retracing keeps the past as folds of the present, just as the very complex ways that politics and media reestablished the Franco-Algerian War's significance. It is these cracks and joints concerning an early twenty-first century judgment of the war that Richet's *Mesrine* features never elude, but include as part and parcel of a surrounding French society, which mutually produces and consumes such a double feature. In fact, with 2,274,424 tickets sold in seven weeks,[4] *Killer Instinct* was the most-attended drama in France in 2008 and won the César awards for best director (Jean Paul Richet) and best actor (Vincent Cassel).

Before beginning our reading of the film through the lens of the scission, a brief investigation of the film's use of genre (primarily gangster) aids our study, as its conventions in many ways amplify the Franco-Algerian War's presence in a mainstream public field. I will then examine the ways in which three specific sequences that relate to the Franco-Algerian War and its aftermath establish a new perspective that the shameful past informs: violence toward Algerians in war and later in France in part I, *Killer Instinct*, and then the rage against the Anti-Algeria Independence Movement in Part II, *Public Enemy No. 1*. In conclusion, I will return to the scission, this time to consider it with Derrida's vocabulary of the wound as a circumcision, an opening toward the other, an opportunity to deconstruct history. In Richet's films, we find Jacques Mesrine commodified for and by a 2008 public, an icon whose twenty-first century renewal now depends upon the Algerian Revolution's war of memory.

The Franco-Algerian War in a Gangster Film

Genre weighs heavily on the Franco-Algerian War's new cinematic role, and therefore a brief exploration of the films' roots in and homage to the 1970s' American gangster- or mafia-film serves our broader goal of situating Richet's Mesrine. Although present, an exploration of the biopic-genre does not serve this particular study. *Mesrine* as a pastiche draws on several French traditions, including the French *polar*-genre (often defined as a thriller, but police based), and the heist sub-genre. In fact, even in title the Mesrine films evoke this exchange of French and American film traditions—*Public Enemy No. 1* was a 1931 film starring James Cagney as a gangster that propelled other French film noirs.[5] Phil Powrie discusses the *polar* genre with its roots in the 1930s as indicative of a crisis of masculinity in which criminal behavior and its policing suggested the contemporary values of society. Furthermore, as Powrie finds the 1980s' polar film largely nostalgic for the previous evocations of the genre, Richet's Mesrine features illustrate similar impulses, not only for the 1970s generally and its American gangster pictures, but for a previous epoch in French cinema. In fact, Mesrine as a topic of French film always evoked this *polar* potential. Jean-Paul Belmondo, once the number-one box-office actor who was famous for his police and gangster roles in *Le Doulos* (Jean-Pierre Melville, 1962) *Le Voleur* (*The Thief of Paris*, Louis Malle, 1967) and *Stavisky* (Alain Resnais, 1974), bought the rights to Mesrine's autobiography and fellow actor Alain Delon whose most well-known gangster roles include *Le Samouraï* (Jean-Pierre Melville, 1967) and *Le Cercle Rouge* (*The Red Circle*, Jean-Pierre Melville, 1970) also considered purchasing the film rights.

In addition, Graeme Hayes finds that the French heist film and its most well-known 1950s versions—*Touchez pas au grisbi* (*Don't Touch the Loot*, Jacques Becker, 1954) and *Riffifi* (Jules Dassin, 1955)—also relay specific political and cultural sentiments of the production year. His citation of Roland Lacourbe describes the heist film as revitalized by the 2008 Mesrine features: "The heist dramatizes the revolt of the downtrodden man, creating a fictional space for revenge against the agents of legalized oppression in modern society."[6] Mesrine's statements to the press (which are here repeated as film dialogue) express the anarchist sentiment that he steals from the banks rather than individuals. Thus the contemporaneous press (and the press in the film) compare Mesrine to Robin Hood. While Richet's *Mesrine* films most bombastically allude to a cult strain in American films of the 1970s, a grounding in the French heist film and *polar* genre revitalizes the American French exchange.

Although genre studies is equally an aspect of contemporary film-studies, Robert Warshow, one of the first to classify the gangster film, remains relevant. Warshow approaches film-genre from both a descriptive angle, finding similar structural elements, and a functional one, in which the conventional themes are unearthed and a meaning is construed. Although the 2008 *Mesrine* films most obviously reference the late 1970s' and early 1980s' cult mafia films, *Scarface* (Brian DePalma, 1983) and *The Godfather* and *The Godfather II* (Francis Ford Coppola, 1972–4), Warshow's findings concerning *Little Caesar* (Mervyn Leroy,1930), *The Public Enemy* (William A. Wellman, 1931), and *Scarface* (Howard Hawks, 1932) prove the gangster genre's durability and elasticity. We locate a mise-en-scène that portrays wealth through clothes, cars, and excessive night life, and "a particular 'rise and fall' of a central protagonist who" is "both hero and villain personified: a 'tragic hero' found in nearly all gangster features."[7] Jacques Mesrine embodies this gangster archetype; in his violence and spontaneity he is threatening. Yet the film encourages the audience's support and identification with the protagonist, for "his weakness as much as his power and freedom."[8] In this way, such a tragic gangster hero is synonymous with a complex character, an element of the

1970s–80s' wave of gangster films that also drew on the method acting of Al Pacino. Furthermore, the rise and fall of Jacques Mesrine, common knowledge to the public, and underlined in the credit sequence, bring the protagonist and character into the mythical film lineage of the gangster genre.

In consideration of the films' often-ignored references to the Franco-Algerian War and Algerians, Steve Neale's essay "Questions to Genre" leaves room for a twenty-first-century French version, as he describes the genre's evolution and dialectical function.[9] Although, the Mesrine films evoke the iconography and plot structure that generally adheres to the American 1970s' gangster cluster, the very specific concerns of 2008 emerge. In fact, the cult status of Brian De Palma's 1984 version of *Scarface* in immigrant communities of the *banlieue* has even become a cliché—one recalls the *Scarface* t-shirt worn by the just-out-of-prison character from the *banlieue* in the comedy *Case Départ* (*Tee Box*, Lionel Steketee and Fabrice Eboué, 2011). Well before the 2008 films, the recognized name of Jacques Mesrine became a feature of French hip-hop culture and music, the most obvious reference being Black M, whose moniker is short for Black Mesrimes (my rhymes).[10] In fact, Abdel Raouf Dafri, the screen-writer, reveals in an interview his interest in providing the true story of Jacques Mesrine's life to "kids in the ghetto who wear a t-shirt with his name, but do not know the real story."[11] This very specific interest in merging the production with the *banlieue*/hip-hop culture—in which Jacques Mesrine, a white French 1970s' gangster already signified cool—appears to be a goal of the producer; both the screenwriter and director were from such neighborhoods and their previous works addressed these communities with rap music. One way to reach out to the *banlieue* population, that is largely first-, second-, or third-generation immigrants, was through Mesrine's association with a gangster mythology, a cinema mythology that was bred in Hollywood. Another was the production of an album of rap music (though the songs are not used in the film) to be released as a related project.

To end this brief discussion of the beginnings of the gangster genre and its relationship to the *Mesrine* productions, and to introduce my discussion of the contradictory memories and views put forth by the films of the Franco-Algerian War, we should consider how the gangster genre in its conventions and adaptability allows for a paradoxical and ultimately contemporaneous view of the once forgotten war. As I have already mentioned, "the tragic hero" protagonist whose downfall is imminent, demands a complex characterization. Jacques Mesrine's chameleon-like relationship to the war and its memory is in part forgiven as a character flaw. In fact, his altered view in Part II only enhances his mysterious nature, a feature of his charisma. The audience might disagree with the violence of these gestures, or, in the case of crimes against Algerians, despise the racist ideology at the root of such murders. Nevertheless, as in other gangster features, the public will undoubtedly align with the protagonist, admiring his "power and freedom," enhanced by the centered framing of his figure, and near constant presence. Starring actor Vincent Cassel attempts to explain the contradiction of Mesrine's banlieue popularity:

> What surprises me the most, here's a guy who, during the Algerian War, shoots an Arab disrespecting him like a dirty shit and a rat but can today be a star in

the ghetto where the majority of the youth are sons of immigrants.¹² There is an unbelievable paradox, but that, I think, is explained by the fact that Mesrine remains above all the image of a guy who fought against everything.¹³

As any first reading of these sequences demonstrates, Mesrine remains in authority, relating a liberty with violence that law-abiding citizens are denied. In this way, the gangster genre (as well as the autobiographies of Jacques Mesrine) permit cinema these grave acts of injustice toward Algerians and then, as part of the same formula, juxtapose them with an act of revenge. Thus, the gangster genre bolsters the scission between films and social political perspectives. Lastly, the considerable French box-office success (a rarity for films that feature the war) demonstrates the gangster genre and Mesrine as effective vehicles through which to portray the evolution of historical memory.¹⁴

Jacques Mesrine in the Franco-Algerian War

The War in Flashback

While the Franco-Algerian War is an important force in *Mesrine Part I: The Killer Instinct* and *Part II: Public Enemy No. 1,* the war by no means overshadows the film's primary signifier, Jacques Mesrine. The stylized opening credit sequence enhances his glamour, with split and triple screens—there are sometimes three images of the protagonist and his girlfriend at various angles. Furthermore, the late 1970s' mise-en-scène (primarily clothes and cars) recalls the cult 1970s–80s films *Scarface* and *Godfather* (a compliment paid in nearly every review and a reference also made by the screenwriter), preparing the public for a similar infatuation with the criminal protagonist. Therefore, the beginning of the film situates the viewer at the end of the eponymous gangster's life, where looming music anticipates a flashback as much as the protagonist's death. A sudden cut from a row of rifles pointed by police at Mesrine and his girlfriend (Sylvie Jeanjacquot played by Ludivine Sagnier) in their car to the Franco-Algerian War in 1959 satisfies the public's desire to see a film about a legendary gangster in the 1970s, while opening a larger historical query.

The flashback device enhances suspense and reveals information crucial to the plot, but also mimics a thought process, and here implies Mesrine's psychological response to near death. As mentioned in Chapter 2, Maureen Turim finds that the meaning of flashback "derives from the speed with which cinematic editing was able to cut decisively to another space and time."¹⁵ It was several years later employed to describe the post-traumatic symptom of World War I veterans as "battlefield flashbacks."¹⁶ Similarly in the 2008 Mesrine films, a signifier of post-traumatic stress disorder coalesces with a narrative function in the filmic flashback. In fact, by directly following this bookend-teaser with the Franco-Algerian War in 1959, the filmmakers encourage a cause and effect reasoning. More precisely as the following sequence (the only set in Algeria) is chronologically the first of the biopic, the filmmakers suggest that the French military's techniques fractured and infected their young servicemen.

This responds to the current addressed also in Chapter 2's discussion of *Fidaï* (Damien Ounouri, 2012) and throughout Chapter 3; some ground-breaking documentaries featured veterans speaking of their experience (torturing in particular) and its effect on their mental health, and this evolved into fictional depictions of post-trauma from the Franco-Algerian War in the 2000s. Of course the flashback device increases suspense and allows the film to investigate Mesrine's biography, but by specifically cutting to the Franco-Algerian War, the productions reveal a larger national confrontation with psychological dimensions.

Evoking the tensions of the production year, the scene ambiguously addresses torture, not alluding to the techniques most associated with the war policy (waterboarding and electric shocks) that a montage from *La Battaglia di Algeri* (*The Battle of Algiers,* Gilles Pontecorvo, 1966) most famously depicted. The verbal abuse by a *harki,* blows taken to the victims' heads and faces, as well as their bound limbs and nudity reveal torture elements, but do not cross a thin line that would condemn the soldiers from a twenty-first-century perspective. Although the settings chosen by the French military to torture in Algeria were incredibly varied, common elements included "places where victims could not be heard when they screamed from pain … The torture chambers were generally small, stark, and unclean."[17] The brick structure, narrow in close-ups and sharp angles, suggests such an enclosed area, resembling the torture chamber more fully portrayed in *The Intimate Enemy* (Florent-Emilio Siri, 2007). Just as my study of *The Intimate Enemy* reveals, mediatized historical realizations and interpretations in the late 1990s necessitated a return to the trauma through the twenty-first century's first decade in France.

Furthermore, as Bancel and Blanchard note, the torture practiced during the Franco-Algerian War holds particular interest that I would argue in part is driven by the atrocity's spectacular nature. Thus, previous works whose plots were directly concerned with the Algerian Revolution and the post-trauma of soldiers such as *The Betrayal,* Philippe Faucon, 2006, *The Colonel* (Laurent Herbiet, 2006), and *The Intimate Enemy* (Florent-Emilio Siri, 2007) pressure the *Mesrine* films, demanding a possible torture-chamber scene in a gangster film, because of the brief Franco-Algerian War setting. Yet while the previous films depicted the multifaceted subject, and *The Intimate Enemy* most courageously (within limitations) exposed the actions of the French torturer, *The Killer Instinct* only implies such a setting, and refrains from too horrific of a sequence, that early in the film might scar the main character and thus jeopardize the viewer's continued spectatorship. While Mesrine's service in Algeria from inside of the chamber rather than in battle reveals practical budget concerns, such a readdress of the Franco-Algerian War demonstrates the film's involvement in early twenty-first-century France's war of memories— an era in which the once dismissed question of colonization and the Franco-Algerian War became the nexus of a heated national debate. The scene touches on the torture discourse prevalent in the preceding years, but with ambiguity relieves Mesrine and the spectator from the torture portrait of the much less successful *The Intimate Enemy* released three years prior. (*The Intimate Enemy* was pulled from French screens after twenty-four days with only 409,912 tickets sold in comparison with *Mesrine Part I*'s 2,274,424 tickets sold in seven weeks.)

Such a depiction of the Franco-Algerian War as a trigger for numbness to death and a resulting criminality interprets a concept made by Mesrine himself in both of his autobiographies. Mesrine describes his experience in war in his first book, *L'Instinct de mort* (*Killer Instinct*), "I learned to stop respecting life by contemplating death too closely. Little by little I hardened on the inside ... I had buried deep in my heart all human feeling."[18] In his 1969 book *Coupable d'être innocent* (*Guilty of Being Innocent*), we find further contemplation of the war's effect on his decision to enter crime:

> I left the army in 1959, decorated for acts of bravery, but marked forever by the blood, the mud, the suffering and the shit of this useless war ... Unbalanced in my psyche. Having seen too many deaths to respect life. Having seen too many injustices to believe in Justice. Having simply lost a sense of life ... I put myself to work without conviction ... a few months later, I tumbled, from a taste for action and risk, into the gangster world.[19]

While the camera enhances the already iconic status of Jacques Mesrine, and demonstrates his unique personality's creative role in criminal activities, the scene of Mesrine as a silent, cold, young man in war before becoming a gangster interrogates his criminal motivations. Thus, the war scene remains thematically faithful to Mesrine's autobiography; it depicts the estranged emotions and the confused actions of a soldier.

Nevertheless, Mesrine's short description of the war (roughly six pages of a 359-page book and a paragraph of the second) remains fairly abstract, with but one anecdote in which Mesrine frees an Algerian father and son in the desert.[20] What little Mesrine shared about torture (during the war) permitted Dafri and Richet to freely interpret his role as participant and witness. Mesrine writes, "In the basement the suspects submitted to interrogations. I saw these men get themselves tortured, yell about their hate for France, some preferred to die right there rather than to speak."[21] In this short statement, Mesrine himself offers only a summary of his experience with torture during the war. He never relates his function or admits anything. Did he torture? Did he applaud? Did he shoot? Were the injustices in the previous quote, killings? torture? While other events in Jacques Mesrine's autobiography interpreted by the Richet films indicate Mesrine's knowledge of the French military's torture policy, the filmmakers' decision to include a scene that ambiguously suggests a torture chamber without being explicit is highly selective. The allusion of the French military's torture policy implies the brutality, but filmic elements obscure such inferences. Ultimately, the scene of the Franco-Algerian War enhances Mesrine's mystery and allure as his behavior is at once cruel and rebellious and, in historical context, justified. Furthermore, the scene—the first of a flashback—indicates that Mesrine's service and resulting post-trauma are the root of his criminal behavior.

Chivalry in War

The scene's conclusion, in which Mesrine at last comes to the forefront (a manner of building suspense), further obfuscates his service and racism. The older general,

Figures 5.1 and 5.2 *Killer Instinct* (Jean-Paul Richet, 2008)

who has thus far not spoken, orders Mesrine to kill a suspect's sister—she has just been brought in to further bait the suspect into giving a bomb's location. In a medium close-up the camera frames Mesrine's hesitation with a facial expression and a rub of the chin, but when ordered a second time to execute the woman, he decidedly turns his rifle toward the male suspect. In this manner, Mesrine counters a French military order, while committing murder. Although the film implies the military's mistreatment of Algerians as justified by racism (enhanced by the camera's abstraction of Algerian characters), Mesrine's action hints at his disagreement with such a status quo and, through this small act of rebellion, cross-cuts his military obedience with gallantry. Thus the film commences a dance of race and gender, which further defends Mesrine from a scorn that might otherwise abort the public's viewership.

Richet's 2008 productions reconcile a marketing phenomenon, Jacques Mesrine, with a contemporary cultural climate that seeks to understand the Franco-Algerian War through its representation. While Mesrine witnesses the lighter torturing of the suspects by the *harki* (beating, threatening to have sex with the suspect's sister) he never commits these acts or the others, just as the scene begins with the suspects' physical state (nude, handcuffed, kneeling) but does not demonstrate the process of such dehumanization. Furthermore, the *harki*'s demands, "tell us where the bomb is!," and threats in Arabic that accompany the chaos, depict the need to locate a bomb before it kills European civilians (the "ticking bomb" scenario that General Paul Aussaresses employed to justify torture in his 2001 book that elicited controversy).[22] Mesrine only appears in the execution/torture chamber under the stress of saving many more lives—insinuating a debate renewed in the twenty-first century that complicates the moral binary of torture. It is this act of killing on command during the Franco-Algerian War, with the rebellion of executing a man instead of a woman, that informs the contradictory nature of the features and star personality, proving the Franco-Algerian War's rising fictional presence.

Killing an Algerian Pimp

OAS (Secret Army Organization)

Unlike the invented scene concerning Mesrine's service in Algeria, in his autobiography Mesrine does detail his murder of Ahmed, an Algerian pimp, his first killing outside of war. In terms of plot, the previously described scene during the Franco-Algerian War applies a cultural and historical context for the violence that continued toward Algerians in France. Such an important chapter in French history includes the OAS, the group that began in 1960 to obstruct the forthcoming Algerian independence and attempted the assassination of Charles De Gaulle in 1961 and 1962. Raphaëlle Branche describes French society's understanding of the OAS in 1960: "A majority of French people are in favor of the negotiations in light of the cease-fire, and the proponents of French-Algeria are considered die-hards (*jusqu'au-boutistes*), men running against history's current, and the members of the OAS are considered criminals."[23] As such, *Killer Instinct* introduces the French nationalist terrorist group through gangsters; violence, intrinsic to their racist goals and ideology, incorporates Mesrine, though his sights are primarily financial. Nevertheless, Mesrine de facto serves the OAS in *Killer Instinct*, for his gangster boss and friend, Guido (Gérard Depardieu), emphatically declares his guiding belief. "My army, everyone knows it. It comes in three letters, O A S. It hits where it wants when it wants."[24] The OAS continues to be a lightly treaded undercurrent of the diptych. Although such references can be subtracted in a stripped-down plot, they allot the story a richer historical context. In this manner, political statements concerning Algeria revolve around the protagonist, who contributes only through actions with self-interested motives—in this instance he seeks revenge for Ahmed's beating of Sarah, a prostitute that was young Mesrine's first.

Yet if Mesrine the character never promotes the OAS directly in dialogue, his support of Guido and his murder of the Algerian pimp with Guido demonstrate his ties. By drawing visual comparisons with the torture and murder of Algerians during the war, *Killer Instinct* suggests the historical legacy of the French military's torture policy. As soon as the men exit the car, Mesrine and then Guido force Ahmed down with their guns so that they converse on a higher plane; a cut then reveals Ahmed in the same stance as his Algerian counterparts. Like the nameless prisoner/suspects tortured and killed in the war, Ahmed's arms are bound behind his back while he

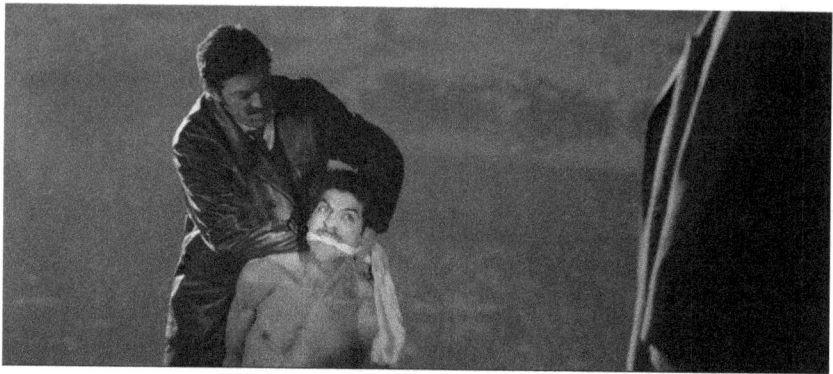

Figure 5.3 *Killer Instinct* (Jean-Paul Richet, 2008)

kneels before the French oppressor. Mesrine talks down to Ahmed before putting a rag around the pimp's mouth and stabbing him in the side several times.

This medium shot of Mesrine next to but above Ahmed (intercut with shots of the knife entering the flesh) reiterates the power dynamic; Mesrine has omniscient agency, and the suffering of Ahmed only enhances his screen power. The ever-present Guido tortures the victim by shining a flashlight in his eyes, beaming support from the OAS, and positing a voyeuristic sadism, which might also apply to the viewing public. The inclusion of this character who voices the severity of his racism and allegiance to the OAS places Mesrine's violence against Algerians in a very specific evolving historic circumstance. Raphaëlle Branche views the OAS as the natural progress of colonial behavior in Algeria, "The colonial situation and its history in Algeria ended in a very specific representation of Algerians. The forms of repression thus testify to an age-old discrimination and a conception of Algerians as a passive group that would only understand force and violence … In this way the colonial state may have possibly produced the organizations that fought against it with terrorist tactics."[25] Our protagonist's actions and his milieus support such a historical interpretation; Mesrine's indoctrination against Algerians in war serves his murder of them again in France, as does the imperialist ideology of the minor but significant character Guido, who also defended the French military's imperialist claims in Indochina.

Nudity

Although the framing downplays the nudity of the tortured Algerians in the war scene (the chaotic camera movement only framing the chest and faces of the Algerian suspects), Ahmed's burial incurs a distanced view of his degrading nudity—when at last Mesrine throws Ahmed into the grave, a high angle long shot reveals the victim's bare backside. As Chapter 3 notes, nudity was an essential element of torturing for the French military during the Franco-Algerian War. The decision to include such a shot of

Ahmed's nude body demonstrates a need to underline the severity of torture, and the remnants of the warfare in Algeria, now years later in France. We do not witness the stripping process, and the motivation is always to avenge the abuse of Sarah, a woman. With distance and darkness, the shot exposing a man's buttocks—still a rarity in film—is funerary rather than sexual. The shot reveals the evolution in mainstream cinema's representation of male-to-male violence, a brutality that brings the protagonist's actions closer to the unforgivable and unjustified, complicating his glorification.

The burial further inscribes the Algerian's expendability and the icon's power; we see the dark outlines of Mesrine and Guido shoveling soil in a stable long shot, before looking finally at the body, almost covered in dirt. The practice of burying Algerian suspects alive was a French military procedure—though torture and death by gun fire were more common.[26] Although we do not witness such a tactic in the brief scene of Mesrine's war service and although his autobiography never describes such behavior, one can be certain that Jacques Mesrine realized the repetition in his murderous gesture and the colonial dimensions of the French burying an Algerian alive when writing in 1977. In concerns of its cinematic representation in 2008, the sequence allegorizes and critiques what had been a popular view of the Franco-Algerian War. The French government, who did not label the "events" a war until 1999, as well as the popular press, buried not only the economic reality of North African communities in France who were expunged to *banlieues* in low-paying jobs with little chance of advancement, but also the roots of such malaise in the Franco-Algerian War, all aspects of the aforementioned invisible years (1962–92), as labeled by Bancel and Blanchard. In this context, we find Richet's Mesrine films in a discourse that critiques the invisible years from a more advanced stage of the memory process. The murder of Ahmed, Mesrine's first killing outside of war, functions symbolically by demonstrating that the mentality and silence that allowed the torture and killing of Algerians in warfare remained in French culture during the surrounding years. However, the film compromises on behalf of a box-office favorite protagonist; gallantry toward women befuddles Mesrine's violence toward Algerians. In addition, Mesrine's silence in the midst of a racist, nationalist rhetoric renders his motivations elusive. Furthermore, in nearly every scene and in most shots, his image, centered and powerful, dominates the spectator. In this way, the severity of Jacques Mesrine's crimes against Algerians in *Mesrine Part I: Killer Instinct* does not recoil a multicultural public in the 2000s.

The two examples of murdering Algerians in *Killer Instinct* portray the ways in which racism and the brutality of warfare informed French behavior post-Empire. Nevertheless, chivalry and gallantry aided by a starring character/actor mitigate such violence, for a macho protection of women motivates Mesrine's two murders of Algerians. As my description of each of the scenes demonstrates, both of the murders of Algerians in *Killer Instinct* are historically precise: the first murder, legal and carried out by and for the French state abroad; the second a live burial representing the military's ideology and technique as continued in French criminal life. Yet a new-found consciousness of the terror of the Franco-Algerian War and its influence on contemporary France reveals the aura of the torture chamber. Thus when the veteran tortures and kills an Algerian in France, the film demonstrates how the racist, imperialist, ideology of the French military in Algeria shaped French behavior toward immigrants afterwards leaving them vulnerable to attacks. These two scenes are but fragments of a much longer narrative that glamorizes the protagonist and his violent whims as part of a rebel, outlaw character. In fact, though the films depict the torture of Algerians in these two instances, they mirror the autobiography by exploring more fully Mesrine's torture in high security prisons (QHS, Quartiers de haute sécurité). As such when Richet's 2008 Mesrine does make political statements, they apply to the treatment of inmates and never concern Algerians.

L'Ennemi Public No. 1

The Scission between Films

There is a very real break between *Part I: Killer Instinct* and *Part II: Public Enemy No. 1*. The films were released one month apart (October 19 and November 22) and not initially screened together, and while they were sold together as part of a DVD set, they are separate discs and are also sold individually. One cannot overlook a marketing strategy that producer, Thomas Langmann, envisioned in which one finds the influence of the successful American television series *The Sopranos* (1999) that encouraged French filmmakers to work in television platforms and extend their cinematic gangster visions—Olivier Assayas's *Carlos* in 2010 provides another example. More specifically the Mesrine diptych reveals the influence of Francis Ford Coppola's *Godfather I* and *II*—though the producer instead cited a diptych his father directed, *Manon des sources* (*Manon of the Spring*) and *Jean de Florette* (Claude Berri, 1986), as his inspiration. Some directors who considered the project found two features excessive (Mathieu Kassovitz, for example); but the double feature included double paychecks (1.5 million per film) and this incentive might have influenced Jean-Paul Richet's decision.[27]

Aesthetically, the scission between films potently cuts the viewer's attention with the narrative, enforcing a before and after perspective. This cut pervasively aligns with the titular character's mysterious, elusive, and contradictory nature and mimics his subversive reasoning in terms of the Franco-Algerian War. Jacques Derrida's critique of Philip Sollers's *Numbers* in which he illustrates the scission applies to this space cut between Part I and Part II of the 2008 *Mesrine* features:

> This "scission" marks the text's interruption (*"when the text is interrupted, folds back upon itself"* …) and also marks the arbitrary insertion of the letter opener by which the reading process is opened up indifferently here and there, the cutting edge of writing which begins with the reading of some sentence clipped out from there or here, the chancy but necessary repetition of the already-thereness of some (other) text, the sharp edge of decision in general, of decided decision, of decision undergone as well as decision deciding … the passage from nothing to "here," from here to "there," … Such a decision is a castration, at least acted out or feigned, or a circumcision.[28]

This citation, to which I will return several times, portrays the dimensions of the scission, for the interruption describes the filmmaker's process as it "marks the insertion of the letter opener" as well as the ways in which this scission alters the reading (or in this case viewing) process. If Part II starts more or less chronologically where Part I ended (1973), the opening credits, the separate DVD and/or entrance fee reintroduce Mesrine and imply his change since his assassination of Algerians—key elements of Part I. Furthermore, this film set more than a decade after the Franco-Algerian War ended, imparts a different view of the war and a France impacted by a growing population of Algerian immigrants. Yet in spite of the cut (the castration, the circumcision), and abrupt spacing, the films remain part of the same body of work. Thus Part II of the Mesrine biopic proffers a very different sentiment toward the Franco-Algerian War and its historicism, but nonetheless builds on the representation of racism, indifference, and repression portrayed in Part I. As such a distinct study of Part II and the scission made between the two understandings of the war's impact in France force a reconsideration of the criminal acts put forth in *Killer Instinct*. These scenes and attitudes survive as a "necessary repetition of already there-ness," the inescapable already there-ness of the Franco-Algerian War in 2008.

Reversal

The most bloody scene of Part II, in which Mesrine enacts revenge toward a journalist who had dishonored his character, places Part I's carnage of Algerians in relief. Although Jacques Mesrine remains the focal point of nearly every scene, Part II reverses his enemies and friends and through them shifts his proper position. This even occurs in language; in Part I, Mesrine's boss and friend, Guido, who aids the murder of Ahmed the Algerian pimp, speaks favorably for the OAS and employs demeaning pejorative racial terms for North Africans (*bicot* and *bougnoule*). In Part II, however, Mesrine's primary accomplice is the ultra-leftist Charlie Bauer, who, like Mesrine, was against imprisonment (their primary political endeavor), always supported Algerian Independence, and dismisses the OAS as *fachos* (among other pejorative vulgar terms).

Thus Mesrine opposes his previous political surroundings; where he allied with Guido to plan the murder of Ahmed, because of his hatred of Algerians and belief in French-Algeria, he now mines Bauer's furor at the extreme right for assistance in the murder of Jacques Dallier, a journalist for *Minute*, an extreme right magazine still in publication. (The film names the journalist who survived, Jacques Tellier, rather than Jacques Dallier.) Obviously, the victims of Mesrine's torture are similarly reversed: one an Algerian, the other a French nationalist. Although Mesrine commits essentially the same acts of torturing and leaves his still-living prey for dead, his victims and accomplices alter his own less-developed political position and, within a plot line, suggest character development. Film form highlights similarities in these acts, a car ride of nearly three minutes into the countryside (with the same somber and menacing musical theme) commences both torture-murder sequences, and in both Jacques Mesrine sits at the car's helm accompanied by his helper in the front passenger seat and soon to be victim in the back. Furthermore, just as the racist jokes of Guido and Mesrine situate the viewer in the proper mentality of the early 1960s' France in Part I, the car ride with the journalist Jacques Dallier voices the right wing's nationalist claim to Algeria in Part II.

The Paris Massacre of October 17, 1961

When Jacques Dallier, the right-wing journalist, mentions the Paris Massacre, he congratulates the knowledgeable audience and inspires their anger toward his character, aligning the public further with the protagonist, "The police of October 1961, they knew where to put the *bougnoules* ... The cops, they had Papon. Papon was a good boss."[29] Consciousness of the once censored and buried history of the October 17, 1961 Paris Massacre had recently taken on mainstream historical import during the tangible years (1992–2002); Jean-Luc Einaudi exposed the atrocity of the Paris police killing many who took part in the FLN's peaceful march to end the Arab curfew in *La Bataille de Paris—17 octobre 1961* (1991).[30] The mayor of Paris, Bernard Delanoë, then became the first government official to acknowledge the tragedy, commemorating the atrocity with a plaque in Paris in 2001. Several films then resulted that brought further attention the state crime and its cover-up, such as *Caché* (*Hidden*, Michael Haneke, 2005) and *La Nuit Noire: 17 octobre, 1961* (*Black Night: October 17, 1961*, Alain Tasma, 2005). Such brief footnotes to history in a successful mainstream release whose market was neither intellectually, nor pedagogically geared demonstrate both a broad awareness of this history in 2008 and a need to reiterate the facts. The car ride with Dallier resembles what Derrida calls folds, for although Part II presents a very different attitude toward the Algerian Revolution, this interpretation of history necessitates a repetition of "the already-thereness."

When Dallier utters Papon's name twice, the script resituates Jaques Mesrine's icon status with a timely awareness of the history of French racism, for Maurice Papon, in addition to being the chief behind the Paris Massacre in 1961, had previously ordered the deportation of 1,600 Jews under the Vichy government (1942–4) and had served in the Franco-Algerian War. The national memory process is apparent; Maurice Papon was tried and found guilty for crimes against humanity in the "tangible years" 1998, and his name thus became a powerful cinematic reference, working very similarly in Michael Haneke's *Caché*.[31] Papon's name signifies the massacre's atrocity and encourages the ignorant to do their history homework, while demonstrating the censored Paris Massacre's twenty-first century impact. Moreover, the references to the Paris Massacre reinforce Mesrine's repetition of torture in *Killer Instinct*. As the previous quote of Raphaëlle Branche indicates, the nationalist, imperialist attitudes that permitted colonization, and the French military's behavior during the war of decolonization, fueled sentiment and behavior in France. The memory of the Paris Massacre of 1961 in *Hors-la-loi* (*Outside the Law*, Rachid Bouchareb, 2010) enacts a site of the Algerian independence experience. *Public Enemy No. 1*'s utterance of the Paris Massacre of 1961 instead previews a screen retribution, with both a historical (1979) and a contemporary context (2008).

Figure 5.4 *Public Enemy No. 1* (Jean-Paul Richet, 2008)

The Cave

The location of Dallier's torture and near murder most emphatically invokes a subversion of French-Algeria; a cave reverberates with the cruelty of France's colonization of Algeria and *enfumades* (in the nineteenth century, the French army asphyxiated thousands of Algerians by driving them into caves and burning a fire at the entrance). In *A History of Violence in the Early Algerian Colony*, William Gallois reveals the paradox of French military documentation, which proves the typical occurrence of decimating families, tribes, and villages while expressing such procedures as exceptional and heinous. He demonstrates that the *enfumades* appear ubiquitous to General Thomas Robert Bugeaud's campaigns in 1832 and 1845:

> The very awfulness of those massacres and the public excoriation of the French military in the metropole have tended to see them as atrocious outliers in the history of the early colony. Yet to a student of French campaigning they seem relatively typical and nondescript.[32]

An increased awareness of these frightening historical associations combine with the soon-to-be-victim's brief biased discussion of French-Algeria to evoke the terror at the root of French colonization in Algeria. The journalist's political positions and historical shorthand suggest no emotional comprehension of colonization's cruelty, and his gruesome torture minutes later for the awakened 2008 public wreaks of revenge. As such, the cave setting, far from Paris as evidenced by the car ride, dark, candlelit, with suspenseful music, applies elements of the horror genre to the obscure memory of French colonial massacres.

Mesrine's Personal Revenge

Richet's *Mesrine* features' attack of colonial ideology is tightly wound, and the scission between films allows for the contemplation of Jacques Mesrine's previous acts and his character's internal retaliation. The films' photography and lighting keep Jacques Mesrine/Vincent Cassel dominant, and in order to guard the public's fascination with an ambiguous protagonist, the narrative mitigates his previous crimes against Algerians. As I have already stated, the depiction of the Franco-Algerian War aligns with a new interest and understanding of the French military's torture policy, as well as its effect on French soldiers/veterans. In addition, with the murder of the Algerian pimp, the abuse of French immigrants in France during the 1960s acquires visible, spectacular proportions. Thus the public's relief at the torture of Jacques Dallier derives from this new understanding of French history represented on screen by the previous murders of Algerians. The scission between Part I and Part II, which is at the very least an intermission, and the distinct packaging that separates the films, distance the protagonist and public from this shameful past.

The revenge that Jacques Mesrine seeks also liberates his former racism, and suggests a self-critique, which ultimately condemns France's imperial conquest. Although Mesrine published *L'Instinct de mort* in 1977 and his torture of Jacques Tellier took place in 1979, certain passages reflect on the colonization of Algeria and a judgment: "Those that we called rebels fought to obtain their independence and reconquer what my ancestors had taken from them a century before. I went then to participate in an absurd war with the certitude that it is never those who start it (war) that fight it."[33] This indication of Jacques Mesrine's historical frame of mind in 1977 reveals his reasoning when choosing a cave for the torture and near-murder of a right-wing extremist journalist, for these words, written during a period in which the Franco-Algerian War was largely ignored by popular discourse, display a foresight into the national regret and anger to come. The awareness of the racism in which colonization is rooted and the ways in which war abuses the young men who sacrifice physically and emotionally illustrate the text's resonance with the wars of memory in 2008. These lines can be lifted from their original context to give voice to the larger multicultural French society of 2008 (which the film aimed to attract), demonstrating again the suitability of Jacques Mesrine as an early twenty-first-century subject. The films reverse the cave as a symbol of colonial cruelty to subjugate the French nationalist to his own prescribed horrors.

The Franco-Algerian War that opens the Mesrine films' chronology endures in the torture of Jacques Dallier in Part II. As the mise-en-scène evokes the massacres of Algerians by the French, the blocking and torture encourage this comparison. While the camera's attention to motifs of pain, blood, and wails evokes the horror of the crimes, the protagonist's power and dominance complicate his responsibility. We watch the journalist strip and be handcuffed (a process we did not witness in the killings of Algerians) and during the most extreme physical beating, complete with extreme close-ups that the two previous murders lack, Mesrine tells Dallier, "I will show you what we did in Algeria,"[34] before gagging him exactly as he did Ahmed, the Algerian pimp in Part I. This statement and gagging underline the new victim's racial reversal—these are not featured in the 1984 film version of the same near mortal crime—and the scene's historical charge plays to a targeted immigrant and immigrant-allied audience.

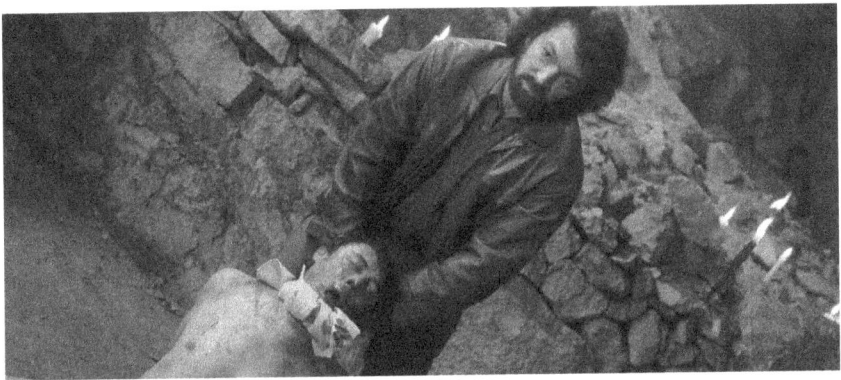

Figure 5.5 *Public Enemy No. 1* (Jean-Paul Richet, 2008)

As the surrounding media information woven into this analysis reveals, France thoroughly reconsidered the Franco–Algerian War in the decade preceding Richet's Mesrine films; in summary the French government officially labeled the conflict a war in 1999, historians such as Raphaëlle Branche and Benjamin Stora generated new interest in the secrets of the war, French generals and veterans admitted to torturing, and writers such as Didier Daennickx and Jean-Luc Einaudi helmed an exposure of the censored Paris Massacre of October 1961. Also indicating the ways in which Algeria provoked national millennial questions in French history was Article 4 of a 2005 law that aimed to impart a more favorable view of colonization (especially of North Africa) in the public classroom.[35] After a large debate and a declaration signed by notable historians, the law was overturned suggesting a national ambivalence of how to remember colonization in Algeria lay within a desire to expose the once hidden truth. Like the surrounding Article 4 debate of 2005 and its eventual rejection, the *Mesrine* films' differing views of Algeria in one conflicted, contradictory, character signify the wars of memory; these films as cultural artifacts emblematize "a society in interaction with its past, but also in search of a sense of the present and the anguishes of the future."[36] Moreover, the term "wars of memory" in its precise era also defines the films' scission. Through a cut in its center, the diptych provides spectators with two views of the Franco-Algerian War and its history: one in which the OAS thrives and punishes immigrants; another in which the OAS is subjected to punishment. Inevitably, the preference given to the latter through chronology, and the level of extreme violence, attaches to a post-2000 understanding of Algerian independence. Nevertheless, the existence of these different scenes and the mysterious protagonist's varied stances reveal a memory process by which contemporary France participates and interrogates its proper history for entertainment purposes. By invoking elements of French history, the films locate a contemporaneous struggle to organize a variety of memories, beliefs, and approaches.

Conclusion

Although I have already proven the films' separation and unity, and the ways in which the films' historic references and intratextual visual allusions consider the Franco-Algerian War and its legacy, Jacques Derrida's concept of the circumcision holds more powerful implications for the contemporary public of these filmic texts. While Derrida employs circumcision to allude to a self-contained duality (*Circumfession*), his frequent term generally applies to a wound that generates both difference and belonging, externally and internally—all aspects of the 2008 *Mesrine* features' relationship to each other, which we have already explored. However, Derrida's reading of Paul Celan's *Einem der vor der Tür stand* (*Standing before the Door*), which finds the wound as an opening to the reader, applies particularly to the spectatorship of Richet's Mesrine features. In fact, if we consider the Mesrine diptych as Celan's poetic text, and viewing the film as a reading, the scission alters the viewer's relationship to the film. He writes of the word "circumcise" in the poem's context:

> This word to be circumcised, this word of *someone's* to be circumcised, this word to be circumcised for someone, this word which must thus be given, and given *once* circumcised, we may understand this word as an opened word.
>
> Like a wound, you will say ... Opened, first of all, like a door: opened to the stranger, to the other, to the neighbor, to the guest, to whomever.[37]

Viewing Richet's Mesrine films, with their specific historical references to the OAS and the Paris Massacre of 1961, we find French history cinematically opened, and any spectator invited to deconstruct the French violence toward Algerians, as well as its ricochets and advances in moving images. With space, the scission or circumcision of the Mesrine diptych, like the circumcised/opened word in Paul Celan's poetry, provides a doorway through which the viewer may enter and interpret. By the year 2008, the Franco-Algerian War and the 1961 Paris Massacre at last were common to French vernacular. Yet this unique space of familiarity and its relationship to current events, as well as temporal distance from the once censored violence, welcomes spectators to further reflect on the nature of nationalist ideology.

The intertwined discussion of the biblical shibboleth, after which Derrida entitled his work on Celan's poetry, also evokes France's and French cinema's relationship to the harsh reality of the Franco-Algerian War–era. In Judges Chapter 12, the surviving Ephraimites due to a biological difference cannot say properly the word *shibboleth*, a word originally meaning a stalk of grains. The Galeadite guards force those entering to attempt its pronunciation in order to identify and kill any Ephraimites aiming to return to their ancestral land. Derrida writes, "the Ephraimites experienced their inaptitude to pronounce what they nonetheless knew ought to be pronounced *shibboleth* not *sibboleth*."[38] Officially alluded to as events, or a conflict, and not labeled a war until 1999, the Franco-Algerian War previously wore signs of such literal unpronounceability. In addition, interpreting pronunciation metaphorically, we find an inability to address the war culturally and visually, for despite many knowledgeable persons' efforts, an invisibility in mainstream culture prevailed for over forty years.

The concept of the shibboleth sheds light on the Mesrine features, not because they were unique or the first to depict the Franco-Algerian War and its aftermath, but because the scission clothed in an icon's trappings and the gangster genre's conventions opens the public's doorway wider, cutting the Franco-Algerian War-legacy with multiple interpretations, and hereby rendering it more accessible/pronounceable for a mainstream public. As a return of memory reveals French cinema and its spectators revisiting the Algerian Revolution as a mise-en-scène and as a subject, *Mesrine Part I: Killer Instinct*, and *Part II: Public Enemy No. 1* inscribe and then reinscribe the national wound, opening the spectator to connections in the past, and exposing their striking contribution to present tensions. In this way, through the scission, the Mesrine diptych biopic reveals an acceptance of the (if negotiated) historical reality of the Franco-Algerian War and its legacy, an acceptance that connotes a national belonging. Derrida writes, "And this doorway is nothing other than circumcision as *shibboleth*, the place of decision for the right of access to the legitimate community, the covenant or alliance."[39] The spectator by self-inscribing the circumcision in viewing Richet's *Mesrine*'s films allies with a conflicted past whose reverberation is felt throughout the French culture of the 2000s. Ultimately, *Mesrine Part I: Killer Instinct*, and *Part II: Public Enemy No. 1* depict their titular protagonist's relationship to Algeria as torn and secondary, a scission that breathes consequentiality and tolerance into the war of memories.

6

The Revolution through Utopian Dialectics

Une si jeune paix (*So Young a Peace*, Jacques Charby, 1965) and *Loubia Hamra* (*Bloody Beans*, Narimane Mari, 2013)

Through both production, style, and loose plot, Narimane Mari's *Loubia Hamra* (*Bloody Beans*, 2013) embodies a twenty-first-century view of the Algerian Revolution that blurs national borders and historical eras. The film stars improvising street children of the beach suburbs of Algiers reenacting and rewriting their version of the Algerian Revolution that took place fifty some years before. Guided and inspired by colorful props and clues, the children embrace the ocean as an arbiter of time and space; this collaboration between youth and nature gives birth to a new vision of the Algerian Revolution. In this world run by children, eating and dancing on the beach replace the historic violence. Yet echoes of *Une si jeune paix* (*So Young a Peace*, Jacques Charby, 1965) complicate Mari's symbolism. In fact, this first Algerian fiction picture (made largely in homage to the intellectual icon of Algeria, Frantz Fanon) also stars children who play war against one another, though in the months directly following the Evian Accords rather than fifty some years later. Never visiting the ocean or beach, the orphans of the 1960s stage their battles within the confines of the orphanage and its surrounding landscape, a mise-en-scène that evokes imprisonment. Although the principal difference between the two films lies in the nonactor cast's experience and innocence regarding war, the portrayal of space that connotes trauma's proximity relays vast changes in the geographical screen imagining of Algeria. Plainly, by studying the settings of both films' play revolution, we locate the reality and idealism of early independent Algerian geography, and more fully comprehend its confusion half a century later. Algeria's first independent film reveals a national postwar trauma and Mari's twenty-first-century revisitation suggests the growing dissolution and multidirectional postmemory of the Revolution. The confident naïveté of children playing war yokes *Bloody Beans* to a film made fifty years prior and as such demands an investigation of the altered view of Algerian space.

In this chapter, I will first define and apply Michel Foucault's term "heterotopia" to the geography of *So Young a Peace*. I will next parse and employ an extension of heterotopia to describe *Bloody Beans*, what David Harvey labels spatiotemporal utopian dialectics. The mise-en-scène of both films embodies the politics of their production; in first identifying closed configurations in *So Young a Peace* that represent a new Algerian society, we identify *Bloody Beans'* intertextual references and comprehend the subversion possible in the twenty-first century. In consideration of the first Algerian fiction film in which children reenact war, we locate the implications of the later child troop's expanse of beach and ocean, a cinematic dissolution of history and nation. The doubled imagining of Algeria as a war playground finds the tightly wound construction of time and space unraveled. In this way, *Bloody Beans* explores the endurance and permanence of history, as well as its mythological afterlife.

Film as Heterotopia, *Une si jeune paix*

Michel Foucault first developed the term heterotopia to describe the semiotic function of language, but later in 1984 employed heterotopia as a geographic theory. In "Of Other Spaces: Utopias and Heterotopias," he defines and differentiates the linking terms:

> There are also, probably in every culture, in every civilization, real places—places that do exist and that are formed in the very founding of society—which is something like counter-sites, a kind of effectively enacted utopia in which the real sites, all the other real sites that can be found within the culture, are simultaneously represented, contested, and inverted.[1]

When Foucault refers to counter-sites of societal import as heterotopias, he includes the movie theater, with the jazz bar and bordello. Foucault also labels another cinematic image, the mirror, a heterotopia. He writes, "The mirror is, after all, a utopia, since it is a placeless place"—one that reflects something it is not, but that remains part of the same reality as an object. He continues, "It exerts a sort of counteraction on the position that I occupy."[2]

The reappropriation of the colonizer's spaces resulted in such heteropias in post-Revolution Algeria. Historically, Algerians (and namely the state) did claim all of the colonizers' abandoned physical structures, such as schools, post offices, banks, homes, called *bien vacant* or truly vacant, as well as government buildings, reversing and enacting their original meanings as a natural reinscription of societal space. In this way, deterritorialization and reterritorialization interact and typify the post-Revolution Algeria that many texts and films of the era represent. As locations serve social roles, they map the boundaries of the new nation, its cities, and neighborhoods, illustrating the social geography of their human subjects. In particular, *So Young a Peace* reveals a multifaceted, heterotopic value, engendering many types of in-between spaces; the post office, the orphanage, the soccer field, the cemetery all emblematize (and later in this film, contradict) the utopian ideals of the newly independent Algeria. In fact, the film begins with an intertitle "three months after independence" revealing the children's mimicking of war as the "representation, contestation, and inversion" of society described by Foucault. Ultimately, the disturbed children's interactions trouble even when affirming a nationalist agenda.

Orphans

While the majority of the war's primary participants were adults, the child population that contributed and endured the war was significant. In fact, the data collected by Abdellaziz Bouisri and François Pradel De Lamaze demonstrate how childhood trauma affected the country's outlook; 43 percent of Muslim-Algerians in 1954 were aged between 0 and 14, and in 1966, 56 percent of the Algerian population was between the ages of 0 and 19.[3] *So Young a Peace* appropriately depicts the child survivors as Algeria's future and their orphanage as the locus and paradigm of the new nation's urgent situation, a crisis-heterotopia (a term that Foucault defines as "reserved for individuals who are, in relation to society and to the environment in which they live, in a state of crisis"[4]). The grieving, traumatized children need attention desperately, and their compulsion to repeat the war is symptomatic of their traumatism. In *Beyond the Pleasure Principle*, Sigmund Freud expands on repetition compulsion by first recalling his infant grandson's need to master his mother's leaving for short intervals; the toddler throws small objects calling out "gone!," and then fetches them, shouting "there!" ("fort" and "da" in German).[5] While Freud perhaps chose this example for its banality, it very specifically applies to the orphans of *So Young a Peace*. The children formulate a situation comparable to that in which they lost their parents, attempting to understand their own survival, and perhaps even resurrect their families—a completely unconscious gesture that seeks to prove mastery over loss. This post-trauma that we read as national, especially as the film is considered Algeria's first fiction feature, organizes the narrative and equally informs every aspect of the mise-en-scène; the crisis-heterotopia spills into the larger heterotopia, namely postwar Algeria.

Closed configurations largely determine heterotopias, as such separating and closeting from the larger society permits a very selective mimicking. In the primary orphanage of *So Young a Peace*, such isolation requires an enormous gate and a tall stone fence that an orphanage employee guards. Although the gate does not deter the children from sneaking out, it separates the orphanage and surrounding garden from Algiers—unknowing citizens may walk by the gate and sign, but will see neither the children within, nor the building and garden that they occupy. In fact, the gate dominates an establishing shot of the orphanage territory, before a tracking shot follows Mustapha and Ali to a garden entrance. In this gated garden space, physical trauma encapsulates the children; a one-armed girl carrying her one-armed doll; a boy who struggles to walk with an artificial limb; and Mustafa, our protagonist, who is unable to climb out of his window or up walls because of a crippled hand. Foucault's reading of the cinema (a two-dimensional space meant to project three dimensions) appears especially relevant. If (as Foucault states) the Persian garden originally represented the four parts of the world and its navel, the orphanage garden occupied by children and a teacher evokes the heterotopias of the garden and cinema at once.[6]

The manicured nature indicates a society's ideals and even its reterritorialization, while the children's voices and disabilities speak to a reconstructed society existing out of view. A multitude of traumas indicate both the wholeness of the alienated group and the specificity of each character's isolated tragedy; close-ups of different maimed body parts and several isolated flashbacks interrupt the chronological narrative, portraying the national trauma while insisting on the uniqueness of each child counterpart.

In fact, *So Young a Peace* in style connotes Italian neorealism and its documentary aura (applied and transformed further by Gillo Pontecorvo for *La Battaglia di Algeri* [*The Battle of Algiers*] a year later).[7] Yacef Saâdi, who founded Casbah Film to promote Algeria as a setting for European coproductions, picked Pontecorvo after asking Roberto Rossellini, revealing how Italian directors and neorealist cinema appeared as a role model for new Algerian productions that sought to publicize a socialist ideology. Charby's brand of neorealism indicates the new state's role in its first production, but also locates an appropriate marriage of style and theme, previously paired in another tragedy of a child's post-trauma, Roberto Rossellini's *Germania anno zero* (*Germany Year Zero*, 1948), in which a surviving German child commits suicide. However, the reality of a grieving child population imported the visual power of children to awaken empathy. Matthew Connelly postulates that "perhaps the FLN staged the scenes of children crying beside their parents' corpses" in clips taken by *muhjadeen* that were then central to American reporting.[8] While the FLN mined such scenes for emotional impact and political purposes, the actuality of children whose families' lives were determined by war rendered the optics more effective.

On a literary front, the Algerian context references Frantz Fanon's final posthumously published book *Les Damnés de la terre* (*The Wretched of the Earth*) in which a general treatise on war trauma outlined in the introduction is verified by specific, individual case studies included before the conclusion. Although less known, the film more specifically relates Jacques Charby's anonymously edited *Les Enfants d'Algérie: Témoignages et dessins d'enfants réfugiés en Tunisie, en Libye et au Maroc* (*The Children of Algeria: Testimonies and Drawings of Refugee Children in Tunisia, Libya, and Morocco*), a collection of the children's witness accounts of the war, that were recorded principally in Arabic and then transcribed and translated into French, accompanied by the their illustrations.[9] The French police had arrested Jacques Charby as a *porteur de valises*, who then escaped and fled to Tunisia[10] where he interacted considerably with Fanon. The Algerians seeking refuge in Tunisia included many orphaned children under Fanon's psychiatric care.[11] The children inspired Charby to anonymously publish a book in Italy, with the goal of awakening the French public to the orphans' needs. In this manner, Charby's interest in orphans intersected with Fanon's therapy and writing, and the translated interviews of *The Children of Algeria* follow a format similar to that found in *The Wretched of the Earth*. Fanon's ideology and methodology also influenced Charby's film style; Guy Hennebelle writes in a review of the film in *El Moudjahid*: "Charby sends us to Fanon and to the multiple pathological cases described in *The Wretched of the Earth*."[12] Cinematically, neorealism provided a vehicle through which to pair social views with the seldom represented truth of post-Revolution Algeria. All of the children cast were traumatized orphans of the war.[13]

Most significantly, the protagonist of the film, Mostefa, played by Mostefa Bellaïd himself, had previously provided his terrifying witness account and survival in the book: French soldiers killed his parents in front of him, shot him in the left leg, and, when he tried to escape, burned his left hand and arm.[14] Mostefa concludes his passage violently, expressing the impossibility of repentance toward the French: "I will burn them as they burned me … I will never forget those who burned me even if they say they are sorry I will not forget them."[15] When reading of the criminal behavior toward children and their survival, we locate trauma at the root of such hatred and divisions. Interestingly, in the text, the child Mostefa Bellaïd spares other children, "I will not burn a child, as they have done nothing to me."[16] However, Charby does not apply Mostefa's exception to his film, where violence against children by children questions the intergenerational effects of war and, less overtly, the internal consequences of nationalism. Charby ultimately adopted his lead actor but a stable home in Europe never quelled the survivor's sorrow. Mostefa Bellaïd committed suicide at the age of 50, a post-face not intended by the director.

Orphan Art

French directors for the liberation movement had already recorded Fanon's process with orphans and had in a sense made a cinematic version of the book *The Children of Algeria*. As previously discussed, René Vautier, Yann Le Masson, and Olga Poliakof's experimental documentary *J'ai huit ans* (*I Am 8 Years Old*, 1961) pictures the orphans and the art they made to exorcize their trauma, as prescribed by their psychologist Fanon.[17] (Images of their art are reprinted in Chapter 2.) The children's art hangs on the orphanage walls throughout *So Young a Peace*, the fruits of Fanon's technique of art therapy as recorded in *The Children of Algeria*.[18] Fanon himself realized that such artistic expression of witnessing war holds a patriotic dimension that can be utilized for propagandistic purposes. In fact, Boukhatem Farès, an adult patient through whom Fanon developed his art therapy, became an artist for the ALN, creating works that the FLN "subsequently presented to representatives of friendly foreign delegations."[19] By including children's artistic accounts of the Revolution on the walls, the film publicizes Algeria to foreign viewers, an aspect of the intended public (in 1965, *So Young a Peace* screened at Cannes Film Festival and won a prize at Moscow Film Festival). Furthermore, as *I Am 8 Years Old* had already featured the orphans' art, the grief dominating the experimental short reverberates within the feature-length narrative. In fact, the mural behind the boys at their desks can be identified as a war scene with parachutists and tanks (no victims are visible), one that closely resembles several of the paintings in the 1961 short, and those that were first featured in the book *The Children of Algeria*. Critically reading Charby's nationalistic impulses, art augments the use of children for political effect in both texts. However, in consideration of the children's loss, the primitive renderings restate their age and trauma, invoking Fanon with collective sorrow and its accompanying patriotism.

In the scene's establishing shot of the classroom, the bottom of a mural painting begins just at the students necks'. By placing their heads directly on the bottom border

Figure 6.1 *So Young a Peace* (Jacques Charby, 1965)

of the chaotic art, the framing suggests the children's emanating thoughts as well as the fearsome memories' inescapability. Within the mural's frame, the art continues a strategic dual emphasis on the colonized psychological pain as well as the people's victory, thus visually depicting de- and reterritorialization at once. In consideration of Mostefa Lacheref's opinion that Algeria's early cinema mired the people in war by solely depicting revolution narratives, we find the child-painted murals maintain the past war in Algeria's present. Furthermore, the camera's framing, exterior to the mural's, evokes an Algeria unable to transcend its recent history, one that the filmic illustration visually cements.

Whereas the boys are seated in their memory of the past war, a map of Africa hangs on the wall behind their teacher, emblematizing far-reaching knowledge, boundaries, and objectivity.[20] Elements of pan-Africanism in the classroom reflect a government agenda under Ben Bella that was essential to Frantz Fanon's discourse. At the All African People's Congress in 1958, Fanon, as an Algerian delegate, notably expressed his view that, "Algeria was the guide territory and was leading what would become a continent-wide revolution."[21] There are no names of countries or cities on the map; thus the oneness of the isolated continent appears stronger than the high contrast hues in black and white film that relate borders. The shot-reverse-shot in the classroom between misbehaving boys in front of their own depiction of the war and their militant teacher in front of a map of Africa, evokes the specific post-trauma of colonization and war, and the healing sought in the concept of continental solidarity and strength. A child's painting of Fidel Castro highlights Algerian participation in the nonalignment movement (Cuba served as an example for the FLN), demonstrating the ways in which the education policy reflects state ideology. Such decorative artifacts display the utopian message of pan-Africanism in the early 1960s. However, these optimistic outlooks serve to enclose the orphans and the viewer, a perspective that concludes with the tragic consequences of war and the ideology of reterritorialization.

Wretched of the Earth

Although Fanon's work with the orphans is less documented, *So Young a Peace* echoes the cases of those Algerians studied in *The Wretched of the Earth*—like the orphans of the film, these displaced individuals suffer from a similar confusion that results in an aggressive repetition of war trauma. In one case, an Algerian man attacks all his fellow Algerians believing that they are disguised as French: "All these people who call themselves Algerian are French ... and they don't leave me alone ... I will kill them without exception."[22] While the orphans of *So Young a Peace* remain in a collective, in naming the other Algerian orphanage that wins a soccer match against them the OAS, they rely on a similar binary that labels other Algerians French and enemy. (The two teams alternate this naming, but keep their groupings distinct, proving their lack of signification.) Fanon's two case studies concerning children alert the reader to his interest in orphans and the psychology of traumatized children. A murder of a European child by two Algerian boys (aged 13 and 14) demonstrates a need to vindicate the adult deaths of Algerians on what they deem as an appropriate level, someone their size.[23] When Fanon writes about the "Behavior troubles of young Algerians less than 10 years old," he speaks more generally of a group of orphans with sadistic tendencies not unlike those depicted in the film. *So Young a Peace* thus re-presents Fanon's concern for the orphans and their post-traumatic agitations as a patriotic call to justice and healing.

Before the soccer match, Mustafa exclaims to his teammates that they will win because of their jerseys—all made in the likeness of the Algerian flag. However, when they arrive, the opposing team (which appears to come from a French Catholic orphanage as a French priest is their chaperone) wears the same patriotic jersey. This uniform attaches the players to a nationalist beginning entrenched in warfare and colonialism that results in its child size reproduction (an image that brings greater irony to the conclusion of *Les Folles Années du Twist* [*The Crazy Years of the Twist*, Mahmoud Zemmouri, 1986] as discussed in Chapter 3). However, countering the nationalist formula, the orphanages have no clear enemy—ultimately the visiting team wears their jerseys inside-out, further internalizing and reversing the blanket symbol. The anger over losing fuses with their trauma when they call the winners from the winning orphanage the OAS—which perhaps derives from the Frenchness of the rival Catholic orphanage.[24] Soon afterwards, the orphanages exchange the floating signifiers OAS and FLN thus replaying the trauma that they have endured, and emphasizing the binary intrinsic to their pained and misled understanding of war. Representing the power of the signifiers, children alter the sign labeling Mostefa's orphanage "Les enfants de la Revolution" to read "Les enfants OAS." The small Algerian flag remains painted to the side, and in this manner pairs the OAS with its antithesis under the heading of children. When further below the same sign, Abder (one of the boy leader's names) is equaled to imbecile (Abder=imbecile) the semiotics prove empty, a boy is as stupid, as the OAS is pro-Algerian, the shot, shows the progression of play and

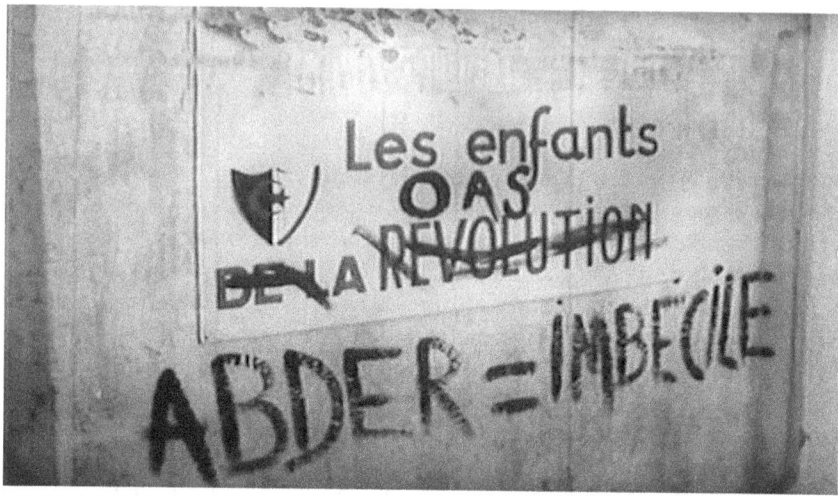

Figure 6.2 *So Young a Peace* (Jacques Charby, 1965)

physically captures the emptying of historical signifiers, which for the emerging generation signify but loss and anger.

Forests and the Cemetery

The boys' claiming of destroyed French war vehicles vandalized by the OAS demonstrates the extent of which the revolutionary war still pervaded the Algerian landscape after its demise, and how these visions, as those reproduced by film, might lock the imagination of its citizens in the past. The orphan boys skillfully cross a fence guarded with barbed wire to play among the French army's abandoned military tanks. Long shots display the children's intense physicality and fierce interaction shouting and firing their air guns, excited by the once loaded weapons. One sign still propped on a tank reads "O.A.S. Salan" (Raoul Salan was the founder of the OAS who had directed the putsch attempt in 1961, and who was imprisoned after his plot to undermine Algerian independence). Like the graffitied orphanage gate sign, the words loaded with historic import and contemporaneous significance infuse the children's innocent gestures with the threat of death and its seriousness. Again the fence and barbed wire enhance the heterotopia by guarding the boys' game from the eyes of others, which allows for the reversal and emptying of the (invented) dichotomy, and which here stages a neosociety on war remnants.

However, a long shot framing six pairs of boys' wrestling in the forest most effectively displays the youth ownership of Algerian soil. The boys' dance-like, improvised, but clearly choreographed contestation suggests the psychological trauma of colonialization embedded in Algerian earth. The forest trees also posit a graphic match to the boys in the garden of their orphanage, where trees similarly frame the circular space they inhabit, and in which a distant fence rests behind the pillar-like

Figure 6.3 *So Young a Peace* (Jacques Charby, 1965)

Figure 6.4 *So Young a Peace* (Jacques Charby, 1965)

trees. Foucault describes such an arrangement of items that enclose a heterotopia: "the site is defined by relations of proximity between points or elements; formally, we can describe these relations as series, trees, or grids."[25] Indeed, in both the orphanage garden and the forest, the landscape contains the boys as they fight needlessly for its ownership; the surrounding trees and gate relegate their fighting to the two-dimensional grid of the screen. In this way, the film pictures the orphans in a heterotopia, whether the reclaimed space is within the orphanage or out. In both instances, the quiet capital in the distance contrasts with and modifies the gated boy-society. This community and their mimicked war are known only to those within its borders, one of the micro-units in the larger macro-society of Algiers.

Foucault discusses the cemetery as a heterotopia distanced from the city's center: "the other city where each family possesses its dark resting place."[26] In this instance, a Muslim cemetery (which also has a gated entrance) reinforces the recent death toll and an Algerian claim to the earth. The boys walk slowly through the site before sitting to discuss their war strategy on the tombs. One boy, Ali, becomes serious when he recognizes a martyr's grave from its surrounding protective gate. This parallel to the orphans' framing, always within a border, suggests their own proximity to death and the war's psychic toll. A close-up underlines this boy's wisdom; the gate that connotes a war death causes his discomfort as he realizes that the game has begun to move past metaphor. The cemetery setting similarly warns the spectator, so that, when Mostefa and others throw rocks at Ali fleeing, the denial and violence carry a new gravity.

More subtly, however, the boys reterritorialize the cemetery, a place of mourning, as their own proper site of war; driven by post-traumatic repetition, the boys reclaim the buried martyrs as a strand of their own empty battle. In this way, by creating a neowar society, the alienated orphans prolong the Revolution, allowing for an opportunity to avenge their parents' death, and symbolically prevent it. The heterotopia thus contains elements of a heterochrony, for the boys arrive at "an absolute break with traditional time."[27] That this break with time into the recent revolutionary past might allow their parents to continue living, evokes a common element of post-trauma stress disorder, just as flashbacks to and dreams of the traumatic event may permit one contact with those already lost. The very specific arrangement of the crisis-heterotopia engenders

Figure 6.5 *So Young a Peace* (Jacques Charby, 1965)

The Revolution through Utopian Dialectics 141

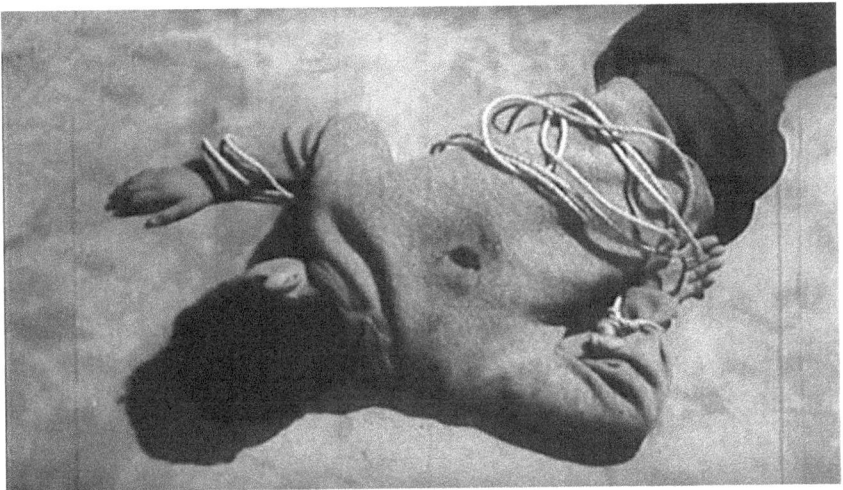

Figure 6.6 *So Young a Peace* (Jacques Charby, 1965)

the heterochrony, and a Manichean Algerian Revolution continues in an unseen space. Thus the game of "fort-da" continues.

The film's conclusion presents the tragic results of such reclamation; after the boys' faux trial, one shoots and kills one of his opponents. At this point, the orphans' sides are blurred, Ali leads the trial, and Mostefa who is now an "OAS" prisoner is bound by rope and imprisoned in an armoire. Nearing the end of Ali's patriotic speech (memorized probably as part of the school curriculum and repeated with some difficulty), one boy, among the fifty or sixty gathered, suddenly and without warning shoots the "OAS" prisoner-orphan who stands before the child judges. The surrounding silence intensifies the sound of the bullet, and brings poignancy to the concluding five camera shots. The camera, the spectator, and the eyes of the young trial public first rest with disbelief on the shooter, before locating Mostefa, who abruptly liberates himself from the closet to investigate the sound. In this medium close-up shot, the armoire's frame which squares Mostefa's chest and face reminds the viewer again of the orphans' captivity in a neosociety that celebrates nationalism and war. The camera then reveals the subject of Mostefa's glance, a boy's corpse face-down, ropes wrapped loosely around his body, emblematic of his prisoner-status in a mortal game.

Silence continues to reign in the following shot of Mostefa, a near extreme close-up (the kind that introduced Mostefa's flashbacks earlier in the film), in which he again stares motionless with disbelief at the results of the child war. As extreme close-ups often imply the framed subject's mental activity, the shot depicts Mostefa's mapping of cause and effect. Furthermore, as the framing cuts off his mouth, our attention rests on his furrowed brow—a facial expression that with a slight angle illustrates dismay. The last shot finds the orphans in a theatric mise-en-scène; in a semi-circle the boy orphans look down at the body, while the camera completes the circle with a claustrophobic sense of enclosure. Trauma of the larger war and

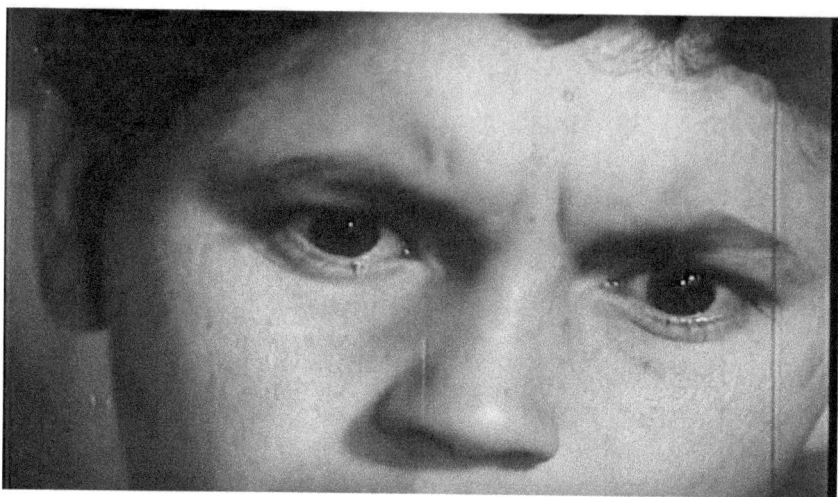

Figure 6.7 *So Young a Peace* (Jacques Charby, 1965)

its ideology birthed the orphan microwar, which then unleashed its unique private trauma, unseen and bordered. Hope for their escape lies in the weighty silence and the downward stare, the creased brow of the protagonist suggesting that thought may guide future actions without guaranteeing it. In addition to a stage, the boys' positioning suggests a ritual, the camera's space including the viewer in the spiritual exercise and thought process.

A quote by Frantz Fanon is then superimposed on the still, "Et il y a des enfants et des enfants à garnir des sourires" (And there are children and children to decorate with smiles). The quote at last places Frantz Fanon's name in the film, and thus the theorist within a rare child context. However, the words otherwise contrast sharply with the image, for neither the trauma nor the murder of children garners smiles. Still, by remembering that both the victim and assailant are but children who in other circumstances innocently create joy, one comes to excuse the events that stem from pain and ignorance. Furthermore, Frantz Fanon's name read on top of such a sorrowful scene recalls the intellectual icon's own aid toward orphans and Algerians more generally. In the context of post-Revolution Algeria, the quote paired with the accident and grief inspires viewers to remember their own civic responsibility to such orphans (as already noted, the director himself adopted the actor in the lead role), infusing what can in the twenty-first century be read as a pessimistic tale with its original, patriotic context of nation-building. With distance in time, the Fanon quote and the orphans suffering lack their plea and urgency. In fact, scholarship seldom references Frantz Fanon's relationship to Algerian orphanages primarily present in his last book *The Wretched of the Earth*. The film produced by the new Algerian government, perhaps even believing it to have a nation-building message concerning the effects of the French torture and abuse, appears now in the midst of the protests surrounding the 2019 presidential election, to speak against the training of patriotism, which for many has grown empty. The film today reads less as a guide to the specific post-traumatic behavior of children following the war, and more generally as a statement against the inculcation of children in a nationalist ideology. Without foreseeing Algeria's future, Charby himself commented on both the universal and the specific message of *So Young a Peace*, "it is on the one hand a universal denunciation, while on the other it attracts attention to this terrible problem of orphans after the war."[28]

When we return to *So Young a Peace* with a full awareness of its circumstances and epoch, we find the heterotopia constricting with vigor. The camera and mise-en-scène limit the boys' space, and enforce a visual captivity. While they are diegetically "out of view" as in a heterotopia, the camera surveys them within these borders—which in some instances appear theatrical, as if on stage with a backdrop. The walls and borders that enclose the boys in their supreme heterotopic structure, the orphanage, also follow them to the soccer field, the cemetery, and the forest. In this manner, they have no reprieve from their microsociety; without the regard or commentary of others, the post-traumatic repetition quickly prevents contact with the external present. This unique feature by a French director neither evokes the complexities of murders by the FLN nor the importance of the varied cultural identities and languages. Nevertheless, it is subversive in a twenty-first-century context because it emphasizes the problems of nationalism for a young traumatized population; the film painfully and original displays the internal decay of traumatized youth and the ways in which such PTSD may be hidden within social services. In fact, it is precisely such trees, walls and beams, that Narimane Mari's *Bloody Beans* dissolves, asking heterotopias why children and history should be enclosed.

Loubia Hamra, a Dialectical Spatiotemporal Utopia

Fifty-one years after the Algerian Revolution, and forty-eight years after *So Young a Peace*, *Bloody Beans* alternatively pictures paths paved by children in which history and film intersect in atypical geographic configurations.[29] In David Harvey's *Spaces of Hope*, the geographer declares the shortcomings of heterotopias; although Foucault "destabilizes" the discourse, he does not envision a liberation of time and space. Harvey concludes, "The task is then to define an alternative ... a spatiotemporal utopianism—a dialectical utopianism—that is rooted in our present possibilities at the same time as it points toward different trajectories."[30] According to Harvey, a spatiotemporal utopianism refers most specifically to opening the constructs that delineate space and time, and thereby broadening our concept of reality, a task that *Bloody Beans* undertakes. In fact, if we employ Harvey's terminology to cinema, dialectic spatiotemporal utopia applies easily to experimental, but narrative films—Assia Djebar's film *La Nouba des femmes de Mont Chenoua* (*The Nouba of the Women of Mont Chenoua*, 1977) also exhibits this tension between chronology and its demise, in which Algeria as an articulated space presents a discombobulation. In fact, a familiarity, or even an anchor in normalcy, augments our perception of such deviations, reflecting a dialectical tension with the bordered time and space of the status quo.

In terms of *Bloody Beans*, the vast possibilities of ocean and intertwined children's bodies also refract the twentieth-century-screen Algerian Revolution that read time and people as divisible quantities. Thus, the abstract 2013 "play" Revolution that pictures neither violence toward nor the trauma of children retains the painful orphans' war of 1965 at its core. While the expression of nation denies the walls of history and territory, it reinvokes them as part and parcel of a rejection. Even a synopsis of the loose aleatory plot includes signifiers of the Algerian Revolution: A cast of children playing on the beach locates and stops an OAS member beating his wife in a beach house. The children then wander through a cemetery before capturing a French soldier. After becoming friends with their captive, they hide from a bomb. Although the children think their French friend is hiding with them, they discover his corpse on the beach when they exit the shelter. In spite of such overt references to the Algerian Revolution, the child cast and fluid mise-en-scène never bind the film to historicity. The director Narimane Mari, French of Algerian heritage, acts as an architect (a term I will explore fully later) constructing an imagining of the Revolution beyond the confines of heterotopias— a claustrophobia that proves disastrous in *So Young a Peace*. In this manner, *Bloody Beans* liberates the Algerian Revolution from its former context and screen depictions, while remaining conscious of its beleaguered history.

Futuristic Child Society

Images of children intrinsically comment on the state of their surrounding society; children represent family and concern for the future. As previously stated, for this reason children are often characters and even protagonists in neorealist and neo-neorealist films as they effectively represent social concerns.[31] Neither realist nor neorealist, the low production value and nonactor child cast of *Bloody Beans* connote documentary elements concerning contemporary Algeria— perhaps for this reason the film was mislabeled as a documentary at The Copenhagen International Documentary Film Festival CPH:DOX. The camera's near full attention to the approximately 8–12-year-olds suggests the age dynamic in Algeria; as of 2017, 29.49 percent of Algeria's population is under 14 (while the child population during the Revolution was certainly greater than today, the age of today's Algerians severely counters the average age of the governing population, 62 years).[32] Furthermore, the children's beach lifestyle, an imaginative reterritorializing, also alludes to Algeria's lack of housing.[33] The children's poverty, perhaps suggested by their wandering status, but evoked more concretely in dialogue with complaints of eating only beans, lightly implies the economic constraints on a young population. In this manner, the film rewrites homelessness, poverty, and a lack of governance as imaginative openings that beckon children with the freedom to roam.

The red beans of the title, translated more ironically in English as bloody beans, are playful rather than tragic; their only real fault is the resulting gas and farting, a favorite joke among children that provokes their laughter in the opening sequence. The beans prove more irreverent to the war's memory, for the torture the children prescribe to their French soldier prisoner is to eat them, the red suggesting blood, as they feel that they have suffered the torment of both eating beans for countless meals and the consequential gas. Such use of beans reimagines the severity of torture that caused much blood loss and bloodshed as a simple meal. Yet, effacing the truth of the torture policy without a historical mise-en-scène eludes critique, for the child cast enforces a reading of their reenactment as play. The audience thus forgives the children's mistake and is relieved by their innocence. The troop has already befriended the French soldier (one of the film's only adults) when they torture him with a bowl of beans—in fact, at dawn they dance around him on the beach and command him in French to tell his friends in Paris that he has friends in Algiers. The dawn beach scene thus replaces the torture commonly practiced by the French military in the war, and alluded to if not pictured in previous Algerian Revolution films, a practice historically associated with night. The film supplants torture with a meal served to the guest of honor at a beach party, and the mise-en-scène modifies this sentiment of friendship with the optimism of early daylight and colorful balloons. *Bloody Beans* thus reconstructs perhaps the most common connotation of the Algerian Revolutionary War and the most common symbol of its severity. Furthermore, now Algerians torture the French military, rather than the reverse (however the French actor playing the soldier is also Algerian, just as the actors playing French soldiers in the majority of Algerian films). Nevertheless, the word's original signification endures, anchoring the film's fantastic flight to a spatiotemporal neverland with the gravity of the past.

Moreover, the score of *Bloody Beans* encourages such an atemporal reading; mysterious electronic dance music by a French group Zombie Zombie superimposes a futuristic element on their historic play of the Revolution. Fifty years earlier, horns and drums in *So Young a Peace* resembled the not-yet composed Morricone score of *The Battle of Algiers*, a style of the era that invoked a militaristic masculinity. By contrast, the sparse and eerie sound-design of *Bloody Beans* fuses with the unfurling natural landscape and the mass of children's active and intertwined bodies, blending the past and present with what signifies the future for an early twenty-first century public. In less experimental moments driven by beats, the score recalls a European night club, a discothèque scenario that would not involve children. The modern dark edge of the dance music does not segregate gender or sexuality; attached to the roaming Algerian youth, the music represents mobility and freedom from genre. These electronic sounds in a natural setting exhibit a yearning for society's reconstruction.

Child grouping

The Mediterranean Sea and its beaches contradict the concept of closure that the most well-known cinematic visions of the Revolution evoked (notably in the *casbah* of *The Battle of Algiers*, and the desert and mountains of *Les Hors-la-loi* (*The Outlaws*, Tewfik Farès, 1969) and *Chronique des années de braise* (*Chronicle of the Years of Fire*, Mohammed Lakhdar-Hamina, 1975). However, more precisely, *Bloody Beans* radically subverts *So Young a Peace*, as the film recycles and refurbishes the concept of children reenacting their version of the Revolution. As in all Algerian films about the Revolution, and similar to my discussion of Ali in *Cartouches Gauloises* (*Summer of '62*, Mehdi Charef, 2006),the children of *Bloody Beans* appear as nomads; they travel from "one point to another" and their lives are the "intermezzo."[34] Although these children, fifty-one years from the Revolution and fourteen from the Algerian civil war of the 1990s, show no legible signs of trauma, their grouping nonetheless recalls Charby's representation of the Algerian terrain dominated by children. Montages of the children build a collective just as the *moudjahid* films: a montage of extreme close-ups of the eyes of the children emphasizes seeing and disguise, while another montage of the children posing individually as statues at a cemetery (soon to be discussed) captures their play with signifiers of death. The final sequence is also a montage of the children, floating in the ocean. These montages advance the group's importance and diminish the individual (ten consecutive shots of eyes, nine consecutive shots of children as statues, all fourteen floating in the sea). Part and parcel of an overarching visual theme of Algerian children in Algerian nature shifts the previous heterotopic reterritorialization of closed configurations to unleash a cinematic rejection of the grid of poles, people, and trees that enclose children.

Three vocal female participants represent difference within this grouping. Through the girls, Mari grapples with gender roles in both present-day Algeria and the Algerian Revolution, as well as its memory—a stark contrast to *So Young a Peace* in which girls perform but a very minor spectator role following the boy leaders at soccer games and mock trials. The three girls do serve a status quo domestic role as food providers when they bring the boys bananas to eat on the beach (the beach serves as a kitchen and dining area in addition to a bed). However, the girls also supply important information on the OAS and the French military, including their whereabouts. Furthermore, the girls challenge their allotted role in dialogue, one stating "that women are not just to make dinner, they fight wars too." (A similar conversation ensues later in the film when the children embark to find the French general.) Thus, girls demanding, arguing, and inserting themselves, replace the cheering extras of *So Young a Peace*—in consideration of all of the cinematic portrayals of the Algerian Revolution, the girls of *So Young a Peace* most notably contrast with the near silent disguised bombers in *The Battle of Algiers*.[35] Though the group is male dominant (fourteen boys to three girls), Mari frames each child with similar attention, and nearly equal screen time. Although the premise of *Bloody Beans* cannot expose the depths of the true contributions by women to the independence cause, a thread that harkens from Assia Djebar's *The Nouba of the Women of Mont Chenoua* remains. The girls struggle to be taken seriously as soldiers, and their participation in spite of sexism encases the child reimagining of the Revolution in a gendered discourse. More importantly, such an understanding of women fighters in the Algerian Revolution proves to be an element of the child society's cohesive whole. In summary, *Bloody Beans* presents the Algerian Revolution as a confrontation of sexism and inequality, one that diminishes neither the contribution of females nor their solidarity in the fight for independence.

Cemetery Part II

Like *So Young a Peace*, *Bloody Beans* relies on the cemetery space to invoke death in the present. However, unlike the Muslim cemetery of the 1965 picture that paid tribute

Figure 6.8 *Bloody Beans* (Narimane Mari, 2013)

to the many Algerian fatalities of the independence cause, in 2013 the children visit unattended Christian graves, the camera isolating and framing several crosses and statues of notable Christian icons. As such, *Bloody Beans* contemplates the distanced exoticism of Algeria's Christian colonial past. The improvising children of *Bloody Beans* prove their agency, not only over their French prisoner, or the plot, but over the cinematic artifice. The camera captures overt *mise-en-abymes*, the child cast's flashlights supply primary lighting and the children freely style themselves, creatively dressing in costumes and applying make-up before entering the cemetery. Standing as sculptures on the tombs, and staring directly into the camera glare, the flashlights and throbbing techno music project a dance pulse onto death. This sequence that lasts six minutes and contains little to no dialogue illustrates the children's disrespect of mortality and ignorance of history—traits that empower a loose but antifrontier narrative. The cemetery of *So Young a Peace* proves to be a heterotopia as Foucault describes, a city outside the city for the dead. Indeed, the mise-en-scène of *So Young a Peace* reflects the children's true repetition compulsion and its post-traumatic roots in an unconscious attempt to delay the parental deaths. In juxtaposition, for the cast of *Bloody Beans* the cemetary lacks ancestral or familial funerary associations. The camera thus follows the children to counter the cemetery's original significance with new possibilities of play.

Furthermore, the beach/ocean expanse that begins and concludes *Bloody Beans* replaces the confines of the reterritorialized orphanage fraught with references to Fanon's ideology in *So Young a Peace*. The first shot of *Bloody Beans* finds a boy jumping into the ocean onto the sand, introducing the in-between space (so common to nomads), and the play in locating the touching of sand (stability) and water (chance

Figure 6.9 *Bloody Beans* (Narimane Mari, 2013)

and uncertainty). The film's geography and relation to time continually grapple with the security of borders, dismantling the solid configurations that fail to protect the orphans of *So Young a Peace*. The shots that follow find a collection of boys of different sizes, jumping, floating, and swimming, all in a space that is both beach and ocean, and neither. The boys touch and stand upon a miniscule island of rocks, taking turns to flip backwards into the water, communicating jovially, proving they can stand together, but yet seeming as comfortable in the water as on this fraction of shared earth. After four minutes, we find our nomad group sleeping on the beach, establishing a community/family, by touching their legs, heads, arms, and chests, as they cross and settle on and under one another. The travelling shots of the fourteen boys merge with views of the ocean and the sound of seagulls; the Algerian landscape becomes a shelter without walls that projects calm onto a nomad status.

Bloody Beans concludes by returning to the importance of the Mediterranean Sea, a geographic border that the film challenges as its characters dwell at its cusp. A montage of the children floating in the film's final minutes strengthens motifs found in the previous montages of their faces and figures. This closing montage begins abruptly after a steady camera finds the children in a long shot sitting in a circle around the corpse of their French prisoner and new friend, Bernard—his death unexplained, but implicitly the result of a bomb from which the children fled. With low minor notes resounding from the eerie electronic score, the distanced shot of their gathering suggests a ritualistic mourning. The use of French and French literature directly after this shot picturing collective grief might be interpreted as sorrow and reconciliation on the part of Algeria toward France, a taboo subject for both nations. However, the film stylistically, as well as the poem and the author chosen, complicate such a reading with broader associations of the French avant-garde that strove to escape such facile categorization.

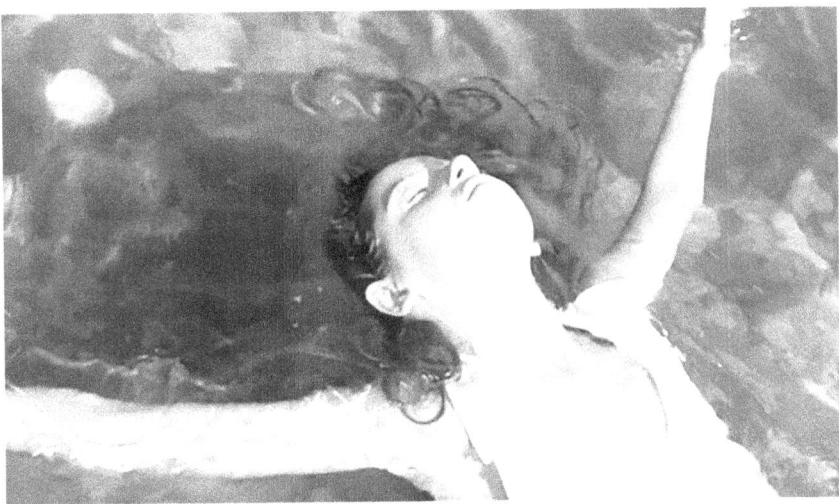

Figure 6.10 *Bloody Beans* (Narimane Mari, 2013)

In fact, an audio-track in which each of the children reads several lines of Antonin Artaud's poem, "Petit poème aux poissons de la mer" ("Little Poem to the Fish of the Sea," 1926) accompanies a montage composed of unsteady close-ups of the individual children, each floating peacefully with their eyes shut (though sometimes laughing). Previously, we have witnessed the children as screen collaborators, selecting and applying their costumes and makeup; using props such as balloons, hats, and wigs; freely improvising dance and dialogue; and lighting the scene with their flashlights. However, in the finale's unpolished poem recitation, one strongly feels the director's inclinations. At last the children's improvisation falls silent as their voices struggling to read in French match the near-stillness of their bodies. The shots of the children do not change in sequence with an accompanying voice, thus it is not necessarily the voice of the child pictured that accompanies the image—this disjuncture of sound and image fragments the individual portraits and enforces a view of the children as a group. Much like the rock island of the first sequence, floating face-up represents an in-between space, for the children dwell neither in nor outside of Algeria, yet distinctly remain defined by a geographic realm. Furthermore, foreshadowed by their previous poses as statues in the cemetery, the children, with their eyes shut, appear both in and outside of dreaming and death. Ultimately, the children appear as half-being half-ocean, what is visible of their wet skin glistens in the shining sun, and Algeria appears as nature to be shared by children.

Artaud's lesser-known poem, "Little Poem to the Fish of the Sea" poses the question of whether one should be or obey, suggesting that the two are incompatible. The poem written as a dialogue between a narrator and a pool of fish, was largely inspired by Lewis Carroll and even references Alice as a character, appropriate for a fantastic project starring children, despite being written by the author of the *Theater of Cruelty*. In fact, the inclusion of the French poem by the influential dramaturge diminishes the children's perceived agency—despite its linguistic simplicity, without an advanced French education, the children could not have taken part in selecting Artaud's poem. When the narrator of the poem asks the fish if it is better to be or to obey, the fish respond that they have died because of their refusal to obey. The narrator makes the judgment: "The fish are dead / Because they preferred to be / to go to the end without knowing anything / of what you call obeying."[36] Mortality becomes a playful acting exercise with geographic dimensions; the sonic superimposition of the text on their half-submerged faces allegorizes the children as rebellious fish, while positing a creative alternative to artistic and historic constraints. *Bloody Beans* presents French first as the language of the enemy, then as a language of cultural exchange and friendship, and in conclusion as the language of rebellion and its accompanying art. The awkward child voices reading in French inject an aspect of the *mission civilisatrice*; one may access high culture through French, and the film *Bloody Beans*, despite its Algerian funding and credits, and Algerian-Arabic dialogue, remains attached to this cultural sphere. On the other hand, by ending her film with an outcry and promotion of rebellion, Mari dares other filmmakers to confront their country (whether it be France or Algeria), and the history that binds them. To this extent, French and Artaud represent a further ellipsis in time and space; the French language serves many purposes and is especially distant from the orders of French soldiers found in early Algerian film.

Furthermore, the pairing of Antoinin Artaud's poem with the montage of floating children, as well as the potent use of the French language to subtly critique the state and previous filmic interpretations of the Revolution, did not anger Algerian authorities as they failed to recognize the sophisticated revolt. The figure of Artaud, and the body of work for which he stands, immediately connote rebellion against the status quo, as Artaud sought to break the fourth wall of the theater and confront the ineptitude intrinsic to living. Unsurprisingly, The Copenhagen International Documentary Film Festival CPH:DOX, latched onto this reference congratulating the film and themselves for their prior literary knowledge: "We celebrate this film for its embrace of Antonin Artaud's statement: 'It is better to be than to obey.'"[37] By citing Artaud, Mari places her film in his company of both rebellion and *francité*, which also makes the film's message more legible and marketable for a festival circuit as well as for a French viewership. However, the reference understood by the educated elite does not undermine the spatiotemporal utopian dialectics; in fact, it further destabilizes the film's nationality, whose transnational Algerian-French status is epitomized by the Mediterranean Sea.

To this extent we may describe the director Narimane Mari with David Harvey's laudatory term "architect," a profession that "shapes and preserves long-term social memories and strives to give material form to the longings and desires of individuals and collectives."[38] Indeed, this first feature-length film by Mari addresses the Revolution as a historic symbol, while countering the previous representations of the war's atrocity with improvisational fantasy. However, Mari most radically confronts previous depictions and historical accounts by portraying friendship between the Algerians and the French, and by evoking sorrow after a French soldier's death. We find transnational productions of the twenty-first century more generally able to depict friendships between French-Algerians and Algerians—*Summer of '62* most obviously deserves a comparison because the protagonist and his friends are of school-age, while *The Colonel, The Betrayal, The Intimate Enemy,* and *Djinns* among other twenty-first-century productions, depict working relationships between Algerians and the military, as well as their complications. Yet the improvisational, experimental format and the child-cast of *Bloody Beans* permitted a revision of the war whose plot centers on such a friendship.

OAS/Pig

A rubber pig mask charged with twenty-first-century importance visually represents the historic OAS in basic terms; the French eat pork, the Algerians do not. Nevertheless, such masks were not known to be worn by the French terrorist organization during their significant years, and thus a contemporary French meaning disrupts any historical structure. As part of the film's exposition, the children's conversation defines the OAS as the French who kill each other. In an unstylized medium shot, the children then start using the word pigs to describe the French (e.g., "they all look like pigs"), revealing an accepted slang-term in their group culture. One girl describes a particular OAS member in detail—a general who has no need to eat beans as he has an abundance of chocolate. Food then highlights differences in nationality and class as they are combined: chocolate the dream food that must be stolen from the unjust, beans, the demeaned Algerian diet. Although the dialogue never mentions the consumption of pork, the pig's association with non-Muslims derives from such *haram* food choices. Therefore, when the first group of children approaches the general's home to steal chocolate, previous dialogue has foreshadowed the vigorous pig snorts that infiltrate the sparse score. These snorts shift the film toward the experimental and prepare the audience for a man wearing a pig mask whose threat is enhanced by the handheld camera's low angle. Both humorous and eerie, the rubber pig mask primarily signifies the OAS and at this point, the French; the mask symbol thus ridicules the terrorist group and troubles history. As *Bloody Beans* was released in 2013, the initial public most immediately associated the mask with the *Bloc Identitaire* that was formed in 2002.[39] The most well-known of French anti-immigrant groups use a swine as their primary symbol, and in their most visible years, 2003–10, wore pig masks at xenophobic protests against Halal restaurants, and in publicity, as part of a larger pro-pork campaign that served *soupe identitaire* (soup made with pork) at homeless shelters.[40]

However, the rubber pig mask as employed by the *Bloc Identitaire* holds larger, spectacular significance, as the *Saw* horror movie franchise, American but also popular in Europe, is contemporary to the group's years of importance (the original *Saw* film premiered in 2003). In this way, Jigsaw, the mastermind killer of the *Saw* features, originally infused the *Bloc Identitaire*'s humorous tone with a hegemonic violent threat. The choice of a pig mask is achronological and quickly evokes the continuum of pro-French-Algeria sentiment and its relation to anti-immigrant fervor. While the Algerian setting evades France, the pig mask alludes to the French political climate with a humorous gesture; the ridiculousness of the pig sounds coupled with dark keyboard tones intimates horror, a genre that frequently draws on comedy.

The French pig speaks only in the soundtrack's snorts, which rise with intensity as the scene progresses but revert to a haunted depressed squeal as the scene concludes—exposing the lack of language as a sign of his impotence. On the other hand, children exercise agency and prove their strength in number when chanting in both Algerian Arabic and French, "Vive l'Algérie!" and "Dégage!" Without physical confrontation, it is mere words that ultimately destroy the pig's fist-wielding spirit. Eventually disparaged by their united front, the masked man wanders to the beach and disappears into the landscape. Although the OAS made deadly attacks in the months surrounding the Evian Accords,[41] *Bloody Beans* dismantles their terrorism, with a theater piece in which the children are victorious. Obviously, the masked man's descent from the roof toward the ocean simplifies the end of a terrorist organization (which still has supporters) and the immigration of thousands. Yet the twenty-first-century symbolism of the anti-immigrant and anti-Muslim movement, as well as the the euphoric public outcry, erase the specific categorization of time and space. The pig mask and sound design in this experimental Algerian Revolution setting free meaning to rewrite evil as ridiculous, ultimately supporting all fronts that fight against colonialism's legacy and its inherent racism.

Like all filmmaking, the artistic and technical practice concretize an idea, as such planning and financing are intended to serve a larger visionary goal. In my interview with Malek Bensmaïl, the director attested that the Algerian state and its entertainment boards (ENTV) restrict their funding to pictures that uphold the revolutionary mythology of Algerians as a monolingual people, unified and victorious with the FLN. For this reason, he was forced to work with the French state again (INA) to produce *The Battle of Algiers, A Film in History* (2017).[42] In 2008, his film *China Is Still Far* could not pass such scrutiny to receive full Algerian funding. Perhaps given the experimental nature of *Bloody Beans*, the film escaped such probing. While the filmmaker used, in part, her own production company, Aller-retours, based in Algeria, but whose name emblematizes the director's/producer's travels to and from Algeria and France, she, in conjunction, received funding from the Algerian Cultural Association. For this reason Mari considers the film Algerian, though she also states that the CNAP (Centre National des Arts Plastiques) in Paris contributed to the project, as well an additional French production company, Centrale Électrique.[43] In Mari's opinion, Algerian funding is temperamental; while *Bloody Beans* received Algerian support, a year and a half later the committee included some different members who did not fund her second Algerian project, *Le Fort des fous* (*The Oven for Crazies*, 2017), which she ultimately filmed in Greece. Mari therefore believes that timing and chance are as important as the nationalism of the narrative.

While there are many factors that affect such funding decisions, one cannot deny that in spite of *Bloody Beans*' distinct reimagining of war, in which a French soldier becomes a friend and is mourned, certain characteristics of nationalistic productions concerning the war remain intact. In fact, *Bloody Beans* neither suggests the fatalities caused by the FLN nor implies the party's enforcement in Algerian communities.

Signified by loud sounds and hiding, the bomb remains somewhat mysterious, as the OAS, the French military, and the FLN bombed during the war. Nonetheless, the children and the French soldier are innocent, and thus the film casts blame on an outside party. Furthermore, however whimsical the narrative may be, the Algerian children remain unified and motivated by a need to disempower the OAS and the French military, not unlike the 1960s' and 1970s' features of *moudjahid* cinema. The child group initially works collectively to defeat the OAS, a group depicted as a pig without language. Ultimately, the complications of depicting a French soldier as compassionate to Algerian children may be mitigated by casting an Algerian actor in the role.

On the other hand, the Algerian children, who may be considered the de facto FLN of *Bloody Beans*, force their French prisoner to eat beans as a torture or torture-revenge, and this light approach reassigns revolutionary symbolism to natural quotidian objects. Similarly, rather than the harsh, unfair rule of the French military found in *moudjahid* productions, the film proceeds with little visual information regarding the severity of the French occupation of Algeria. In fact, the only visual signifiers of the French military are in bits of costume, the captured soldier's camouflage and his general's undershirt, white and simple but with epaulettes. Truly, if one party dominates the other, it is the children who win, but by sheer number and without force—neither side inflicts violence on the other, and the film remains suitable for the cast's age group. As Harvey writes, "The architect struggles to open spaces for new possibilities and future forms of social life."[44] Mari recasts the physical closure of the heterotopic post-Revolution films, liberating nature in lieue of reclaiming it, thus the Algerians of *Bloody Beans* live joyfully in the interstitial earth-sea. To an extent, *Bloody Beans* continues a visual opening of Algeria and the future of its revolutionary symbolism that began at the finale of *China Is Still Far* (Chapter 2). In *China Is Still Far*, the children we had previously seen studying the Revolution in the classroom are now at the beach on a field trip joyfully exploring their country's boundary and its natural opening to others. Three years later, the Algerian children of *Bloody Beans* refuse the confines of the school structure and weave their terrain and its painful history into a game.

Conclusion

At the conclusion of *Spaces of Hope*, David Harvey investigates the murky territory between the universal and the particular, as well as their dependence on one another. In terms of Algeria and nationalism, it is the universal claims against colonization that brought the personal, specific crimes against French-Algeria, which in turn generated international activism and supported pan-Africanism. Jacques Charby seized this relationship; in *So Young a Peace*, the very specific situation of orphans after the Algerian Revolution battles the universal beliefs in innocence, opportunity, and family that children automatically represent. In the twenty-first century, with distance, and outside of the new state ideology, the film offers a vibrant universal truth and particularity; patriotism and post-trauma combine to demonstrate the mortal effects of war's repetition compulsion, warning against future violent postcolonial movements (such as the Black Decade). Returning to this scenario fifty years later, *Bloody Beans* unsettles Algerian nationalism further, French and Algerian-Arabic, as well as the translation that occurs within such dialogue and recitation, support a visual transgression of the geographic borders. Ultimately, Mari's film pronounces significant markers of Algeria and history in order to simultaneously unravel and reinstate their relevance; the Algerian Revolution symbolizes a distance between peoples that the OAS confrontation upholds and that the interaction with the French soldier blurs.

Yet must film concede such arrangements with previous depictions in order to confront the past? And perhaps in order to make the most radical existential step in receiving Algerian state funds and credits, even while dissolving their traditions? How can Algeria rewrite the Revolution without evoking history or territory? Harvey writes:

> We can always aspire to make our own historical geography but never under historical and geographical conditions of our choosing, then the leap from the present into some future is always constrained, no matter how hard we struggle to liberate ourselves from the three basic constraints of (1) where we see it from, (2) how far we can see, (3) where we can learn it from.[45]

Such points relate the architect's/filmmaker's challenge of building a new historical geography, but with given materials. In *Bloody Beans*, the universal ideals illustrated by the hope and innocence of children and by the vast expanse of beach and ocean, are still mired in the particularism of viewing Algeria fifty years after its independence on film. *Bloody Beans* evokes new spaces free of ownership, a concept not possible in the post-independence cinematic imaginary, which sought to reterritorialize. Nevertheless cinematography, with its perimeters, restricts a setting, even while conjuring the limitless landscape. Ultimately, *Bloody Beans* strides toward the future, liberating the Algerian Revolution from its previous screen legends. However, negotiations with both Algeria's history and film history, align the experimental film with its neorealist predecessor, *So Young a Peace*. The traces of the orphans' struggle enhance the emancipation of the Algerian Revolution's screen meaning.

Conclusion

On February 8, 2018, the French Conseil Constitutionnel (whose members traditionally include past presidents) amended a decision concerning the Algerian Revolution that reflects the internationalism embedded in the recent films about the war. Article 13 of the 1963 law awarded a pension to French citizens who suffered violence related to the Franco-Algerian War—now, fifty-five years later, all other injured nationalities (including Algerians) will have the right to such French funds. Certainly, by 2018, the population able to claim their pension has diminished, and many who live in Algeria and fought for the FLN already receive compensation from the Algerian state.[1] Nevertheless, the council's decision implements France's desire to forge a stronger foundation with Algeria, which begins by excavating Algeria's de/colonization and admitting historical blame. This book has revealed elements of the Algerian Revolution in cinema that are analogous to the law's revision. The transcinema of the twentieth century, with its autonomous productions that primarily depict one nation's perspective, extends now to a cinema that resituates shared memories in the twenty-first century. Algeria and France today regularly coproduce films concerning the war including those studied within this book such as *Algérie Tours/détours* (Oriane Brun-Moschetti and Leïla Morouche, 2006), *Cartouches Gauloises* (*Summer of '62*, Mehdi Charef, 2007), *La Chine est encore loin* (*China Is Still Far*, Malek Bensmaïl, 2008), *Hors-la-loi* (*Outside the Law*, Rachid Bouchareb, 2010), *Fidaï* (Damien Ounouri, 2012), and *Loubia Hamra* (*Bloody Beans*, Narimane Mari, 2013). Thus moving images represent people of mixed citizenship and heritage that seek to understand history and its consequences in contemporary society. Furthermore, Abdelkader K, the man that challenged the constitutionality of the original 1963 law, still suffered from gun-shot wounds he had endured at eight years of age.[2] The topic of children harmed and/or orphaned by the war was present throughout Algeria's campaign for independence. In fact, this forceful theme attached to the scholarship of Algeria's intellectual icon Frantz Fanon, grounds the first Algerian fiction feature (by French director Jacques Charby) *Une si jeune paix* (*So Young a Peace*, 1965). The Revolution's damage to children finds new expression in these twenty-first-century films, most notably Mehdi Charef's seemingly autobiographical feature (he was but ten years old at independence) *Summer of '62*, which provides a voice for such child survivors of war now near the end of their lives. It is with optimism and renewal that this monograph's study ends with the experimental 2013 feature, *Bloody Beans*; time and distance permit the war's symbolic play. Such utopian endeavors join the two countries, rather than recapitulating nationalist myths and reiterating sincere wounds. In addition, the children's relationship to the Algerian Revolution reveals both patterns and lapses, interrogating the nature of history.

Now, in the summer of 2019, months of peaceful protests have at last forced Abdelaziz Bouteflika from his fifth reelection campaign. At last the longest running Algerian president will give way to a new leader and perhaps a new government, which will affect the moving images of the war produced by state funds and those that might be filmed in Algeria. With Algeria facing the unknown, it is difficult to predict how the future state will alter their position and/or funding concerning portrayals of the Revolution. Malek Bensmaïl was not able to procure Algerian funds for his documentary *La Bataille d'Algers un film dans l'histoire* (*The Battle of Algiers: A Film in History*, 2017), and the ONM (National Organization of the *moudjahidine*) continues to fund biographical projects that idealize revolutionary martyrs—for example, Ahmed Rachedi's *Mostafa Ben Boulaid* (2008), *Krim Belkacim* (2014), and *Lofti* (2015). Nevertheless, the government partnership and its display of the 2009 coproduction agreement appears as a natural aspect of an active current; facts previously absent from the Algerian film narrative of the Revolution emerged through transnational productions made both before and after this initiative. In this monograph's corpus, the friendships of Algerians and French-Algerians in *Summer of '62* and *Bloody Beans* and the Algerian fratricide and the war in France in *Outside the Law* surface as the most obvious examples. These aspects of the films coproduced by the Algerian state derail the nationalistic foundation of the industry and locate a new opening in Algerian funding. The more transgressive productions appear through a loophole, as the state is unable to place an experimental feature in the same parameters; *Bloody Beans* transcends such uniform ideologies and presents the Algerian children befriending a French soldier and reciting French verse. Though less treated due to the comparative pairing nature of my chapters, *La Trahison* (*The Betrayal*, Philippe Faucon, 2005) reveals not only a harki's allegiance to Algerian independence, but his conflicted emotions and contradictory actions, as well as that of his French colonel. The Algerian government's contribution to such films illustrates an acceptability of partnerships with France and French people, deriving from a growing, if still partial, ability to alter the official reading of the Algerian Revolution.

While at the beginning of 1970s, French cinema severely critiqued the French military's policy in an anticensor current—*Avoir 20 ans dans les Aurès* (*To Be 20 in the Aurès*, René Vautier, 1972) and *R.A.S.* (*Nothing to Report*, Yves Boisset, 1973)—by the end of the decade Pierre Schoendoerffer offered a conservative rebuttal—*La Crabe tamboure* (*The Drummer Crab*, 1977) and *L'Honneur d'un capitaine* (*The Honor of a Captain*, 1982). The twenty-first century balanced these perspectives by projecting a self-reflective torturer who suffers from his actions. These depictions respond not only to Raphaëlle Branche's exposition of the once forbidden military files, but to the public confessions of former generals (Paul Aussaresses and Jacques Massu in 2000) and the outcry against them. Thus twenty-first-century French cinema not only depicts the soldiers committing the atrocities, but, with a distance of now forty plus years, seeks to understand the mental state and military direction that led to so many young men's entanglement. The same distance that permits a multilayered defense of the torturers in *L'Ennemi intime* [*The Intimate Enemy*, Patrick Rotman, 2002] also opens a critique of the atomic bomb tests, clothed in a horror film in *Djinns*. While the horror genre paints the soldiers' actions and the looming atomic test as mortifying and cruel, the concept of the Algerians' revenge through jinns minimizes the responsibility of the French army and defense team. Forces beyond the French men's control in part absolve them from blame.

The Algerian Revolution's entrance into the horror genre, like its inclusion in the gangster genre with the Jacques Mesrine biopic diptych, demonstrates the once *événements'* growing importance as a lieu of war history in French popular culture. With the largest North African population in Europe, several generations of Algerians live in France. This multicultural richness represents a new epoch of internal transnational currents, and the Algerian Revolution has at last infiltrated a popular mainstream exchange. Richet's Mesrine diptych includes one scene set during the Algerian Revolution, portrayed as a step in the criminal's training. Yet such a scene (as others studied in this monograph) evokes a paradigm shift in French society's view of the Franco-Algerian War; what was once invisible and outside of the public sphere resides now at the heart of French society. Following the Mesrine films precedent, *Djinns* (*Stranded,* Hughes and Sandra Martin, 2010) defies the previous limits of the Algerian Revolution on film, resetting the shameful era of French history within genre conventions. The tropes of horror, whether they be sparse music or extreme angles, just as the tropes of the gangster flick in guns and dialogue, now modify the atrocity of the French military's presence in Algeria, as well as its afterlife of extremist right-wing support. Such twenty-first century films never fully address the massacres, torture, and severity practiced by the ALN, a decision that might be considered sympathetic toward the French. Furthermore, the films' portrayal of the war's duress mitigates the young French men's criminal behavior. Fundamentally, the Algerian Revolution in genre films indicates that an evolution in sentiment has taken place, and that new historical evidence and distance oblige a self-critique that neither exonerates nor condemns.

Generally, Jacques Derrida's theories of the specter and of the scission apply most readily to the twenty-first-century Algerian Revolution filmic discourse; both theories parse and confuse elements of time, as recent cinema revisits previous dominant historical views. The theorist's understanding of the specters inherent in moving images suggests the transversal space in which the twenty-first-century films about the Franco-Algerian War era surface. The screen's ability to simultaneously dominate the film public's present, while revealing the past in which it was filmed and implying the future absence of the subject, projects the Franco-Algerian War as a moving symbol. The war, whose present relevance fills the screen, incarnates the past (including its once censored invisibility) and reveals its evolution as a specter. While *Djinns* most significantly relates the ghosts of the Algerian Revolution on screen with its diegetic jinns, all of the other films depicting the Algerian Revolution in the twenty-first century share this temporal confusion, which is oftentimes portrayed by the flashback and flash-forward device (*The Intimate Enemy, Djinns,* the Mesrine biopic). In the case of *Bloody Beans*, the set's lack of association with a fixed time unearths spatiotemporal, utopian dialectics that present the Algerian Revolution as an achronological signifier. The specter of the war, which suggests the past, present, and future at once, emanates from and into the future of the two nations. Such a future surpasses the death and torture with which the war is commonly associated and eclipses early Algerian film's unified nomads in the countryside.

Therefore, Derrida's concept of the scission, a cut on the body that represents loss but which opens space for the possibility of dialogue, applies not only to the Jacques Mesrine biopic to which I have applied the concept. Certainly the French military's self-critique in film depicts a cut made by the war, and an opening, in cinematic confession, which encourages a public reckoning. In fact, all of the films in this discourse reframe a view of the past and question the previous understanding of the Algerian Revolution, while providing an altered perspective in which communication between the once warring enemies is now feasible and restorative. Such curative processes in film may derive from production, but may also stem from narratives that feature redemptive exchanges and collaborations. In this way, recent cinema not only projects the still tender wounds of the Algerian Revolution, but equally bestows a therapeutic process for the internal scars.

Appendix

Timeline: Algeria and France, 1827–2019

1827 The fan affair or *l'affaire de l'éventail* (which by some accounts was not a fan but a flyswatter) involved a conversation in which the ruling Turkish dey asked to be reimbursed for a sum owed by the French army. When the French diplomat, Pierre Deval, responded with pejorative anti-Muslim terms, the dey lightly hit him with the fan.
1830 The French conquest of Algeria begins, first by seizing Algiers.
1832 The spiritual and military leader Abdelkader ibn Muhieddine unites Algerians against French imperialism.
1834 Algeria becomes a French military colony.
1841 General Thomas Robert Bugeaud begins his campaign against Abdelkader, and defeats an army sent by the Ottoman Sultan. *Enfumades* or trapping escaping Algerians in caves with fire and thus causing their asphyxiation was used as common torture technique.
1847 The French state determines that any land not cultivated by Algerians can be utilized for French settlers.
1848 France officially recognizes Algeria as part of France. *Algérie-française* is open to all European settlers, who will then be awarded French citizenship.
1870 The Crémieux decree grants Jewish Algerians automatic French citizenship; Decree 137 confirms that Algerian Muslims cannot attain French citizenship.
1881 France defines three departments of *l'Algérie française*: Algiers, Oran, and Constantine.
1926 The Algerian Messali Hadj, after training in the French army and settling in France with a French wife, establishes L'Étoile Nord-Africaine and begins to organize against French colonization.
1937 Messali Hadj forms the PPA (Parti du peuple algérien).
1939 As World War II begins, many Algerians in need enroll in the French forces.
1942 Vichy France (led by Philippe Pétain who cooperated with Nazi Germany) loses control of Algeria, which then becomes a base for the free French forces.
1943 Ferhat Abbas communicates a manifesto for independent Algeria that the free French administration rejects.
1945 On September 8, in Sétif, the Allied forces organize a march to celebrate victory. Many seeking Algerian independence and asking for the pardon of Messali Hadj join the march. The march turns into a massacre (between 6,000 and 20,000 die) and inspires many to band together and fight for independence.

1946 The first Indochina War commences in 1946 between French forces and Viet Minh opponents, and concludes with a French loss on July 21, 1954. The French army relied heavily on colonial troops, including Algerians.

1947 All Algerian citizens are granted the right to French citizenship, yet restrictive measures prevent the majority of Algerians from voting.

1954 The FLN (Front de Libération Nationale) plans thirty attacks on the Catholic All Saints Day, November 1. This date called *Toussaint Rouge* can be understood as the beginning of the Algerian Revolution. All independence parties other than the MNA (Mouvement National Algérien) are now united with the FLN.

1955 The French government creates *l'état d'urgence* or state of emergency in order to combat the growing independence movements in Algeria. The French government reinstates *l'état d'urgence* two more times during the Franco-Algerian War, in 1958 and in 1961–2.

1956 The French discover Edjelleh and the Hassi Messaoud oil fields, and begin production two years later. By 1959, *Algérie française* had become the world's tenth largest oil producer.

1956 The Battle of Algiers begins in September as the FLN strategize with bombing. The French military claims victory a year later.

1958 In May, some French generals stationed in Algeria fear Algerian independence and thus stage a putsch. The French government then makes a plea to Charles de Gaulle, who returns to power with the condition of altering the constitution, and commencing the Fifth Republic.

1960 On February 13, the first French atomic bomb (coded as *Gerboise bleue*) is detonated as a test in the Algerian Sahara near Reggane.

1961 On January 8, the French government holds a referendum on Algerian independence (*le droit de l'autodétermination*), which many French-Algerians oppose. Some who violently oppose Algerian independence found a terrorist organization the OAS (Organisation Armée Secrete).

1961 The French government and GPRA (Gouvernement Provisoire de la Révolution Algérienne) begin negotiations toward independence. OAS attacks including a failed coup d'état on April 22 continue.

1961 On October 17, the FLN hold a pacific march through Paris to oppose the curfew in place for North Africans. The police under Maurice Papon kill many Algerians, drown some in the Seine, and brutally arrest thousands.

1962 On February 8 in Paris, violence in large part due to the police disturbs a peaceful protest against the OAS organized by the communist party and unions. Nine die at the Charonne metro station.

1962 Heads of Algeria's GPRA and Charles de Gaulle sign a formal cease-fire agreement in the Evian Accords, the annexes of which allow France to continue atomic bomb testing on Algerian soil until 1967. Most Europeans in Algeria flee the violence and depart for France.

On July 3, Algerian independence is declared and Ahmed Ben Bella is elected Algeria's first president.

1962 On August 22, in Petit-Clamart, the OAS makes their most famous attempt to assassinate Charles de Gaulle. The president, his wife, and son-in-law narrowly escape machine gun fire in a Citroën DS 19.

1965 Houari Boumediene, minister of the interior under Ben Bella, seizes power in a coup d'état during the filming of *The Battle of Algiers*.

1967 A meeting between Houari Boudmediene and Charles de Gaulle prolongs the arrangement made in the annexes of the Evian Accords, to allow chemical weapon testing on Algerian territory for five additional years.

1976 The reformed Algerian Constitution declares Algeria as socialist, Islam as the state religion, and Arabic as the sole national language.

1984 The family code in Algeria, which draws in part on Shariah law, legalizes polygamy (though seldom practiced) and confines women to a minor's status.

1988 Widespread protests throughout Algeria, largely populated by youth, take place from October 5 through the October 11. The police and military intervene with violence, and at least 500 die.

1989 The National People Parties' Assembly allows parties besides the FLN to campaign for elections; FIS (Front Islamique du Salut) registers as a party.

1991 After FIS won 55 percent of local elections the preceding year, the party wins 188 seats in the first round of general elections. The FIS victory of the second round seems certain and thus the federal government cancels the second round.

1992 Violence escalates, and a man associated with FIS murders politician Mohamed Boudiaf and at least forty others at an event.

1997 Maurice Papon undergoes a criminal trial for deporting Jews to concentration camps under the Vichy government between 1942 and 1944. The trial also exposes how Papon, when he was the head of the French police, oversaw the massacre and arrest of Algerians on October 17, 1961.

1999 The French National Assembly recognizes that the events in Algeria between 1954 and 1962 constitute a true "war."

1999 After all opposition candidates withdraw, Abdelaziz Bouteflika is elected president. A lengthy process of secret negotiations between the FLN and FIS quells the violence. Many members are pardoned. An estimated 100,000 Algerian lives were taken during the Black Years (1992–2000).

2000 General Paul Aussaresses admits to the use of torture to *Le Monde*, and then repeats his claims to the American television show, *60 Minutes*. The next year, he publishes his account, *Services Spéciaux: Algérie, 1955–1957* (*The Battle of the Casbah: Terrorism and Counter-Terrorism in Algeria, 1955–1957*).

2001 Mayor of Paris Bertrand Delanöe presents a plaque at an official ceremony to recognize the lives that were lost on October 17, 1961.

2002 The Amazigh language becomes a national language of Algeria that may be taught in schools.

2003 In March, Jacques Chirac is the first French president to visit Algeria since 1962. By June, after a nine-year halt due to the Black Years, Air France recommences passenger flights to Algeria.

2005 Article 4 of a law passed by the national assembly of France asked French high schools to "acknowledge and recognize in particular the positive role of the

French presence abroad, especially in North Africa." After widespread protest, the law was repealed in 2006. Algerian president Bouteflika spoke directly against the article.

2006 Algeria pays back an eight billion dollar debt to the Paris club (an organization composed of officials from major creditor countries), demonstrating its improving economic status.

2006 President Bouteflika says that France's rule of Algeria was one of the "the most barbaric form of colonization in history."

2007 Newly elected French president Nicolas Sarkozy speaks in Algeria, but refuses to apologize for the colonial past, saying that there were victims on both sides and that both nations should look toward the future.

2012 President François Hollande visits Algeria. Although he does not apologize for the colonial past, he does recognize the pain inflicted by French colonialism.

2013 At a gas plant in Amenas, Algeria, three men of an Islamist al-Qaeda linked group take hostages. After four days, the Algerian special forces intervene and free 167 people. Targeting foreigners, the Islamists kill 39 people, one of whom is French.

2014 Fighters linked to the Islamic State behead a French tourist Hervé Gourdel in Djurdjura National Park of Kabylie after demanding that France withdraw militarily from Iraq and Syria.

2015 In 2015, France suffers a series of terrorist attacks by radicalized French nationals. Most notably, twelve die at the offices of the satirical weekly, *Charlie Hebdo,* and 130 at a rock concert at the Bataclan in Paris—over 350 are injured.

2016 Amazigh joins Arabic as an official language of Algeria in the 2016 Algerian constitution.

2017 Emmanuel Macron visits Algeria as part of his presidential campaign, and apologizes to Algeria, calling colonialism barbaric and a crime against humanity.

2018 On February 8, 2018, the Conseil Constitutionnel of France amends a 1963 decision that awarded pensions to French citizens who suffered violence related to the Algerian Revolution. Now all other injured nationalities (including Algerians) will have the right to apply for such French funds.

2019 In February, generations of Algerians nationally protest Abdelaziz Bouteflika's presidential campaign for a fifth term. Bouteflika, who had suffered a stroke in 2013, had not spoken publicly in years. On March 11, Bouteflika withdraws from the election, though national protests continue demanding a new government.

Notes

Introduction

1 "J'ai un énorme respect pour les martyrs, pour nos aînés, qui se sont battus pour que je sois libre, libre de dire, mais il nous faut sortir de l'Histoire pour assumer notre présent. Pour les honorer, nous devons exercer nos libertés." ("Entretien. Kamel Daoud: 'Je mène une bataille contre une pensée unanimiste dominante,'" *El Watan*, February 20, 2017).

2 "La colonisation fait partie de l'histoire française. C'est un crime, c'est un crime contre l'humanité, c'est une vraie barbarie. Et ça fait partie de ce passé que nous devons regarder en face, en présentant nos excuses à l'égard de celles et ceux envers qui nous avons commis ces gestes. Mais 'en même temps,' a-t-il poursuivi, 'il ne faut pas balayer tout ce passé. Et je ne regrette pas cela parce qu'il y a une jolie formule qui vaut pour l'Algérie: la France a installé les droits de l'homme en Algérie. Simplement elle a oublié de les lire'" ("En Algérie, Emmanuel Macron qualifie la colonisation française de 'crime contre l'humanité.'" *Libération*, February 15, 2017).

3 As this is an English language text, I will give the title first in its original language (excluding chapter headings). In subsequent references I will refer uniquely to the English title. The filmography will then include the title in both the original language and in English translation. For the films *Djinns* and *Fidaï*, I exeptionally refer to their French translation of Arabic and Arabic titles respectively. These two titles indicate levels of lingual and cultural translation that my analysis explores.

4 "Nous avons dépassé en barbarie les Barbares que nous venions civiliser." (Stora, *Algeria, 1830–2000*, 18).
Louis-Philippe named a special commission of eight members to visit Africa and to then report on the state of the countries. The commission stayed in Algeria for around three months and published a volume of 476 pages. Yacono, "La Régence d'Alger en 1830 d'après l'enquête Des Commissions de 1833–1834."

5 Daoud, *Meursault, Contre-Enquéte*.

6 Throughout this book, I refer to citizens of European descent who lived in Algeria during the French occupation as French-Algerian. Others may use the term *pied-noir*.

7 Meursault is the main character of *The Stranger* who kills a nameless Arab and is given the death penalty. Camus, *L'étranger*.

8 Daoud further proved his freedom of expression in spite of threats and critique, when he more radically blamed Islam in a first-person statement concerning the sexual assault of women by North African immigrants on New Year's Eve in Cologne. Daoud, "La Misère Sexuelle Du Monde Arabe."

9 Rahal, "Comment faire l'histoire de l'Algérie indépendente?," 3.

10 Bensmaïa, *Experimental Nations*; Deleuze and Guattari, *Mille Plateaux*.

11 Harvey, *Spaces of Hope*.

12 I am here referring to the Algerian films, *Zabana!* (Saïd Ould Khelifa, 2015) as well as Ahmed Rachedi's *Mostafa Ben Boulaid* (2008), *Krim Belkacim* (2014), and *Lofti*

(2015), which were produced by the Algerian government's ONM (Organisation nationale des moudjahidine; that promotes the memory of the Algerian Revolution.
13 Le Sueur, *Uncivil War*; Malley, *The Call from Algeria*.
14 Silverstein, *Algeria in France*.
15 Bancel and Blanchard, "La colonisation," 139.
16 Stora, *La Gangrène Et L'oubli*.
17 Branche, *La Torture et l'armée pendant la Guerre d'Algérie*.
18 Aussaresses, *Services Spéciaux*.
19 These first tests in 1960 were all named after a desert rodent. *Gerboise Bleue, Blanche,* and *Rouge*, spelled out the colors of the French flag before *Gerboise Verte*.
20 Bensmaïa, *Experimental Nations*.
21 "Conformément à la logique implacable de la colonisation, l'Algérien est quasi absent partout. Que ce soit au sein du public du cinéma, ou au sein de la profession elle-même" (Megherbi, *Les Algériens Au Miroir Du Cinéma Colonial*, 13). Some other publications that directly address cinema in colonial Algeria that are cited elsewhere in this monograph include: Dadci, *Dialogues Algérie-Cinéma* and Slavin, *Colonial Cinema and Imperial France, 1919–1939*.
22 Bennington and Derrida, *Jacques Derrida*; Fioretos, *Word Traces*.

1 The Twentieth-Century Screen Geography of the Franco-Algerian War

1 A few books that study the Franco-Algerian War in twentieth-century films include: Armes, *Postcolonial Images*; Dine, *Images of the Algerian War*; and Stora, *Les Imaginaires de guerre*; see also "La Guerre d'Algérie à l'écran," issue 85 of *Cinéaction* featuring Mouny Berrah, Guy Hennebelle, and Benjamin Stora, 1997.
2 Silverstein, *Algeria in France*, 7.
3 Denis, *Le Cinéma et la guerre d'Algérie: La Propagande à l'écran (1945–1962),* presents an exhaustive research on the military films produced in these years.
4 "Les soldats français n'ont du soldat que l'uniforme. On les voit toujours soigner, construire, enseigner ... La légende explique: 'Vous êtes les meilleurs éléments de contact avec la population'" (Stora, *La Gangrène et l'oubli*, 43).
5 Garreau, *Archives secrètes du cinéma français*.
6 Stora, *La Gangrène et l'oubli*, 45. Emma Kouby's "A War of Worlds over an image of war" thoroughly treats the Fox Movietone footage and the reception of five stills from the short published in *L'Express*.
7 Denis, "Métaphores cinématographiques en situation coloniale."
8 Alleg, *La Question*.
9 Alleg was born in London and moved to Algeria at the age of 18. He wrote for the *Alger républicain*.
10 Jean-Paul Sartre wrote a review of *La Question* in *Les Temps Modernes,* the journal he founded largely to disseminate his own essays, and signed a petition against this ban with other well-known authors (André Malraux, Roger Martin du Gard, and François Mauriac) that further spread *La Question*'s renown.
11 Sartre, *Being and Nothingness*, 453.
12 Le Sueur, *Uncivil War*, 9.

13 "There is the evidence, there is the horror, our own: we will not be able to see it without pulling it out from ourselves and crushing it" [Voilà l'évidence, voilà l'horreur, la *nôtre*: nous ne pourrons pas la voir sans l'arracher de nous et l'écraser] (Sartre, "Vous êtes formidables," in Sartre, *Situations, V*, 67).
14 Baugh, "Sartre, Derrida and Commitment the Case of Algeria," 44.
15 "Dans la conscience du colonisé,"… "la perception qu'il a du colonisateur" (Fanon, *L'an V*, 51).
16 "Capitalistes parisiens, propriétaires fonciers d'Algérie … Reste qu'ils s'accordent sur un point: museler le peuple" (Sartre, *Situations, V*, 108).
17 Le Sueur, *Uncivil War*, 11.
18 Hong, *Cold War Germany, the Third World, and the Global Humanitarian Regime*, 148.
19 Jules-Rosette, "Jean-Paul Sartre and the Philosophy of Négritude," 265–85.
20 Senghor, *Anthologie de la nouvelle poesie nègre et malgache de langue francaise*.
21 "It was to the credit of Senghor that he was not stifled by the peremptory arguments and the vision of this first theoretician of negritude whom he had aroused: he had asked Sartre for a cloak to celebrate negritude; he was given a shroud." Mudimbe, *The Invention of Africa. Gnosis, Philosophy and the Order of Knowledge*, 1988: 84–5.
22 Mudimbe, "A Conversation with V.Y. Mudimbe with Faith Smith," 969.
23 Ungar, "Making Waves," 34–46.
24 Of the two known copies of *Une nation, l'Algérie*, one was destroyed and the other lost.
25 Vautier, *Caméra citoyenne*, 35.
26 Sartre, *Situations, V*, 81.
27 At the projection on January 25 at the Forum des Images in Paris, Marceline Loridan-Ivens confided that among the rushes that hadn't been edited were "some scenes of lynching and power struggles between the Algerians themselves. But we were against colonialism, added the director, and we didn't want to show the contradictions of these people who had fought on the good side, that which would have diminished their importance. Today I regret it a lot" [Lors de la projection du 25 janvier dernier au Forum des Images à Paris, Marceline Loridan a confié que parmi les rushes qui n'ont pas été montées figuraient "des scènes de lynchages et des luttes de pouvoir entre les Algériens eux-mêmes. Mais on était contre le colonialisme, a ajouté la cinéaste, et on ne voulait pas montrer les contradictions de ces gens qui avaient lutté du bon côté, ce qui aurait amoindri leur rôle. Aujourd'hui je le regrette beaucoup"] ("Algérie, Année Zéro de Marceline Loridan Ivens et Jean-Pierre Sergent").
I presented my upcoming article, "A Prism of Ambivalence and Censorship: The Algerian Revolution in *Chronique d'un été* and *Algérie Année Zéro*" at the Society of Cinema and Media Studies conference in Seattle in 2018.
28 "le même technique que celle que les Nazis utilisaient avec leurs prisonniers" (Vautier, *Caméra citoyenne*, 102).
29 Marker, "Self-Censorship and Chris Marker's *Le joli mai*."
30 Bonner quotes Ilan Avisar who notices that the film "does not concentrate on the genocide against the Jews," and "never mention[s] Germans or Germany either." In interviews, after hinting several times that *Nuit et brouillard* was about the Algerian War by claiming the film warned of future atrocities, Resnais at last said in 1980, "The whole point was Algeria" (Bonner, "The New Executioners").
31 Connelly, *A Diplomatic Revolution*, 137.
32 Hong, *Cold War Germany, the Third World, and the Global Humanitarian Regime*, 149.
33 Connelly, *A Diplomatic Revolution*, 133–136.

34 Hong, *Cold War Germany, the Third World, and the Global Humanitarian Regime*, 151. The DEFA and the state television broadcaster (*Deutscher Fernsehfunk*) also produced films on Algerian refugees and orphans in Morocco and Tunisia, including *Ahmed weine nicht* and *Sorah und Ali* (p. 365).

35 Mohammed Harbi hesitantly employs the adjective totalitarian to describe the FLN, and their attempt to create a "contre-état." According to Harbi, the murderous, competitive nature of the rival independence groups stemmed from the collision of democracy and authoritarianism. The FLN never explored the plurality in government that the PCA (Parti Communiste Algérien) or the MNA may have provided. Harbi, "Culture et démocratie en Algérie."

36 Gérard Phillippe backed out of his original agreement to dub. The copies distributed internationally by DEFA were also in German and Arabic.

37 "L'armée est ainsi le people, comme le peuple est ainsi l'armée."

38 Hong explains that nurses were dressed in military fatigues in this film and other FLN propaganda. "The Algerians hoped that such images would reinforce the legitimacy of their cause and counteract the French propaganda, which depicted Algerian militants as a terrorist fringe group" (Hong, *Cold War Germany, the Third World, and the Global Humanitarian Regime*, 149).

39 In 1957, René Vautier headed the École de formation du cinéma in Wilaya 1, Zone 5. The school produced four television shows that socialist countries stations played including *L'École*, *Les Infirmieres de l'ALN*, and *L'Attaque des mines de l'Ounza*. Ahmed Rachedi, who did survive the war and continues to produce Algerian films, was trained by Vautier.

40 Dadci, *Première Histoire*, 247. Ahmed Bedjaoui also finds several inaccuracies in Vautier's accounts. (*Cinéma et guerre de libération*, 63–6).

41 Irwin Wall explains that bombing of Sakiet Sidi Youssef and the consequential civilian deaths were "a public relation disaster for France," and helped to sway the United States (*Les États-Unis et la Guerre d'Algérie*, 111–12).

42 Ould-Khelifa, "Le Moudjahid Pierre Clément est mort."

43 In *La Belle Vie* (*The Beautiful Life*, Robert Enrico, 1964), we find an SCA cinébus on the streets of Paris, promoting and recruiting the military, selling books by generals, soldier dolls, and ashtrays. In this instance, bystanders look into the opened bus at films of soldiers abroad.

44 Salmane, *Algerian Cinema*, 18.

45 "Tout citoyen peut donc parler, écrire, imprimer librement" (Vautier, *Caméra citoyenne*, 9).

46 Salmane, *Algerian Cinema*, 18; Bovier and Fluckiger, "René Vautier et le cinéma ouvrier."

47 "La France de 1962 fourmille de petits organismes culturels: ciné-clubs, sections de comités d'entreprises amicales, sections de syndicats, comités de défense, groupes, groupuscules et chapelles. Ces organismes sont privés. Ils sont libres, chez eux, de dire et voir ce que bon leur semble. Ils sont placés en dehors du circuit de l'argent, de l'état du profit et échappent ainsi, ne serait-ce que partiellement, à ces contraintes qui étranglent la liberté d'expression" (Le Masson and Poliakoff, "Manifeste pour un cinéma parallèle").

48 *5-8 2-B* (Guy Chalon, 1959); *S.P. 89098* (Philippe Durand, 1959); *Le Retour* (Daniel Goldenberg, 1961); *J'ai huit ans* (René Vautier, Olga Baïdar-Poliakoff, and Yann LeMasson, 1961); *Parfois le dimanche* (Ado Kyro, 1961); *Demain l'amour* (Paul

Carpita, 1962); *Fille de la route* (Louis Terme, 1962); *La Quille* (Jean Herman, 1963); *27 mois après* (Jean-Claude Bourlat, 1963).
49 Vautier, *Caméra citoyenne*, 122.
50 "Nous n'étions et nous ne voulions pas être des substituts de militants algériens" (Vautier, *Caméra citoyenne*, 103).
51 Vautier, *Caméra citoyenne*, 104.
52 Fanon conceives of the new Third World Man who will not look to Europe for models. "Let us decide not to imitate Europe; let us combine our muscles and our brains in a new direction. Let us try to create the whole man, whom Europe has been incapable of bringing to triumphant birth" (*Les Damnés de la terre*, 113).
53 "le symbole puissant du mal du cinéma algérien" (Maherzi, *Le Cinéma algérien*, 79).
54 Marie trans. Neupert, *The New Wave*, 16.
55 Jauffret, *Soldats en Algérie, 1954–1962*, 27.
56 Ibid., 80.
57 Di Orio, "Total Cinema."
58 Croombs, "*"La Jetée* in Historical Time."
59 Sharpe, "Gender and the Politics of Decolonization in Early 1960s French Cinema."
60 The declaration appeared in the leftist magazine *Vérité-Liberté*.
61 Vautier, *Caméra citoyenne*, 97.
62 Vautier writes that instead of producing a film concerning the Algerian Revolution Alain Resnais went to Germany to make *L'Année dernière à Marienbad*: "C'est en voyant ce film, alors que j'avais eu vent des projets d'Alain Resnais sur la guerre d'Algérie, que je me suis dit: la censure a gagné … (la censure)elle a créé des réalisateurs français "bienséants"—analysez le mot: cela veut dire bien assis." ["It was when I saw this film, when I had heard about Alain Resnais' projects on the Algerian war, that I said to myself: censorship won … (censorship) it created proper (*bienséant*) French directors, analyze the word: it really means well situated."] (Vautier, *Caméra citoyenne*, 27).
63 Liogier, "1960; Vue d'Espagne, La Nouvelle Vague Est Fascist."
64 Brody, *Everything Is Cinema*, 85.
65 See Damien Carron's book titled *La Suisse et la guerre d'indépendance algérienne (1954–1962)* and the television documentary *Les Coulisses suisses de la guerre d'Algérie (The Swiss Backstage of the Algerian War)* by Pierre-André Thiébaud, 2013.
66 During the talks between the FLN and France in March of 1961, the mayor of Evian was killed when the OAS bombed his home.
67 "'Toujours souriant au-dessus de moi, Jacquet m'avait branché la pince au sexe" (Alleg, *La Question*, 33). Interviews reveal that Godard actually forced actor Michel Subor to undergo such physical pain for realism. Perhaps this explains why the actor is not sexually demeaned, or tied to a board; Godard may not have wanted to humiliate the actor and/or be accused of homosexual tendencies.
68 In an interview with *Paris-Presse*, Godard, further illustrating the film's political context, calls the film "Gaulliste" and states that it is the FLN not the French we witness torturing in detail: "Sin embargo, creaia haber hecho un film gaullista," says J. L. Godard, director de *Le Petit Soldat*, "prohibido por la censura francesca" (pp. 13–14). Translation of an article by Paul Giannoli in *Paris-Presse* found in Liogier, "1960; Vue d'Espagne: La Nouvelle Vague est fascist," 144.
69 The commission asks equally, in the sequence during which the actor Belmondo is put in a bathtub and experiences abuse from the killers, the following words be cut:

1. "during the Algerian War"
2. "in the military service"

[La commission demande également, dans la séquence au cours de laquelle l'acteur Belmondo est mis dans une baignoire et subit certains sévices de la part des deux tueurs, la coupure des mots suivants:

1. "pendant la guerre d'Algérie"
2. "au service militaire"] (Garreau, *Archives secrètes du cinéma français*, 123).

70 "A l'époque de votre libération je n'étais pas très conscient ... Que voulez-vous, *Le Petit soldat* c'est le film d'un jeune bourgeois français avec toutes les limites que cela comporte." (Hennebelle, *CinémAction*, 279).
71 Though the screenplay dates the action as passing in 1962, the film does not allude to a specific date.
72 Greene, *Landscapes of Loss*, 48.
73 Bertin-Maghit, *Lettres filmées d'Algérie*.
74 Flood, "Torture in Word and Image," 48.
75 "il traduit la méconnaissance—puisqu'on ne voit rien—et permet la reconnaissance— parce qu'on apprend tout: à l'image de ce que fut, pendant la guerre d'Algérie, la connaissance qu'on put en avoir, entre les actualités visuelles, imposées par la censure, et les informations orales diffusées clandestinement" [it reflects ignorance—since we see nothing—and allows recognition—because we learn everything: in the image of what was, during the Algerian war, the knowledge we could have, between visual news, imposed by censorship, and oral information disseminated clandestinely] (Claude Bailblé, Michel Marie, and Marie Claire Ropars-Wuilleumier, *Muriel*, 316).
76 "*Muriel* n'est pas un film sur l'Algérie, mais un film où il est question d'Algérie comme une pensée gênante que chacun cherche à oublier" (Boudjedra, *Naissance du cinéma algérien*, 27).
77 "Les Resnais, les Marker, les Autant-Lara et autres cinéastes courageux doivent, pour voir leurs films distribués, choisir l'ambiguïté. Leurs secrètes intentions n'ont, c'est le moins que l'on puisse dire, aucune chance d'être comprises par le public" (Le Masson and Poliakof, "Manifeste pour un cinéma parallèle").
78 Yacef, *Souvenirs de la Bataille d'Alger*.
79 Armes, *Postcolonial Images*, 39.
80 To an extent Ahmed Bedjaoui blames this monopoly for the struggles of Algerian film, writing of cinema post the nationalization, "We know what follows: deprived of all industrial infrastructure, cinema was going to see long-standing jobs and trade skills disappear, with theaters in remission and a stalemate that persists fifty years later." [On connaît la suite: privé de toute infrastructure industrielle, le cinéma allait voir disparaître des métiers et des savoir-faire forges de longue date, avec des salles en sursis et une situation d'impasse qui perdure, cinquante ans après] (*Cinéma et guerre de libération*, 96).
81 Ould Khettab, "Algerian Cinema a New Wave Is Emerging"; Chabani, "Salle de cinéma Sierra maestra à Alger."
82 Daulatzai, "The Battle Everywhere," *Fifty Years of the Battle of Algiers*, 38–64.
83 Le Sueur, *Algeria since 1989*, 19–20.
84 "Le film italo-algérien *La Bataille d'Alger*, de Gillo Pontecorvo est interdit totalement par la commission de contrôle des films en 1966" ["The Italian-Algerian *The Battle*

of Algiers by Gillo Pontecorvo is censored completely by the government censor in 1966"] (Garreau, *Archives secrètes du cinéma français*, 255).

85 Caillé, "The Illegitimate Legitimacy of *The Battle of Algiers* in French Film Culture," 377.
86 "In 1968 the Algerian and French governments set a quota on migrants of 35,000 per year, which was reduced to 25,000 in 1971. Although Algeria suspended all migration to France in 1973, an estimated 7,000 Algerians nonetheless continued to migrate illegally each year at the end of the 1970s. In the mid-1970s, both France and Algeria offered incentives to migrants to return home, one of them being guaranteed housing. Although figures were hard to obtain, it appeared that few responded to these gestures" (Metz, *Algeria*).
87 "Pourquoi vous n'avez pas vu 'La Bataille d'Alger.'"
88 *La Bataille d'Alger*, "Projetée Dans Une Salle Parisiennee."
89 "Des Inconnus brisent les vitres du studio Saint-Séverin."

"ANFANOMA is the acronym for the Association Nationale des Français d'Afrique du Nord, d'Outre-Mer et de leurs Amis, led by Colonel Pierre Battesti from 1958 to 1973. ANFANOMA was soon joined by a proliferation of cultural associations, which were frequently structured around the repatriates' area of residence in Algeria and which sought to recreate the memories and culture of the colonial community." (Barclay, "Introduction," 124).

90 Caillé, "The Illegitimate Legitimacy of *The Battle of Algiers* in French Film Culture."
91 David Porter's *Eyes to the South: French Anarchists and Algeria*, and Catherine Simon's *Algérie les années pieds rouges*, describe how the post-independence government forced the young French left to reassess their investment in Algeria.
92 Bedjaoui, *Cinéma et guerre de libération*, 103.
93 Beaugé, "Guerre d'Algérie: le poignard de Le Pen" and Soullier, Torture en Algérie." Also the documentary, *La question: Le Pen et la torture* (*The Question: Le Pen and torture*) by José Bourgarel.
94 Heynemann's feature-length film was not the first filmic adaptation of *La Question*. In 1961, Mohand Ali Yahia, an Algerian film student in East Berlin, made a short film, *Die Frage*, based on the book.
95 "Pierre Schoendoerffer, une carrière au service de l'image." In fact, in 1956 in Afghanistan, Coutard shot his first film, *La Passe du diable* (*The Devil's Pass*), codirected by Pierre Schoendoerffer and Jacques Dupont.
96 Abdulrazak, "Arabization in Algeria," 31.
97 Derrida develops the term in one of his last publications, *Le Monolinguisme de l'autre, Ou, La Prothèse d'origine*.
98 Stora, *Les Imaginaires de guerre*, 178.
99 Zinet's other acting credits that contrast ironically with his role in *Le Coup de Sirocco* include *Dupont Lajoie* (Yves Boisset, 1974) in which he shoots a racist French man to avenge his brother's murder in the final shot, and several of René Vautier's short films about the working conditions of Algerians in France (*Les Trois Cousins* and *Les Ajoncs*, 1970).
100 Le Sueur, *Algeria since 1989*, 19–20.
101 Weil, *Le Sens de la République*.
102 Less experimental but following in *La Nouba*'s footsteps, *Barberousse mes sœurs* or *Barberousse my sisters* (Hassen Bouabdellah, 1985) interviews former female

Algerian prisoners after watching *Serkadji* (Hadj Rahim, 1982), a fiction feature that depicts male prisoners at the same prison.
103 There has been much speculation on Djebar's use of classical Arabic in the film, and whether it was in fact due to the funding of the Algerian state. However, Ahmed Bedjaoui, the producer of the film, at the NEH Institute on North African Women's Voices in the Arts, said that this decision was in fact the influence of her partner at the time who worked in classical Arabic. In a 2008 interview, Djebar explains how the film reveals as the language of emotion. De Medeiros, "An Interview with Assia Djebar."
104 Roberts, "Constrained Militants."
105 Khanna, *Algeria Cuts*, 123–9.
106 Bedjaoui, *Cinéma et guerre de libération*, 193.
107 Malti, *Histoire secrète du pétrole algérien*; Lewis, "France in a Fuel Supply Shift, to Pay More for Gas."
108 Soufi, "Les Archives algériennes en 1962."
109 "Le refus de nous rendre nos archives équivaut à nier l'existence de l'Algérie avant 1962. Elles sont la trace matérielle de notre Histoire" (Soufi, "Les Archives algériennes en 1962").
110 *Les Sacrifiées* (*The Sacrificed*) by Okacha Touita, *Liberté la nuit* (*Liberté the night*) by Philippe Garrel, and *Cher Frangin* (*Dear* Brother) by Gérard Mordillat were exceptions.
111 "Surtout, derrière le voile de cette réalité exposée, se sont réveillées des voix anonymes, recueillies ou ré-imaginées, l'âme d'un MAGHREB unifié et de notre passé" (intertitles from *Zerda or the Songs of Forgetfulness*.).
112 Bedjaoui writes that a television series of ten episodes was the original project commissioned. After two years of editing the format changed. Bedjaoui, *Cinéma et guerre de libération*, 170.
113 This passage is taken from the already mentioned East German production *Allons z'enfants de l'Algérie* (Karl Gass, 1962). Such filmic commentary on France's atomic test in Algeria is not found in French-funded moving pictures until *Djinns* (2011).
114 Gauch, "Impasses of Algerian Cinema."
115 The film *Youssef* thus dialogues with revolutionary history in a manner not dissimilar to *Les Martyrs reviennent cette semaine* (*The Martyrs Come Back This Week*) by Arabophone author Tahar Ouattar, who in this 1974 novel talks about how citizens fear that the revolutionary martyrs will return from the grave and judge their actions.
116 Martínez, *La Guerre civile en Algérie, 1990–1998*. Mundy challenges Martínez's thesis as simplistic in *Imaginative Geographies of Algerian Violence*.
117 Austin, "Against Amnesia."

2 The Algerian Revolution in Three Transnational Documentaries

1 Central Intelligence Agency. The World Fact Book, Africa: Algeria.
2 Bensmaïa, "The War That Haunts France," 9.
3 "Cette fois, la racine principale a avorté, ou se détruit vers son extrémité; vient se greffer sur elle une multiplicité immédiate et quelconque de racines secondaires qui prennent un grand développement. Cette fois, la réalité naturelle apparaît

dans l'avortement de la racine principale, mais son unité n'en subsiste pas moins comme passée ou à venir, comme possible" (Deleuze and Guattari, *Capitalisme et Schizophrénie*, 12). See also Deleuze and Guattari, *A Thousand Plateaus*.
4 Guy Austin's *Algerian National Cinema* is the first of this nature and remains a primary resource, with a short study of *China Is Still Far*.
5 In "Concepts of Transnational Cinema," Will Higbee and Song Wee Lim dissect the interplay between postcolonial and transnational, concluding that a *critical* view of transnational cinema "is also always attentive to questions of post-coloniality, politics and power, and how these may, in turn, uncover new forms of neocolonialist practices … It scrutinizes the tensions and dialogic relationship between national and transnational, rather than simply negating one in favour of the other" (p. 9).
6 Oriane Brun-Moschetti explained this: "Leïla est d'origine algérienne et pourrait prétendre avoir la double nationalité (elle voudrait d'ailleurs entreprendre cette démarche, c'est juste une question de temps)" ("Re: *Algérie tours, détours*," E-mail to Nicole Beth Wallenbrock, April 24, 2014).
7 "Si notre film permet de cerner l'implication et l'impact de ce cinéaste pendant la guerre et après l'Indépendance, c'est surtout l'occasion de faire revivre le dispositif des *Cinépops* … Nous avons choisi de passer des films du répertoire algérien car montrer ces films permet de tester la résistance, le sens et l'impact des images face au temps, suivant les régions et les générations et de capter la sensibilité, le vécu et l'intérêt des spectateurs" ("Sur la route de Cinépops").
8 "Sur la route de Cinépops."
9 To give a precise date and place to this well-documented event: December 28, 1895 in the basement of the *Grand Café* in Paris, the *Salon Indien*.
10 To demonstrate the state's investment in cinema studies as part of the public school curriculum (from grade school through high school), one finds a brief explication on the Minister of Education's website: "L'art cinématographique et plus largement la sensibilisation aux arts et techniques des images et des sons proposent, en collaboration étroite avec le ministère de la Culture, depuis le début des années 80, un corpus complet articulant les composantes pratique, culturelle et théorique:
   Des enseignements de lycées, appuyés sur des programmes évalués au baccalauréat; Des formes plus légères de sensibilisation: ateliers, classes culturelles au collège et à l'école primaire; Des dispositifs originaux, initiés par le CNC, permettant l'accès accompagné aux œuvres dans un réseau de salles de cinéma: école et cinéma, collège au cinéma, lycéens au cinéma." ("Cinéma et Audiovisuel").
11 Armes, *Postcolonial Images*, 6.
12 Armes and Malkmus, *Arab and African Film Making*, 3.
13 Katherine Groo explores how the little seen expedition films (from Egypt and Tunisia) should be considered in the larger Lumière catalogue. She writes, "Drawn from human expositions and expeditions to non-Western corners of the globe, these films also manifest the colonial impulses that underpin the Lumière project and allow me to interrogate the difference that visual imperialism makes" ("The Maison and Its Minor Lumière(s), Film History, and the Early Archive," 29).
14 The Algerian State created the *Cinémathèque Algérienne* (now the *Cinémathèque à Alger*, an important institution set up for the preservation and the history of Algerian film in 1965. Originally the theater had two screens: one with 350 seats (*Le Club*) and the other with 450 seats (*Le Français*) for films in their original language. The *Cinémathèque Algérienne* would often borrow French films from the *Cinémathèque Française*, which would also program features from around the world.

15. "coloniser c'est ... éduquer les indigènes, les faire évoluer vers le stade de notre civilisation, ... la barbarie primitive aura cédé devant la civilisation" (Girault, *Principes de colonisation et de législation coloniale*). Costantini, *Mission civilisatrice*, 100.
16. "Pour ceux qui n'a jamais vu un écran, et qui pense que les images sont vivantes ... Il faut faire de l'apprivoisement, il faut gagner sa confiance ... pour l'obliger aussi à bénéficier d'un apport que lui offrent les temps actuels sur les plans sanitaire, social, moral, et économique" (The text of Paul Muritti, the head of the SDC in Algeria, cited by Maherzi, *Le Cinéma Algérien*, 49).
17. Forgacs, "Italians in Algiers," 350–64.
18. Deleuze and Guattari, *A Thousand Plateaus*, 16. "La mémoire courte comprend l'oubli comme processus; elle ne se confond pas avec l'instant, mais avec le rhizome collectif, temporel et nerveux" (Deleuze and Guattari, *Capitalisme et Schizophrénie: Tome 2*, 24).
19. I use the term *lieu de mémoire* as a general reference to a place of collective historical and intellectual importance. Though not my primary focus in this chapter, I am aware of the contribution of Pierre Nora and the problems raised by this work's geographic and historic limitations. Nora, *Les Lieux de mémoire*.
20. "J'ai trouvé l'idée de remettre le titre en français, une manière humoristique qui donnait à comprendre que nous avons encore un chemin à parcourir pour rejoindre ce savoir-là, en tout cas cette Chine du savoir" (Interview on DVD of *China Is Still Far*, Arte, 2009).
21. The fascinating connection and lineage in style between Jean Rouch and Malek Bensmaïl is not the subject of this chapter. However, *Building Bridges: The Cinema of Jean Rouch* provides a varied selection of articles which seek to explain the problematic of a direct cinema style in Africa framed by a French director, and the many ways that Rouch's films complicate and surpass some assumptions.
22. "Il fait plus qu'interroger l'Histoire. Il parvient à montrer son processus de decantation." Le Pastier, "*La Chine est encore loin*," 35.
23. "Tout touche et active la pensée au prisme de la bonne intelligence à l'œuvre. Cadres, lumières, paysages viennent en toute beauté célébrer la vivacité de l'obstination humaine." (Wideman, "*La Chine est encore loin*").
24. Austin, *Algerian National Cinema*, 118.
25. Remaoun, "L'intervention institutionnelle et son impact sur la pratique historiographique en Algérie," 6. In two years, the Algerian Revolution will be the exclusive subject of history class for 5e.
26. In 2016, a box containing numerous artifacts (letters, drawings, photos) concerning Algerian refugees in Tunisia (many of whom were orphans) was found in Essonne, France. The contents became part of an exposition at the Algerian Cultural Center of Paris in the spring of 2018, "Enfants algériens réfugiés en Tunisie (1957–1962)."
27. "Le fou cartographe serait celui qui tente de faire coïncider sans reste une forme délimitée sur la carte terrestre par un tracé de frontières et un nom propre, avec son appartenance à une communauté humaine, et à la limite, avec son être même" (Mouillard-Fraisse, *Les Fous cartographes*, 150).
28. A citation from Stora that summarizes his use of psychoanalytic terminology to describe a national mood, "Tout un ensemble subtil de mensonges et de refoulements organise la 'mémoire algérienne.' Et cette dénégation continue à ronger comme un cancer, comme une gangrène, les fondements mêmes de la société française" Stora, *La Gangrène Et L'oubli*, 8.

29 Branche's doctoral study of the just opened Franco-Algerian War military archives titled *La Torture et l'Armée pendant la Guerre d'Algérie, 1954–1962* unearthed the extremity of the military's torture policy. The same year, former General Paul Aussaresses wrote his unremorseful account of torturing with details, *Services Spéciaux Algérie 1955–1957*.
30 Such books inspired the fiction films about the trauma of torturing on the French soldier, Laurent Herbiet's *Mon Colonel* (2006) and notably Florent-Emilio Siri's *L'Ennemi intime* (2007), which depicts the French soldiers torturing.
31 Marks, *The Skin of Film*, 1.
32 Robert Kohler of *Variety Magazine* writes: Ounouri's artfully made movie—with Jia Zhang-ke's XStream Pictures as co-producer and showing some of Jia's filmic influence—is an act of personal liberation as well. Biz will be contained strictly to the fest circuit. Kohler, "Review: *Fidaï*."
33 Ounouri, "Re: Questions sur *Fidaï*," E-mail to Nicole Beth Wallenbrock, April 7, 2014.
34 Deleuze and Guattari, *A Thousand Plateaus*, 7.

> "Il n'y a pas de langue mère, mais prise de pouvoir par une langue dominante dans une multiplicité politique … une méthode de type rhizome ne peut analyser le language qu'en le décentrant sur d'autres dimensions et d'autres registres." (Deleuze and Guattari, *Capitalisme et Schizophrénie: Tome 2*, 14)

35 "The term flashback was first used in its sense of narrative returns to the past in reference to film, rather than other forms of storytelling … It has been adopted by psychology to refer to the spontaneous recall of a memory image, especially in the context of a war trauma, in which soldiers are said to have 'battlefield flashbacks.'" (Turim, *Flashbacks in Film*, 5).
36 Derrida, *Archive Fever*, 12–13. "alors rappelons-nous aussi que la répétition même, la logique de la répétition, voire la compulsion de répétition reste, selon Freud, indissociable de la pulsion de mort. Donc de la destruction. Conséquence: à même ce qui permet et conditionne l'archivation, nous ne trouverons jamais rien d'autre que ce qui expose à la destruction, et en vérité menace de destruction, introduisant *a priori* l'oubli et l'archiviolithique au Cœur du monument … L'archive travaille toujours et *a priori* contre elle-même." (Derrida, *Le Mal d'archive*, 26–7).
37 Raz Yosef's original use of Jacques Derrida's theory of the *mal d'archive* to discuss Israeli films addressing the 1982 Lebanon War that used news footage inspired this application to *Fidaï*. Yosef, "Traces of War."
38 "On perd, et c'est normal, la réalité de cette époque. Et le langage atteint des limites d'évocation pour des gens qui n'ont pas vécu cette période" (Ounouri, E-mail to Nicole Beth Wallenbrock, August 14, 2015).
39 Derrida, *Archive Fever*, 36. "C'est une question d'avenir, la question de l'avenir même, la question d'une réponse, d'une promesse et d'une responsabilité pour demain" (Derrida, *Le Mal d'archive*, 60).
40 Of the *archontes*: "The citizens who thus held and signified political power were considered to possess the right to make or to represent the law. On account of their publicly recognized authority, it is at their home, in that place which is their house (private house, family house, or employee's house), that official documents are filed. The archons are the first of all documents' guardians. They do not only ensure the physical security of what is deposited and of the substrate. They are also accorded the hermeneutic right and competence. They have the power to interpret the archives.

Entrusted to such archons, these documents in effect speak the law: they recall the law and call on or impose the law" (Derrida, *Archive Fever*, 2) [Aux citoyens qui détenaient et signifiaient ainsi le pouvoir politique, on reconnaissait le droit de faire ou de représenter la loi. Compte tenu de leur autorité ainsi publiquement reconnue, c'est chez eux, dans ce *lieu* qu'est leur maison ... que l'on dépose alors les documents officiels. Les archontes en sont d'abord les gardiens. Ils n'assurent pas seulement la sécurité physique du dépôt et du support. On leur accorde aussi le droit et la compétence herméneutiques. Ils ont le pouvoir d'*interpréter* les archives. Confiés en dépôt à de tels archontes, ces documents disent en effet la loi: ils rapellent la loi et rappellent à la loi] (Derrida, *Le Mal d'archive*, 13).

41 Deleuze and Guattari, *A Thousand Plateaus*, 12. "La carte ne reproduit pas un inconscient fermé sur lui-même elle le construit. Elle concourt à la connexion des champs, au déblocage des corps sans organes, à leur ouverture maximum sur un plan de consistance ... La carte est ouverte, elle est connectable dans toutes ses dimensions, démontable, renversable, susceptible de recevoir constamment des modifications ... C'est peut-être un des caractères les plus importants du rhizome; d'être toujours à entrées multiples." (Deleuze and Guattari, *Capitalisme et Schizophrénie: Tome 2,* 20).

42 Deleuze and Guattari, *A Thousand Plateaus*, 9. "On n'en finit pas avec les fourmis, parce qu'elle forment un rhizome animal dont la plus grande partie peut être détruite sans qu'il cesse de se reconstituer" (Deleuze and Guattari *Capitalisme et Schizophrénie: Tome 2*, 15).

3 The Specter of Torture and Atomic Bombs

1 Ighilahriz and Nivat, *Algérienne*.
2 Branche, *Prisonniers Du FLN*; Rouby, *Otage d'Amirouche, Témoigner pour le souvenir*. Also the documentaries, *Paroles d'un prisonnier d'ALN*, Aggar, *Prisonniers Français du FLN: Algérie 1954–1962*.
3 Bensmaïa, "The War That Haunts France."
4 "Cela fut bien plus sordide que le film n'ose se montrer ... les parachutistes électrocutaient des types englués dans leur merde ... il me paraissait bizarre ce film simple." (Jenni, *L'Art français de la guerre*, 589).
5 Although I have either translated the other film titles to English, or maintained the production's English title, I have decided to keep the French title of *Djinns* throughout the book. The title is a French translation of an Islamic concept/Arabic word.
6 Lazreg, *Torture and the Twilight of Empire*.
7 Morag, *Waltzing with Bashir*.
8 Patrick Rotman, *L'Ennemi intime: Violences dans la Guerre d'Algérie* (DVD Video, 2002).
9 Lazreg, *Torture and the Twilight of Empire*, 185.
10 Ibid., 189.
11 Ibid., 179.
12 *Tom Clancy's Splinter Cell: Double Agent* (Video Game, 2007).
13 Lazreg, *Torture and the Twilight of Empire*, 123.
14 Ibid., 127.
15 Ibid., 134.
16 Freud, *Three Essays on the Theory of Sexuality*, 158.

17 Ibid., 127.
18 Vidal-Naquet, *La Torture dans la République*, 42.
19 Alleg, *La Question*.
20 Lazreg, *Torture and the Twilight of Empire*, 178.
21 Morag, *Waltzing with Bashir*, 16.
22 Ibid., 5.
23 Lazreg, *Torture and the Twilight of Empire*, 120.
24 "Oui, des crimes terribles ont été commis tout au long d'une guerre d'indépendance qui a fait d'innombrables victimes des deux côtés. Et aujourd'hui, moi qui avais sept ans en 1962, c'est toutes les victimes que je veux honorer." Ganne, "Discours de Nicolas Sarkozy à Alger—Afrik.Com."
25 Anderson, *Imagined Communities*.
26 Hirsch, *The Generation of Postmemory*.
27 Laplanche and Pontilis, *The Language of Psycho-Analysis*, 414.
28 Lazreg, *Torture and the Twilight of Empire*, 173.
29 Elsaesser, *German Cinema—Terror and Trauma*.
30 Metz, *Le Signifiant imaginaire*.
31 "Si le titre de film s'inscrit naturellement dans le domaine linguistique, il désigne une œuvre à **caractère pictural; or, il semble que** l'outillage linguistico-littéraire, tout utile qu'il soit, ne permette pas d'appréhender le phénomène dans son ensemble: quelques mots renvoyant à un ensemble complexe de milliers d'images elles-mêmes commentées verbalement – à la fois à l'écran et hors écran." (Rouxel-Cubberly, *Les Titres de film*, 2).
32 "Dans les croyances musulmanes, génie ou démon, généralement hostile à l'homme. (Les djinns jouent un grand rôle dans le folklore)" (Larousse, *Dictionnaire Larousse Poche + 2018*).
33 Said, *Orientalism*, 301.
34 "And We did certainly create man out of clay from an altered black mud. And the *jinn* We created before from scorching fire" (*The Quran* 15:26–27).
35 Bancel and Blanchard, "La Colonisation," 138–9.
36 Ibid.
37 Stora, *La Gangrène et l'oubli*.
38 Barthes, *Camera Lucida*.
39 Derrida and Stiegler, *Echographies of Television*, 115.
40 Ibid., 117.
41 Billaud, *La Grande aventure du nucléaire militaire français*.
42 "After heavy protests from the neighboring African states, France conducted only sub-surface tests after November 1961 and, according to different sources, tested another 10 to 13 nuclear devices in the Hugger Mountains until 1966" (Caland, "French N-Tests in the Algerian Desert | Wise International").
43 Merchet, "Secret Défense—Essais Nucléaires."
44 Hong, *Cold War Germany, the Third World, and the Global Humanitarian Regime*, 151–60.
45 AVEN grew out of a group present since the mid-1990s, the FNAS (la Fédération nationale ancien du Sahara).
46 Chrisafis, "France Finally Agrees to Pay Damages to Nuclear Test Victims."
47 "Quand les appelés du contingent servaient de cobayes."
48 Pluet, "Essai nucléaire à Reggane." Pluet was a friend of René Vautier.
49 Pierre Billaud who had been a key player in the government planning surrounding the Gerboises tests died in 2012. Five years after Billaud's death, *L'Harmattan* published

a collection of his historical accounts, *La Grande aventure du nucléaire militaire français.*
50 *Radiological Conditions at the Former French Nuclear Test Sites in Algeria,* 55.
51 Derrida and Stiegler, *Echographies of Television,* 121.
52 Ibid., 121–2.
53 McMahon, "Untimely Resnais," 226; Gauch, "Muriel, or the Disappearing Text of the Algerian War."
54 Bertin-Maghit, *Lettres filmées d'Algérie.*
55 *Muriel* further displaces audio from image, when later Françoise accidently plays a second of a tape of men vociferously laughing together—we associate the voices with the torture of the Algerian recounted by Bernard.
56 Bailblé, Marie, and Ropars-Wuilleumier, *Muriel.*
57 Wood, *Hollywood from Vietnam to Reagan,* 75.
58 Hantke "The Military Horror Film."
59 Ibid., 715.
60 In *Muriel,* the celluloid evidence of Muriel's death (real and imagined) that Bernard has collected ends incinerated. By contrast, in *Djinns'* conclusion, the camera supports historical testimony.
61 Derrida and Stiegler, *Echographies of Television,* 129.

4 Reclaiming the Screen Algerian Revolution

1 Higbee, *Post-Beur Cinema,* 61–95.
2 Naficy, *An Accented Cinema,* 21.
3 Bensmaïa, *Experimental Nations, or, the Invention of the Maghreb,* 13.
4 Austin, *Algerian National Cinema,* 10.
5 Bedjaoui, *Cinéma et guerre de libération,* 96.
6 Maherzi, *Le Cinéma algérien,* 25.
7 Salmane, *Algerian Cinema,* 28.
8 Austin, *Algerian National Cinema,* 57–8.
9 In *Algerian National Cinema,* Guy Austin summarizes the agrarian film movement, "The *cinéma djidid* was rooted in the 1971 agrarian revolution ... [and] prioritized topics related to social issues such as unemployment, industrialization and the role of women in Algerian society, rather than rehearsing myths of the war against the French" (p. 25).
10 In a different vein, Merzak Allouache's *Omar Gatlato* (1976) broke ground and received popular acclaim as a dark comedy in a neorealist tradition that commented on the sexual frustration and economic turmoil of a young generation instead of reinvoking the revolutionary narrative.
11 Deleuze and Guattari, *A Thousand Plateaus,* 304.
12 Lee, "Mehdi Charef et le cinéma de l'intégration," 190.
13 In two related books, *Cinéma I: L'image-mouvement* (1983) and *Cinéma II: L'image-temps* (1985), Gilles Deleuze develops a strategy of categorization. In short, the movement-image aims for the spectator's immediate sensory reaction, whereas the time-image relies on the viewers' deeper analysis and thought.
14 Deleuze and Guattari, *A Thousand Plateaus,* 380.
15 Jean-Pierre Lledo's documentaries *Algérie, mes fantômes* (*Algeria, My Ghosts,* 2003) and *Algérie, les histoires de ne pas dire* (*Algeria, Stories to Not Tell,* 2007) present

friendships between French-Algerians, Jews, and Arabs in Algeria and the ways in which war devastated such multicultural communities.

16 While this chapter demonstrates the influence of *moudjahid* cinema on coproduction projects of the twenty-first century that portray the Algerian Revolution, Algerian features did not continue to solely employ classical Arabic, and *Omar Gatlato* (1976) set in contemporary Algiers is such an example.

17 Abdulrazak, "Arabization in Algeria," 31.

18 Bensmaïa, *Experimental Nations, or, the Invention of the Maghreb*, 15.

19 While *Liberté la nuit* (*Liberty the night*, Philippe Garrel, 1983) does not depict the independence group fratricide, it features the Franco-Algerian War in (and around) Paris—the narrative includes *porteurs de valises*, the OAS, the FLN, and a French-Algerian. Still auteur sensibilities (black-and-white film, actors' direct address to the camera) combine with a largely French cast and emphasis, preventing the personal film from reaching a *grand public* and/or Algerian audience.

20 Higbee, *Post-Beur Cinema*, 86.

21 "The final scenes of *Indigènes*, set in the present day, depict Abdelkader, the sole surviving North African veteran [of World War II in the film] as an old man while the text superimposed over the final image of the film demands the restitution of colonial veterans' rights in relation to their pensions" (Higbee, *Post-Beur Cinema*, 83–4).

22 "L'abîme entre ses deux films est un exemple éclatant de notre rapport à l'histoire" (Frodon, "Le cinéma français a fait sa guerre d'Algérie").

23 See Amiri, *La Bataille de France* for an indepth analysis of the war taking place in France.

24 Benjamin Stora and Pascal Blanchard both concluded that, "despite the manipulation of the chronology of events of the Sétif massacres for dramatic effect and the exigencies of feature film-making, *Hors-la-loi*'s depiction of events was broadly accurate" (Higbee, *Post-Beur Cinema*, 89).

25 I should also mention several earlier documentaries that presented the Sétif 1945 massacre as a root cause of the Algerian Revolution: René Vautier's *Déjà le sang de mai ensemençait novembre* from 1985 and *Les Massacres de Sétif, un certain 8 mai 1945* by Mehdi Lallaoui and Bernard Langois from 1994.

26 See Harbi, "La Guerre d'Algérie a commencé à Sétif."

27 Although a short sequence from *Chronicle of the Years of Fire* visually mentions the massacre, it is short, distanced, and in flashback.

28 Before the screening, Lionel Luca, a UMP minister for Alpes Maritimes, read the script and claimed the film was anti-French. The premiere was then met with a right-wing protest declaring the film's false depiction of the Sétif massacre.

29 Didier Daeninckx's *Meurtres pour mémoire* (1983) was one of the first books to instigate a larger cultural awareness of the actuality of the police brutality and racism. The historian Jean-Luc Einaudi's 1991 study, titled *La Bataille de Paris—17 octobre 1961*, which reveals how the peaceful march became a police-state devastation received more attention in 1996 during the trial of the former chief of police, Maurice Papon, for the deportation of Jews from the *Vélodrome d'Hiver*. The mayor of Paris, Bertrand Delanoë, spoke at a ceremony in 2001 in which a plaque conveyed an apology and awareness of what had occurred forty years prior.

30 *Le Silence du fleuve* (*The Silence of the River*, 1991); *Une journée portée disparue* (*A Day Gone Missing*, 1993); *C'était le 17 octobre 1961: Opération télécité* (*It Was October 17th, 1961: Operation Telecommunication*, 1999); *Les Enfants d'octobre* (*The Children of*

October, 2000); *Dissimulation d'un massacre* (*The Dissimulation of a Massacre*, 2001); *La Guerre sans nom dans Paris: une nuit d'octobre 1961* (*The War without a Name in Paris: An October Night 1961*, 2001), *Mémoires du 17 octobre* (*Memories of October 17th*, 2002) were all made before October 17 became a fiction film subject. *Ici on noie les Algériens* (*Here We Drown the Algerians*) was made year after *Outside the Law* in 2011.

31 Namely these were taken by Henri Georges, a photographer for *Libération* whose photos were reprinted by *Le Monde* in 2011.

32 Austin, *Algerian National Cinema*, 55.

33 As briefly mentioned, in some respects Bouchareb's *Outside the Law* pays homage to Tewfik Farès's *The Outlaws*. The three brothers who are united by their belief in the FLN cause, in spite of their differences, recall the three Algerian men who escape a colonial prison in Farès's *moudjahid* Western. Furthermore, the plots do not paint the French as the exclusive enemy. The Algerian enemies are the *caïd* (an Algerian official under the French government) and his sons in Farès's *The Outlaws*, and the MNA in Bouchareb's *Outside the Law*. A *caïd* is a also a significant character in *Chronicle of the Years of Fire*, a unique Algerian complicit with the French rule.

34 Bensmaïa, *Experimental Nations, or, the Invention of the Maghreb*, 15.

35 Ibid., 23.

36 Le Querrec, "Les Beurs entre deux rives."

37 Aggar, "La guerre d'Algérie au cinéma cinquante ans d'images entre la France et l'Algérie."

38 Salmane et al. *Algerian Cinema*, 22.

39 The frame reads, "Le veritable sujet du film, c'est le peuple et sa survie quotidienne, son héroïsme ses lâchétés, parfois même son opportunisme ou son indifférence au conflit" [The true subject of the film, is the people and their daily survival, their heroism, their cowardice, and sometimes their opportunism or their indifference to the conflict].

40 However, the French spoken in *The Crazy Years of the Twist* may be interpreted as a marketing decision made by Mahmoud Zemmouri and supported by Mohammed Lakhdar-Hamina. In this case, the funding uniquely from Algeria and the attempts at French distribution made only in post-production complicate our understandings of transnational film and Algeria's perceived autonomy in the 1980s.

41 Hassin et al., "Subliminal Exposure to National Flags Affects Political Thought and Behavior, 19758.

42 Stora, *Algeria 1830–2000*, 53.

43 The death toll from July 5–7, 1962 was high. According to the figures given by Doctor Mostefa Naït, director of the hospital complex in Oran, ninety-five people including twenty Europeans were killed (thirteen stabbed to death). In addition, 161 were wounded. The Europeans told of scenes of torture, pillaging, and above all of abduction. On May 8, 1963, the secretary of Algerian affairs declared at the National Assembly that 3,080 people had been listed as abducted or missing: 18 were found, 868 freed, and 257 killed (throughout Algeria, but especially in Oran). Stora, *Algeria, 1830–2000*, 105–6.

44 "Official slogans such as 'one sole hero, the people' and 'by the people for the people' may attract little attention ... they (these slogans) are reflected in suspicion of the (too) publicly visible *mujahid*, the emphasis on collective above individual action, the perception that the majority who fought have been forgotten by the few who

benefited, or the insistence on the need to tell the war story as a socially useful lesson for younger generations" (Vince, *Our Fighting Sisters,* 246).
45 Jacques Villeret's biological father was Algerian and his birth name was Mohamed Boufroura.

5 A Scission in the Memory of the Franco-Algerian War

1 Bancel and Veyrat-Masson, eds., *La Guerre de Mémoires.*
2 Bancel and Blanchard, "La colonization," 139.
3 Derrida, *Dissimination,* 333.
4 The only higher grossing French films in 2008 were comedies: *Bienvenue chez les Ch'tis* broke records to be the second highest grossing film in France of all time at 20,489,303 tickets being sold in a run of twenty-three weeks; *Asterix aux jeux Olympiques* was at theaters for twelve weeks and sold 6,817,803 tickets. All box office information taken from: CBO Box Office Information, La Référence des professionnels du cinema, http://www.cbo-boxoffice.com/v4/page000.php3.
5 *Casablanca* is in fact a remake of *Pépé le Moko* (Julien Duvivier, 1937). Furthermore, as Benoît Didier convincingly proports, Jacques Mesrine wrote his autobiography and planned his acts with the knowledge and influence of crime literature—a literary genre that also connotes a French-American exchange. Didier, "Faire de sa vie une oeuvre d'art paralittéraire."
6 Hayes, "*Rififi,*" 73.
7 Warshow, The Gangster as Tragic Hero," 86.
8 Ibid.
9 Neale, "Questions to Genre," 157–78.
10 Even in 2003, Bertherat Bruno observes, "Dans la culture des banlieues, dont les groupes de rap sont un symbole, Mesrine est une sorte de héros. 'Les minots rêvent de la carrière de Jacques Mesrine,' assène le groupe Fonky family en conclusion d'une de ses chansons" [In *banlieue* culture, of which rap groups are a symbol, Mesrine is a sort of hero. "The kids dream of Jacques Mesrine's career, yowls the group Fonky Family at the end of one of their songs"] (The song is *Si Dieu veut* on the album *La Furie et la foie*) (Bruno, "Cadavre à la 'une' La télévision et la mort de Jacques Mesrine, ennemi public n° 1 (1979)").
11 "A La Rencontre De ... Abdel Raouf Dafri (auteur de *Mesrine, Un Prophète* et *Braquo*) par Mounir Benali" (A meeting with ... Abdel Raouf Dafri (author of *Mesrine, A Prophet* and *Braquo*), March 7, 2014, https://www.youtube.com/watch?v=O20_wte96Cg.
12 Notice Vincent Cassel's emphasis on sons of immigrants, and not daughters, aligning the gangster-genre with masculinity, even while considering minorities.
13 "Ce qui m'étonne le plus, c'est qu'un type qui, pendant la guerre d'Algérie, shoote un Arabe en le traitant de sale crouille et de raton puisse aujourd'hui être une star dans les cités où la majeure partie des jeunes sont des fils d'immigrés.Il y a là une paradoxe incroyable, mais qui, je crois, s'explique par le fait que Mesrinc garde avant tout l'image d'un type qui luttait contre tout." d'Yvoire and Lavoignat, *Mesrine—30 Ans de cavale dans le cinema,* 237.
14 There are a few examples of the Franco-Algerian War's minor successes with the public, despite a number of investments. Although an independent film dictates a

smaller viewership, Mehdi Charef's *Cartouches Gauloises* [*Summer of '62*] in 2008 sold only 62,240 tickets. Rachid Bouchareb's *Hors-la-loi* (*Outside the Law*, 2010), with a budget of 20.5 million and box-office drawing actors such Jamel Debooze, sold just 381,106 tickets in its first month.
15 Turim, *Flashbacks in Film*, 4.
16 Ibid., 5.
17 Lazreg, *Torture and the Twilight of Empire*, 117.
18 Mesrine, *L'Instinct de mort*, 49–50.
19 Mesrine, *Coupable d'être innocent*, 30-1.
20 A version of this anecdote was part of the film's initial screenplay when the project was to be directed by Barbet Schroeder.
21 "Dans la cave des suspects y subissaient des interrogatoires. Je vis ces hommes se faire torturer, gueuler leur haine pour la France, certains préférant crever sur place que de parler" (Mesrine, *Coupable d'être innocent*, 31).
22 Aussaresses, *Services Spéciaux*.
23 Branche, "FLN et OAS," 330.
24 'Mon armée tout le monde la connaît. Elle se decline en 3 lettres O-A-S. Elle frappe où elle veut quand elle veut."
25 "La situation colonial et sa histoire en Algérie ont abouti à une représentation des Algériens tout à fait spécifique. Les formes de la repression témoignent ainsi d'une discrimination séculaire et d'une conception des Algériens comme un groupe passif qui ne comprendrait que la force ou la violence…Ainsi l'État colonial a-t-il peut-être aussi produit les organisations qui ont lutté contre lui avec l'arme du terrorisme?" Branche, "FLN et OAS," 330.
26 Marnia Lazreg (*Torture and the Twilight of Empire,* 180) gives the account of one soldier who buried a prisoner who was still breathing, in a grave that he had forced the prisoner to dig. Martin Evans ("Harkis," 127) also lists this as a punishment toward harkis in Algeria after independence.
27 d' Yvoire and Lavoignat, *Mesrine—30 Ans de cavale dans le cinema.*
28 Derrida, *Dissemination*, 300–301.
29 "La police d'octobre 61 elle savait remettre les bougnoules … Les flics de l'époque, ils avaient Papon. Papon était un bon chef."
30 Einaudi, *La Bataille de Paris—17 octobre 1961.*
31 The main character of *Caché*, Georges invokes the Paris Massacre in a monologue in which he explains why he believes an Algerian he knew growing up has recently threatened him. "Le 17 octobre en 1961" and "Papon" are among the strands of words.
32 Gallois, *A History of Violence in the Early Algerian Colony.*
33 "Ceux que nous appelions les rebelles luttaient pour obtenir leur indépendance et reconquérir ce que mes ancêtres leur avaient pris un siècle plus tôt. J'allais donc participer à une guerre absurde avec la certitude que ce ne sont jamais ceux qui la déclenchent qui la font" (Mesrine, *Coupable d'être innocent,* 48).
34 "Je vais te montrer ce qu'on fait en Algérie."
35 Boilley, "Loi du 23 février 2005, colonisation, indigènes, victimisations. Évocations binaires, représentations primaires."
36 "une société en interaction avec son passé, mais aussi en quête de sens sur le present et d'angoisses devant le futur" (Blanchard and Veyrat-Masson, *La Guerre de Mémoires,* 21).
37 Derrida and Bennington, "Shibboleth for Paul Celan," 61.
38 Ibid., 64.

39 Ibid., 66.

6 The Revolution through Utopian Dialectics

1 Foucault, "Of Other Spaces," 3.
2 Ibid.
3 Bouisri and Pradel de Lamaze, "La Population d'Algérie d'après le recensement de 1966," 31–4.
4 Foucault, "Of Other Spaces," 4.
5 Freud, *Beyond the Pleasure Principle*, 13–14.
6 "The traditional garden of the Persians was a sacred space that was supposed to bring together inside its rectangle four parts representing the four parts of the world, with a space still more sacred than the others that were like an umbilicus, the navel of the world at its center (the basin and water fountain were there); and all the vegetation of the garden was supposed to come together in this space, in this sort of microcosm." Foucault, "Of Other Spaces," 6.
7 As Guy Hennebelle notes (*CinémAction*, 116–17), *So Young a Peace* also recalls Andrzej Wadja's *Popiół i diament* (*Ashes and Diamonds*, 1958) and Luis Buñuel's *Los Olvidados* (*The Young and the Damned*, 1950), both of which also demonstrate the influence of Italian neorealism.
8 Connelly, *A Diplomatic Revolution*, 133.
9 Charby reversed this process in his film; he wrote the screenplay in French and then asked the children to improvise the dialogue in Algerian-Arabic. Hennebelle, *CinémAction*, 114–15.
10 Charby wrote a book about his prison experience, *L'Algérie en prison*, that was published by Éditions de Minuit in 1961.
11 Cécile Decugis included shots of the orphans in *Les Réfugiés* to be screened for the United Nations in 1957. After losing the vocal track, she rerecorded an audio for a 2011 version renamed *La Distribution du pain*. *Les Réfugiés Algériens* by Pierre Clément and Djamel Chanderli in 1958 features many disturbing shots of children in need while the voice-over explains that children represent 50 percent of the Algerian refugee population.
12 "Charby nous renvoie à Fanon et aux multiples cas pathologiques décrits dans *Les Damnés de la terre*" (Hennebelle, *CinémAction*, 118).
13 In an interview with Hennebelle, Charby said, "I could access two thousand children. I then used three hundred on an on-going basis ... All of the children are really orphans" [Je pouvais disposer de deux mille enfants. J'en ai utilisé trois cents de façon permanente ... Tous les enfants sont réellement orphelins] (Hennebelle, *CinémAction*, 114).
14 *Les Enfants d'Algérie*, 94–5.
15 "Je les brûlerai comme il m'ont brûlé ... Ceux qui m'ont brûlé je leur ferai souffrir je les égorgerai je les oublierai jamais ceux m'ont brûlé même s'ils viennent me dire pardon je leur pardonnerai pas" (*ibid.*).
16 "Je ne brûlerai pas un enfant parce qu'ils m'ont rien fait" (*ibid.*).
17 According to René Vautier's autobiography, Fanon disapproved of their film, as it was an independent effort by French filmmakers that had not been screened by or credited to the FLN. (Vautier, *Caméra Citoyenne*, 165–6.) Although Charby says that Fanon

helped him with the book, *The Children of Algeria* (Hennebelle, *CinémAction*, 115), he died before Charby began *Une si jeune paix*.

18 Hennebelle (*CinémAction*, 114) claims that *I Am 8 Years Old* and *So Young a Peace* both feature the art of the book *The Children of Algeria*.

19 Macey, *Frantz Fanon*, 319.

20 In fact, the book Fanon completed in the year he died from leukemia entitled *Pour la révolution africaine* (*Toward the African Revolution*) can be considered a pan-African manifesto.

21 Macey, *Frantz Fanon*, 366.

22 "Tous ces soi-disant Algériens sont des Français … et ils ne me laissent pas tranquille … Je le tuerai sans exception" (Fanon, *Les Damnés de la terre*, 195).

23 Fanon, *Les Damnés De La Terre*, 201–3. Charby notes that he was unaware of a situation in which Algerian children killed another Algerian child, but that *The Wretched of the Earth* "cites pathological examples even more violent" ("cite des exemples pathologiques bien plus violents") (Hennebelle, *CinémAction*, 115.

24 In Albert Camus's *Le Premier Homme* (*The First Man*), a semi-autobiographical novel concerning the childhood of the protagonist Jacques Cormery, we also witness a child obfuscation of the costumed binary. The main character witnesses a boy in an Arab family dressed as a French paratrooper when returning to Algeria during the war. (p. 73).

25 Foucault, "Of Other Spaces," 6.

26 Ibid.

27 Ibid.

28 "il est d'une part une dénonciation universelle et d'autre part il attire l'attention de l'opinion sur ce terrible problème des orphelins de l'après-guerre" (Hennebelle, *CinémAction*, 115).

29 In David Harvey's *Spaces of Hope*, the free market itself contains such utopian dialectics—the concept and the raw materials.

30 Harvey, *Spaces of Hope*, 196.

31 "There is another reason, unrelated to acting, why children appear in neorealist films, then and now, as often as they do. That is because the essential theme of neorealist cinema is the conflict between the common, anonymous person and the immense societal forces—war, politics, organized crime, the economy—that are completely external to him or her, yet completely determine this individual's existence. The most pitiful victims of such forces, because the most innocent, are naturally children, and therefore it is no accident that important neorealist pictures, Italian as well feature them." (Cardullo, "Neorealism, History, and the Children's Film," 11–12).

32 Central Intelligence Agency, *World Fact Book*.

33 "Enquête. Les Mille et un destins des SDF Algériens—Algérie Part."

34 Deleuze and Guattari, *A Thousand Plateaus*, 380.

35 In its fantastic framework *Bloody Beans* suggests women's role in the Algerian Revolution as found in Nassima Guessoum's documentary, *10949 Femmes* (*10949 Women*, 2014).

36 Original poem:
Les poissons de la mer sont morts
Parce qu'ils ont préféré à être
D'aller au but sans rien connaître
De ce que tu appelles obéir.

37 De Coster, "Algerian Film 'Bloody Beans' Takes Home Best Documentary at CPH:DOX Festival."
38 Harvey, *Spaces of Hope*, 200.
39 For more on the pork association in French film of the early twenty-first century, see: Wallenbrock, "Almost but Not Quite Eating Pork."
40 The *Bloc identitaire* has largely been eclipsed by its younger group *Génération Identitaire* that shares its ideology with the German *Pergida*, another young anti-immigrant group. Likewise the pig symbolism has waned in favor of a lambda, that appears on their t-shirts and propaganda tools. In this way, the new group differentiates itself as more serious.
41 Among others: the June 18, 1961 bombing on the Paris-Strasbourg line that then derailed a train and killed 200, and the massacre of Oran immediately after independence on July 5–7, 1962.
42 Bensmaïl's 2017 film declares that the coup d'état of Boudmediene in 1965 was dissimulated by the simultaneous filming of *The Battle of Algiers*, a fact supported today by many historians (such as James Le Sueur as cited in note 83 of Chapter 1), but which is still controversial in the FLN government.
43 A personal interview with Narimane Mari in 2015.
44 Harvey, *Spaces of Hope,* 200.
45 Ibid., 254.

Conclusion

1 Chanaoui, "En Algérie, Après l'annonce Du Conseil Constitutionnel."
2 Conseil Constitutionnel "Décision n° 2017–690 QPC du 8 février 2018."

Selected Bibliography

Abdulrazak, Fawzi. "Arabization in Algeria." *MELA Notes*, vol. 26, 1982, pp. 22–43.
Aggar, Salim. "La guerre d'Algérie au cinéma cinquante ans d'images entre la France et l'Algérie." *La Liberté Algérie*, 2008, www.liberte-algerie.com/contributions/cinquante-ans-dimages-entre-la-france-et-lalgerie-71062. Accessed May 15, 2019.
Algeria: A Country Study. Washington: GPO for the Library of Congress, 1994.
"Algérie, Année Zéro de Marceline Loridan Ivens et Jean-Pierre Sergent."*Algériades.com: Le guide d'Algérie à l'affiche*, www.algeriades.com/marceline-loridan-ivens-et-jean/article/algerie-annee-zero-de-marceline. Accessed May 16, 2018.
Alleg, Henri. *La Question*. Paris: Les Éditions Minuit, 1958.
"Aménagement de la Cinémathèque Algérienne: un parcours découverte, un exemple de coopération." CNC: Archives Française du film. cnc-aff.fr/internet_cnc/Internet/ARemplir/parcours/Algerie/accueil.html. Accessed June 14, 2019.
Amiri, Linda. *La Bataille de France: La guerre d'Algérie en métropole*. Paris: Robert Laffont, 2004.
Anderson, Benedict R. *Imagined Communities: Reflections on the Origin and Spread of Nationalism*. New York: Verso Books, 1983.
Armes, Roy and Lizbeth Malkmus. *Arab and African Film Making*. London: Zed Books, 1991.
Armes, Roy. *Postcolonial Images: Studies in North African Film*. Bloomington: Indiana University Press, 2005.
Asselin, Pierre. "The Algerian Revolution and the Communist Bloc." *Cold War International History Project*, CWIHP e-Dossier No. 62, February 10, 2015, www.wilsoncenter.org/publication/the-algerian-revolution-and-the-communist-bloc. Accessed May 20, 2018.
Aussaresses, Paul. *Services Spéciaux: Algérie, 1955–1957*. Paris: Perrin, 2001.
Aussaresses, Paul. *The Battle of the Casbah: Terrorism and Counter-Terrorism in Algeria, 1955–1957*. Trans. Robert Miller. New York: Enigma Books, 2004.
Austin, Guy. "Against Amnesia: Representations of Memory in Algerian Cinema." *Journal of African Cinemas*, vol. 2, no. 1, 2010, pp. 27–35.
Austin, Guy. *Algerian National Cinema*. Manchester: Manchester University Press, 2012.
Bailblé, Claude, Michel Marie, and Marie Claire Ropars-Wuilleumier. *Muriel: Histoire d'une recherche*. Paris: Galilée, 1975.
Bancel, Nicolas and Pascal Blanchard. "La colonisation: du débat sur la guerre d'Algérie au discours de Dakar." *La Guerre de Mémoires*. Ed. Nicolas Bancel and Isabelle Veyrat-Masson. Paris: La Découverte, 2008, pp. 137–54.
Barclay, Fiona and Charlotte Ann Chopin, and Martin Evans. "Introduction: Settler Colonialism and French Algeria." *Settler Colonial Studies*, vol. 8, no. 2, 2008, 115–30.
Barthes, Roland. *Camera Lucida: Reflections on Photography*. Trans. Richard Howard. New York: Hill and Wang, 1985.
La Bataille d'Alger. "Projetée Dans Une Salle Parisienne." *Le Monde*, October 21, 1971, https://www.lemonde.fr/archives/article/1971/10/21/

la-bataille-d-alger-projetee-dans-une-salle-parisienne_2472438_1819218. html?xtmc=bataille_d_alger_projetee_dans_une_salle_parisienne&xtcr=1. Accessed January 16, 2012.
Baugh, Bruce. "Sartre, Derrida and Commitment, the Case of Algeria." *Sartre Studies International,* vol. 9, no. 2, 2003, pp. 40–53.
Beaugé, Florence. "Guerre d'Algérie: le poignard de Le Pen."*Le Monde.* March 16, 2012,www.lemonde.fr/afrique/article/2012/03/16/le-grand-blond-au-poignard_ 1669337_3212.html. Accessed June 3, 2019.
Bedjaoui, Ahmed. *Cinéma et guerre de libération: Algérie, des batailles d'images.* Alger: Éditions Chihab, 2014.
Benrabah, Mohamed. *Language Conflict in Algeria: From Colonialism to Post-Independence.* Bristol: Multilingual Matters, 2013.
Bensmaïa, Réda. *Experimental Nations, or, the Invention of the Maghreb.* Trans.Alyson Waters. Princeton University Press, 2003.
Bensmaïa, Réda. "The War That Haunts France." Trans. Jennifer C. Gage. *L'Esprit Créateur,* vol. 54, no. 4, 2014, pp. 6–14.
Bertherat, Bruno. "Cadavre à la 'une': La télévision et la mort de Jacques Mesrine, ennemi public n° 1 (1979)." *Le Temps des médias,* no. 1, 2003, pp. 119–38.
Bertin-Maghit, Jean Pierre. *Lettres Filmées d'Algérie: des soldats à la caméra (1954–1962).* Paris: Nouveau Monde Éditions, 2015.
Billaud, Pierre. *La Grande Aventure du nucléaire militaire français: des acteurs témoignent.* Paris: L'Harmattan, 2016.
Blanchard, Pascal and Isabelle Veyrat-Masson. "Introduction. Les guerres de mémoires: un objet d'étude, au carrefour de l'histoire et des processus de médiatisation." *La Guerre de mémoires.* Ed. Nicolas Bancel and Isabelle Veyrat-Masson. Paris: La Découverte, 2008, pp. 15–49.
Boilley, Pierre. "Loi du 23 février 2005, colonisation, indigènes, victimisations. Évocations binaires, représentations primaires." *Politique africaine,* vol. 98, 2005, pp. 131–40.
Bonner, Virginia. "The New Executioners: The Spectre of Algeria in Alain Resnais's Night and Fog." *Scope,* no. 13, February 2009, https://www.nottingham.ac.uk/scope/issues/ 2009/february-issue-13.aspx. Accessed May 15, 2019.
Boudjedra, Rachid. *Naissance du cinéma algérien.* Paris: F. Maspéro, 1971.
Bouisri, Abdellaziz and François Pradel De Lamaze. "La Population d'Algérie d'après le recensement de 1966." *Population,* March 1971, pp. 31–4.
Bovier, François and Cédric Fluckiger. "René Vautier et le cinéma ouvrier: l'UPCB, une structure de production au service des colonisés de l'intérieur." *Decadrages,* no. 29–30, Spring 2015, pp. 116–41.
Branche, Raphaëlle. "FLN et OAS: deux terrorisms en guerre d'Algérie." *Revue européene d'Histoire,* vol. 14, no. 3, 2007, pp. 325–42.
Branche, Raphaëlle. *Prisonniers du FLN.* Paris: Payot, 2014.
Branche, Raphaëlle. *La Torture et l'armée pendant la Guerre d'Algérie: 1954–1962.* Paris: Gallimard, 2016.
Brink, Joram Ten, ed. *Building Bridges: The Cinema of Jean Rouch.* London: Wallflower, 2007.
Brody, Richard. *Everything Is Cinema: The Working Life of Jean-Luc Godard.* New York: Metropolitan, 2008.
Caillé, Patricia. "The Illegitimate Legitimacy of *The Battle of Algiers* in French Film Culture." *Interventions,* vol. 9, no. 3, 2007, pp. 371–88.

Caland, Julius. "French N-Tests in the Algerian Desert." *Nuclear Monitor,* no. 387–8, March 1993, www.wiseinternational.org/nuclear-monitor/387–388/french-n-tests-algerian-desert. Accessed May 18, 2019.

Camus, Albert. *L'étranger.* Paris: Gallimard, 1957.

Camus, Albert. *Le Premier Homme.* Paris: Gallimard, 1994.

Cardullo, Bert. "Neorealism, History, and the Children's Film: Victor De Sica's *The Children Are Watching Us Reconsidered.*" *Filmhistoria,* vol. 25, no. 1, 2015, pp. 7–17.

Carron, Damien. *La Suisse et la guerre d'indépendance algérienne (1954–1962).* Lausanne: Antipodes, 2013.

Central Intelligence Agency. *The World Fact Book, Africa: Algeria.* Updated September 23, 2019,www.cia.gov/library/publications/the-world-factbook/geos/ag.html. Accessed September 23, 2019.

Chabani, Nacima. "Salle de cinéma Sierra maestra à Alger: une clochardisation à l'extrême." *El Watan.* February 12, 2013, www.djazairess.com/fr/elwatan/403040. Accessed May 30, 2017.

Chanan, Michael. "Outsiders: *The Battle of Algiers* and Political Cinema." *Sight & Sound,* vol. 17, no. 6, 2007, pp. 38–40.

Chanaoui, Zahra. "En Algérie, après l'annonce du Conseil Constitutionnel: 'C'est comme si la France hiérarchisait les victimes.'" *Le Monde,* February 13, 2018, www.lemonde.fr/societe/article/2018/02/13/en-algerie-apres-l-annonce-du-conseil-constitutionnel-c-est-comme-si-la-france-hierarchisait-les-victimes_5256104_3224.html.

Charby, Jacques. *L'Algérie en prison.* Paris: Éditions de Minuit, 1961.

Chrisafis, Angelique. "France Finally Agrees to Pay Damages to Nuclear Test Victims." *The Guardian,* November 26, 2008, www.theguardian.com/world/2008/nov/27/france-nuclear-tests-illness. Accessed March 17, 2017.

"Cinéma et Audiovisuel." *Le portail interministériel de l'éducation artistique et culturelle,* www.education.arts.culture.fr/n-1/enseignements-artistiques/cinema-et-audiovisuel. html. Accessed April 24, 2015.

Connelly, Matthew. *A Diplomatic Revolution: Algeria's Fight for Independence and the Origins of the Post-cold War Era.* Oxford: Oxford University Press, 2006.

Conseil Constitutionnel. "Décision n° 2017–690 QPC du 8 février 2018." www.conseil-constitutionnel.fr/decision/2018/2017690QPC.htm. Accessed February 10, 2018.

Costantini, Dino, ed. *Mission civilisatrice: Le rôle de l'histoire coloniale dans la construction de l'identité politique française.* Paris: Éditions de la découverte, 2008.

Croombs, Matthew. "Algeria Deferred: The Logic of Trauma in *Muriel* and *Caché.*" *Scope: An Online Journal of Film and Television Studies,* vol. 16, no. 1, 2014.

Croombs, Matthew. "*La Jetée* in Historical Time: Torture, Visuality, Displacement." *Cinema Journal,* vol. 56, no. 2, 2017, pp. 25–45.

Dadci, Younès. *Dialogues Algérie-Cinéma: Première histoire du cinéma algérien.* Paris: Imp. Guterberg, 1970.

Dadci, Younès. *Première histoire du cinéma algérien: 1895-1979.* Paris: Éditions Dadci, 1980.

Daeninckx, Didier. *Meurtres pour mémoire.* Paris: Gallimard, 1983.

Daoud, Kamel. "La Misère sexuelle du monde arabe." *New York Times,* February 12, 2016.

Daoud, Kamel. *Meursault, Contre-Enquête: Roman.* Arles: Actes Sud, 2016.

Daoudi, Anissa. "Multilingualism in Algeria: Between 'Soft power', 'Arabisation', 'Islamisation', and 'Globalisation.'" *Journal of North African Studies,* vol. 23, 2018, pp. 460–81.

Daulatzai, Sohail. *Fifty Years of the Battle of Algiers: Past as Prologue*. Minneapolis: University of Minnesota Press, 2016.

De Coster, Ramzi. "Algerian Film 'Bloody Beans' Takes Home Best Documentary at CPH:DOX Festival." *Indie Wire*, November 18, 2013, www.indiewire.com/2013/11/algerian-film- bloody-beans-takes-home-best-documentary-at-cphdox-festival-32874/. Accessed June 29, 2015.

"Décret no 2010–132 du 10 février 2010 portant publication de l'accord-cadre de coproduction et de coopération cinématographique entre le Gouvernement de la République française et le Gouvernement de la République algérienne démocratique et populaire (ensemble trois annexes), signé à Alger le 4 décembre 2007."*Journal Officiel de la République Française*, February 12, 2010, legifrance.gouv.fr/affichTexte.do;jsessionid=357C0F28E7A05130F7880C86A4C7A76C.tplgfr26s_3?cidTexte=JORFTEXT000021817403&dateTexte=&oldAction=rechJO&categorieLien=id&idJO=JORFCONT000021817048. Accessed June 13, 2019.

Deleuze, Gilles. *Cinéma I: L'Image-mouvement*. Paris: Éditions de Minuit, 1983.

Deleuze, Gilles. *Cinéma II: L'Image-temps*. Paris: Éditions de Minuit, 1985.

Deleuze, Gilles and Félix Guattari. *Capitalisme et Schizophrénie: Tome 1, l'Anti-Oedipe*. Paris: Éditions de Minuit, 1972.

Deleuze, Gilles and Félix Guattari. *Capitalisme et Schizophrénie: Tome 2, Mille Plateaux*. Paris: Éditions de Minuit, 1980.

Deleuze, Gilles and Félix Guattari. *A Thousand Plateaus: Capitalism and Schizophrenia*. Trans. Brian Massumi. Minneapolis: University of Minnesota Press, 1987.

De Medeiros, Ana. "An Interview with Assia Djebar." *European Journal of Cognitive Psychology*, vol. 23, no. 4, 2008, pp. 25–8.

Denis, Sébastien. "Métaphores cinématographiques en situation coloniale. Le Cas de la censure française en Algérie (1945–1962)." *1895. Mille Huit Cent Quatre-Vingt-Quinze*, no. 48, 2006, pp. 6–25.

Denis, Sébastien. *Le Cinéma et la Guerre d'Algérie, La Propagande à l'écran (1945–1962)*. Paris: Nouveau Monde Éd, 2009.

Derrida, Jacques. *Dissemination*. Trans. Barbara Johnson. Chicago: University of Chicago Press, 1981.

Derrida, Jacques. "Shibboleth for Paul Celan." Trans. Joshua Wilner. *Word Traces: Readings of Paul Celan*. Ed. Aris Fioretos. Baltimore: John Hopkins University Press, 1994.

Derrida, Jacques. *Le Mal d'archive: Une impression freudienne*. Paris: Éditions Galilée, 1995.

Derrida, Jacques. *Archive Fever: A Freudian Impression*. Trans. Eric Prenowitz. Chicago: University of Chicago Press, 1996.

Derrida, Jacques. *Le Monolinguisme de l'autre, Ou, La Prothèse d'origine*. Paris: Galilée, 1996.

Derrida, Jacques and Geoffrey Bennington. *Jacques Derrida*. Chicago: University of Chicago Press, 1993.

Derrida, Jacques and Bernard Stiegler. *Echographies of Television: Filmed Interviews*. Cambridge: Polity Press, 2002.

"Des Inconnus Brisent Les Vitres Du Studio Saint-Séverin." *Le Monde*, October 22, 1971, https://www.lemonde.fr/archives/article/1971/10/22/des-inconnus-brisent-les-vitres-du-studio-saint-severin_2472612_1819218.html?xtmc=des_inconnus_brisent_les_vitres_du_studio_saint_severin&xtcr=1. Accessed January 20, 2015.

Didier, Benoît. "Faire de sa vie une oeuvre d'art paralittéraire: Quelques réflexions autour de la littérature-Mesrine." *Études Françaises*, vol. 47, no. 1, 2011, pp. 141–55.

Dine, Phillip. *Images of the Algerian War: French Fiction and Film, 1954–1992*. Oxford: Oxford University Press, 1994.

Di Orio, Sam. "Total Cinema: *Chronique d'un été* and the End of Bazinian Film Theory." *Screen: The Journal of Society for Education in Film and Television*, vol. 48, no. 1, 2007, pp. 25–43.

Djamel, G. "Le Drame 'Invisible' Des SDF." *El Watan*, December 12, 2017, elwatan.com/regions/…/le-drame-invisible-des-sdf-12-12-2017-358470_148. Accessed May15, 2018.

Einaudi, Jean-Luc. *La Bataille de Paris—17 octobre 1961*. Paris: Seuil, 1991.

Elsaesser, Thomas. *German Cinema—Terror and Trauma: Cultural Memory since 1945*. Abingdon: Routledge, 2014.

Emie, Bernard. "Lancement à Alger d'une formation professionnelle en post production organisée par l'Institut Français d'Algérie et le Centre Algérien de Développement du Cinéma, en partenariat avec la Femis."*La Fémis*, June 2017, femis.fr/lancement-a-alger-d-une-formation. Accessed June 17, 2019.

"En Algérie, Emmanuel Macron qualifie la colonisation française de 'crime contre l'humanité.'" *Libération*, February 15, 2017, www.liberation.fr/politiques/2017/02/15/en-algerie-emmanuel-macron-qualifie-la-colonisation-francaise-de-crime-contre-l-humanite_1548723.Accessed June 1, 2018.

Les Enfants d'Algérie. Récits et dessins. Témoignages et dessins d'enfants réfugiés en Tunisie, en Lybie et au Maroc. Paris: F. Maspero, 1962.

"Enquête. Les Mille et un destins des SDF Algériens—Algérie Part." Algérie Part, August 9, 2017, algeriepart.com/2017/08/09/enquete-mille-destins-sdf-algeriens/. Accessed August 20, 2017.

"Entretien. Kamel Daoud: 'Je mène une bataille contre une pensée unanimiste dominante.'" Interviewed by Hacen Ouali. *El Watan*, February 20, 2017, www.courrierinternational.com/article/entretien-kamel-daoud-je-mene-une-bataille-contre-une-pensee-unanimiste-dominante. Accessed March 20, 2018.

Evans, Martin. "Harkis: The Experience and Memory of Muslim Auxiliaries." *Algerian War and the French Army, 1954–62: Experiences, Images, Testimonies*. London: Palgrave Macmillan, 2002.

Fanon, Frantz. *L'an V de la Révolution Algérienne*. Paris: F. Maspero, 1966.

Fanon, Frantz. *Les Damnés de la terre*. Paris: F. Maspero, 1968.

Fanon, Frantz. *Pour la Révolution Africaine: Écrits politiques*. Paris: La Découverte, 2006.

Flood, Maria. "Common Vulnerability: Community and Its Presentation in Assia Djebar's *La Nouba des femmes du Mont Chenoua*." *Modern & Contemporary France*, vol. 21, no. 1, 2013, pp. 73–88.

Flood, Maria. "Torture in Word and Image: Inhuman Acts in Resnais and Pontecorvo."*Journal of Cinema and Media Studies,* vol. 58, no. 3, 2019, pp. 26–48.

Forgacs, David. "Italians in Algiers." *Interventions*, vol. 9, no. 3, 2007, pp. 350–64.

Foucault, Michel. "Of Other Spaces: Utopias and Heterotopias." Trans. Jay Miskowiec. *Architecture/Mouvement/ Continuité*, no. 5, October 1984, pp. 46–9.

Freud, Sigmund. *Beyond the Pleasure Principle*. Trans. Peter Gay. New York: W.W. Norton and Company, 1990.

Freud, Sigmund. *Three Essays on the Theory of Sexuality: The 1905 Edition*. Trans. Ulrike Kistner, Philippe Van Haute, and Herman Westerink. New York: Verso Books, 2017.

Frodon, Jean-Michel. "Le cinéma français a fait sa guerre d'Algérie." *Slate*, December 20, 2012, http://www.slate.fr/story/66317/guerre-algerie-cinema-france-vietnam Accessed September 20, 2019.

Gallois, William. *A History of Violence in the Early Algerian Colony*. New York: Palgrave Macmillan, 2003.
Ganne, Antoine. "Discours de Nicolas Sarkozy à Alger—Afrik.Com: L'actualité De l'Afrique Noire et du Maghreb." *Afrik.Com*, December 3, 2007, www.afrik.com/discours-de-nicolas-sarkozy-a-alger. Accessed May 25, 2018.
Garanger, Marc. *Femmes Algériennes 1960*. Paris: Contrejour, 1982.
Garreau, Laurent. *Archives secrètes du cinéma français (1945–1975)*. Paris: Presses Universitaires De France, 2009.
Gauch, Suzanne. "*Muriel*, or the Disappearing Text of the Algerian War." *L'Esprit Créateur*, vol. 41, no. 4, 2001, pp. 47–57.
Gauch, Suzanne. "Impasses of Algerian Cinema: Three Films by Mohamed Chouikh." *Third Text*, vol. 27 no. 2, 2013, pp. 260–77.
Georges, Henri. "Les photos de la repression du 17 octobre 1961." *Le Monde*, October 17, 2011, https://www.lemonde.fr/societe/infographe/2011/10/17/les-photos-inedites-du-17-octobre-1961_1586457_3224.html. Accessed December 15, 2014.
Girardeau, Zérane S. *Déflagrations: Dessins d'enfants guerres d'adultes*. Paris: Éditions Anamosa, 2017.
Greene, Naomi. *Landscapes of Loss: The National Past in Postwar French Cinema*. Princeton: Princeton University Press, 1999.
Groo, Katherine. "The Maison and Its Minor Lumière(s), Film History, and the Early Archive." *Cinema Journal: The Journal of the Society for Cinema and Media Studies*, vol. 52, no. 4 2013, pp. 25–48.
"La Guerre d'Algérie à l'écran." *Cinémaction 85*. Paris: Corlet-Télérama, 1997.
Hantke, Steffen. "The Military Horror Film: Speculations on a Hybrid Genre." *The Journal of Popular Culture*, vol. 43, no. 4, 2010, pp. 701–19.
Harbi, Mohammed. "La Guerre d'Algérie a commencé à Sétif." *Le Monde diplomatique*, March 1, 2005, p. 21.
Harbi, Mohammed. "Culture et démocratie en Algérie: Retour sur une histoire." *Le Mouvement Social*, vol. 2–3, no. 2.219–20, 2007, pp. 25–34.
Harvey, David. *Spaces of Hope*. Berkeley: University of California Press, 2000.
Hassin, Ran R., Melissa J. Ferguson, Daniella Shidlovski, and Tamar Gross. "Subliminal Exposure to National Flags Affects Political Thought and Behavior." *Proceedings of the National Academy of Sciences*, vol. 104, no. 50, 2007, pp. 19757–61.
Hayes, Graeme. "*Rififi*." *The Cinema of France*. Ed. Phil Powrie. London: Wallflower Press, 2006, p. 73.
Hennebelle, Guy. *CinémAction: Chronique de la naissance du cinéma algérien, Guy Hennebelle, un critique engagé*. Ed. Sébastien Layerle and Monique Martineau-Hennebelle. Paris: Éditions Charles Corlet, 2018.
Higbee, Will. *Post-Beur Cinema: North African Émigré and Maghrebi-French Filmmaking in France since 2000*. Edinburgh: Edinburgh University Press, 2014.
Higbee, Will and Song Wee Lim. "Concepts of Transnational Cinema: Towards a Critical Transnationalism in Film Studies." *Transnational Cinemas*, vol.1, no. 1, 2010, pp. 7–21.
Hirsch, Marianne. *The Generation of Postmemory: Writing and Visual Culture after the Holocaust*. New York: Columbia University Press, 2012.
Hong, Young-Sun. *Cold War Germany, the Third World, and the Global Humanitarian Regime*. Cambridge: Cambridge University Press, 2017.
Ighilahriz, Louisette and Anne Nivat. *Algérienne*. Paris: Fayard, 2001.
Jauffret, Jean-Charles. *Soldats en Algérie, 1954–1962: Expériences contrastées des hommes du contingent*. Paris: Autrement, 2000.
Jenni, Alexis. *L'Art français de la guerre*. Paris: Gallimard, 2011.

Jules-Rosette, Benetta. "Jean-Paul Sartre and the Philosophy of Négritude." *Theory and Society*, vol. 36, no. 3, 2007, pp. 265–85.

Khanna, Ranjana. *Algeria Cuts: Women and Representation, 1830 to the Present*. Stanford, CA: Stanford University Press, 2008.

Kohler, Robert. "Review: *Fidaï*." *Variety Magazine*, September 9, 2012, variety.com/2012/film/markets-festivals/fidai-1117948259/. Accessed October 20, 2015.

Kouby, Emma. "A War of Words over an Image of War: The Fox Movietone Scandal and the Portrayal of French Violence in Algeria 1955–1956." *French Politics, Culture, and Society*. vol. 30, 2012, pp. 46–67.

Laplanche, Jean and J. B. Pontalis. *The Language of Psycho-Analysis*. Trans. Donald Nicholson-Smith. London: Hogarth Press, 1973.

Larousse. *Dictionnaire Larousse Poche + 2018: 74000 Définitions, noms communs, noms propres, avec 84 tableaux de conjugaison + un précis de grammaire*. Éd. Anniversaire. Paris: Larousse, 2017.

Lazreg, Marnia. *Torture and the Twilight of Empire: From Algiers to Baghdad*. Princeton: Princeton University Press, 2008.

Lee, Sonia. "Mehdi Charef et le cinéma de l'intégration." *French and Francophone Studies*, vol. 8, no. 2, 2004, pp. 185–91.Le Masson, Yann and Olga Poliakof, "Manifeste Pour Un Cinéma Parallèle." *Positif*, no. 46, June 1962, p. 18.

Le Pastier, Joachim. "*La Chine est encore loin*." *Cahiers du cinéma*, no. 655, 2010, p. 35.

Le Querrec, Guy. "Les Beurs Entre Deux Rives." *Le Monde*, November 1, 1987.

Le Sueur, James D. *Uncivil War: Intellectuals and Identity Politics during the Decolonization of Algeria*. 2nd Ed. London: University of Nebraska Press, 2005.

Le Sueur, James D. *Algeria since 1989: Between Terror and Democracy*. London: Zed Books, 2013.

Lewis, Paul. "France in a Fuel Supply Shift, to Pay More for Gas." *New York Times*, February 4, 1982, p. 00001.

Liogier, Hélène. "1960; Vue d'Espagne, La Nouvelle vague est fascist." *1895: Revue de l'association française de recherche sur l'histoire du cinéma*, vol. 26, 1998, pp. 127–53.

Lyons, Amelia H. *The Civilizing Mission in the Metropole: Algerian Families and the French Welfare State during Decolonization*. Stanford: Stanford University Press, 2013.

Macey, David. *Frantz Fanon: A Biography*. New York: Verso Books, 2012.

Maherzi, Lotfi. *Le Cinéma Algérien: institutions, imaginaire, idéologie*. Alger: Société nationale d'édition et de diffusion, 1980.

Malley, Robert. *The Call from Algeria: Third Worldism, Revolution, and the Turn to Islam*. Berkeley: University of California Press, 1996.

Malti, Hocine. *Histoire secrète du pétrole algérien*. Paris: La Découverte, 2012.

Marie, Michel. *The French New Wave: An Artistic School*, trans. Richard Neupert. Paris: Editions Nathan, 2003.

Marker, Cynthia. "Self-Censorship and Chris Marker's *Le Jolie Mai*." *French Cultural Studies*, vol. 12, no. 34, 2001, pp. 23–41.

Marks, Laura U. *The Skin of Film: Intercultural Cinema, Embodiment, and the Senses*. Raleigh, NC: Duke University Press, 2000.

Martínez, Luis. *La Guerre Civile en Algérie, 1990–1998*. Paris: Karthala, 1998.Massu, Jacques. *La vraie bataille d'Alger*. Monaco: Editions Du Rocher, 1997.

Mathieu, Anne. "Un engagement déterminé contre le colonialisme: Jean-Paul Sartre et la Guerre d'Algérie." *Le Monde Diplomatique*, November 2004, pp. 30–31.

Mcmahon, Laura. "Untimely Resnais: *Muriel's* Disarticulations of Justice." *Film-Philosophy*, no. 20, 2016, pp. 219–34.

Megherbi, Abdelghani. *Les Algériens au miroir du cinéma colonial: Contribution à une sociologie de la décolonisation*. Alger: Enap, 1982.
Merchet, Jean-Dominique. "Secret Défense—Essais Nucléaires: Gerboise Verte, la bombe et le scoop qui font plouf … (Actualisé-3)." *Libération*, February 16, 2010, http://Secretdefense.Blogs.Liberation.Fr/2010/02/16/Essais-Nucleaires-Gerboise-Verte-La-Bombe-Et-Le-Scoop-Qui-Font-Plouf/. Accessed May 1, 2018.
Mesrine, Jacques. *L'Instinct de mort*. Paris: Champs Libres, 1977.
Mesrine, Jacques. *Coupable d'être innocent*. Paris: Les Éditions France-Amérique, 1979.
Metz, Christian. *Le Signifiant imaginaire: Psychanalyse et cinéma*. Paris: Christian Bourgois Éditeur, 2002.
Metz, Helen Chapin. *Algeria: A Country Study*. Washington DC: Library of Congress, 1994.
Morag, Raya. *Waltzing with Bashir: Perpetrator Trauma and Cinema*. London: I.B. Tauris, 2013.
Mouillard-Fraisse, Geneviève. *Les Fous cartographes: Littérature et appartenance*. Paris: L'Harmattan, 1995.
Mudimbe, V. Y. *The Invention of Africa. Gnosis, Philosophy and the Order of Knowledge*. Bloomington: University of Indiana Press, 1988.
Mudimbe, V. Y. "A Conversation with V.Y. Mudimbe with Faith Smith." *Callaloo*, vol. 14, no. 4, Autumn 1991, pp. 969–86.
Mundy, Jacob. *Imaginative Geographies of Algerian Violence: Conflict Science, Conflict Management, Antipolitics*. Stanford: Stanford University Press, 2015.
Naficy, Hamid. *An Accented Cinema: Exilic and Diasporic Filmmaking*. Princeton: Princeton University Press,1996.
Neale, Steve. "Questions to Genre." *Film and Theory: An Anthology*. Ed. Robert Stam and Toby Miller. New York: Blackwell Publishers, 2000.
Neupert, Richard. *A History of the French New Wave Cinema*. Madison: University of Wisconsin Press, 2007.
Nora, Pierre. *Les Lieux de mémoire*. Paris: Gallimard, 1997.
Ouattar, Tahar. *Les martyrs reviennent cette semaine*. Alger: Enag, 2002.
Ould-Khelifa, Saïd. "Le Moudjahid Pierre Clément est mort."*L'Expression*, October 15, 2007, https://www.djazairess.com/fr/lexpression/46385. Accessed June 15, 2016.
Ould Khettab, Djamila. "Algerian Cinema a New Wave Is Emerging."*Middle East Eye*. June 2, 2016, https://www.middleeasteye.net/features/algerian-cinema-new-wave-emerging. Accessed June 15, 2016."Pierre Schoendoerffer, une carrière au service de l'image." Ecpad Agence d'images de la défense, 2012, http://Archives.Ecpad.Fr/Pierre-Schoendoerffer-Une-Carriere-Au-Service-De-Limage/. Accessed June 15, 2016.
Pluet, Nicolas. "Essai nucléaire à Reggane: 150 prisonniers algériens utilisés comme cobayes humains." *Le journal des matins d'Algérie: le journal des débats et des idées*, November 13, 2015, www.lematindz.net/news/19048-essai-nucleaire-a-reggane-150-prisonniers-algeriens-utilises-comme-cobayes-humains.html. Accessed January 21, 2017.
Porter, David. *Eyes to the South: French Anarchists and Algeria*. Chico: AK Press, 2011.
"Pourquoi vous n'avez pas vu 'La Bataille d'Alger.' " *Positif*, no. 119, 1970, p. 73.
"Quand les appelés du contingent servaient de cobayes." *Le Parisien*, February 16, 2010, www.leparisien.fr/une/quand-les-appeles-du-contingent-servaient-de-cobayes-16-02-2010-817293.php. Accessed June 12, 2016.
The Quran. Trans. M. A. S. Abdel Haleem. Oxford: Oxford University Press, 2005.

Radiological Conditions at the Former French Nuclear Test Sites in Algeria: Preliminary Assessment and Recommendations. Vienna: International Atomic Energy Agency, 2005.

Rahal, Malika. "Comment faire l'histoire de l'Algérie indépendante?" *La vie des idées,* 2012, http://www.laviedesidees.fr/Comment-faire-l-histoire-de-l-Algerie-independante.html.hal- 01316091. Accessed March 13, 2019.

Remaoun, Hassan. "L'enseignement de la Guerre de libération nationale (1954–1962), dans les anciens et nouveaux manuels algériens d'histoire. Un enjeu pour l'affirmation d'une culture de la citoyenneté." *Trema: Revue internationale en science de l'éducation et didactique,* no. 29, 2008, pp. 5–19.

Remaoun, Hassan. "L'Intervention institutionnelle et son impact sur la pratique historiographique en Algérie: la politique 'd'Ecriture et de Réécriture de l'histoire', tendances et contre-tendances." *Insaniyat: Revue algérienne d'anthropologie et des sciences sociales,* no. 19–20, 2003, pp. 7–40.

Roberts, Katherine A. "Constrained Militants: Algerian Women 'In-Between' in Gillo Pontecorvo's *The Battle of Algiers* and Bourlem Guerdjou's *Living in Paradise*." *The Journal of North African Studies,* vol. 12, no. 4, 2007, pp. 381–93.

Robin, Marie-Monique. *Escadrons de la Mort, l'école française*. Paris: La Découverte, 2004.

Ross, Kristin. *Fast Cars, Clean Bodies: Decolonization and the Reordering of French Culture*, Cambridge: October Books, 1994.

Ross, Kristin. *May '68 and Its Afterlives*. Chicago: University of Chicago Press, 2010.

Rothberg, Michael. *Multidirectional Memory: Remembering the Holocaust in the Age of Decolonization*. Stanford: Stanford University Press, 2009.

Rouby, René. *Otage d'Amirouche, Témoigner pour le souvenir*. Paris: Charles Lavauzelle, 2004.

Rouxel-Cubberly, Noëlle. *Les Titres de film: économie et évolution du titre de film français depuis 1968*. Paris: M. Houdiard, 2011.

Said, Edward W. *Orientalism*. Harmondsworth: Penguin, 1978.

Salmane, Hala et al. *Algerian Cinema*. London: British Film Institute, 1982.

Sartre, Jean-Paul. *La Nausée*. Paris: Gallimard, 1938.

Sartre, Jean-Paul. *L'Être et le néant*. Paris: Gallimard, 1943.

Sartre, Jean-Paul. *Huis clos*. Paris: Gallimard, 1945.

Sartre, Jean-Paul. *Réflexions sur la question juive*. Paris: Gallimard, 1946.

Sartre, Jean-Paul. *Situations, V: Colonialisme et néo-colonialisme*. Paris: Gallimard, 1983.

Sartre, Jean-Paul. *Being and Nothingness*. Trans. H. E. Barnes. New York: Gramercy Books, 1994.

Senghor, Léopold Sédor, ed. *Anthologie de la nouvelle poesie nègre et malgache de langue francaise*. Paris: Presses universitaires de France, 1948.

Sharpe, Mani. "Gender and the Politics of Decolonization in Early 1960s French Cinema." (Forthcoming with *the Journal of European Studies*).

Sharpe, Mani. "Screening Decolonisation through Privatisation in Two New Wave Films: *Adieu Philippine* and *La Belle Vie*." *Studies in French Cinema,* vol. 17, no. 2, 2017, pp. 1–15.

Silverstein, Paul A. *Algeria in France: Transpolitics, Race, and Nation*. Bloomington: Indiana University Press, 2004.

Simon, Catherine. *Algérie, années pied-rouges: des rêves de l'indépendance au désenchantement (1962–1969)*. Paris: La Découverte, 2011.

Simonet, Thomas. "Filming Inner Life: The Works of Robert Enrico."*Cinema Journal,* vol. 1, no. 1, 1974, pp. 51–9.

Slavin, David Henry. *Colonial Cinema and Imperial France, 1919–1939: White Blind Spots, Male Fantasies, Settler Myths*. Baltimore: Johns Hopkins University Press, 2001.
Soufi, Fouad. "Les Archives algériennes en 1962: héritage et spoliation." *Insaniyat*, no. 65–6, December 31, 2014, pp. 211–37.
Soullier, Lucie. "Torture en Algérie: Jean-Marie Le Pen dément une nouvelle fois." *Le Monde*, February 21, 2018, www.lemonde.fr/politique/article/2018/02/21/torture-en-algerie-jean-marie-le-pen-dement-une-nouvelle-fois_5260134_823448.html. Accessed June 3, 2019.
Stora, Benjamin. *La Gangrène et l'oubli: La Mémoire de la guerre d'Algérie*. Paris: La Découverte, 1998.
Stora, Benjamin. *Algeria, 1830–2000: A Short History*. Trans. Jane Marie Todd. Ithaca: Cornell University Press, 2001.
Stora, Benjamin. *Les Imaginaires de guerre: Images de la guerre d'Algérie et du Viêt-Nam*. Paris: La Découverte, 2004.
"Sur la route de Ciné-pops." *Algérie tours, détours,* www.algerietoursdetours.com/aproposdufilm.html. Accessed June 10, 2014.
Tarr, Carrie. *Reframing Difference: Beur and Banlieue Filmmaking in France*. Manchester: Manchester University Press, 2005.
Turim, Maureen. *Flashbacks in Film: Memory and History*. Abingdon: Routledge, 1989.
Ungar, Steven. "Making Waves: René Vautier's *Afrique 50* and the Emergence of Anti-Colonial Cinema."*L'Esprit Créateur*, vol. 51, no. 3, 2011, pp. 34–46.
Vautier, René. *Caméra Citoyenne: Mémoires*. Rennes: Apogée, 1998.
Vidal-Naquet, Pierre. *La Torture dans la république: essai d'histoire et de politique contemporaines, 1954–1962*. Paris: La Decouverte, 1983.
Vince, Natyla. *Our Fighting Sisters: Nation, Memory, and Gender in Algeria, 1954–2012*. Manchester: Manchester University Press, 2015.
Wall, Irwin M. *Les États-Unis et la Guerre d'Algérie*. Paris: Sobel, 2006.
Wallenbrock, Nicole. "Almost but Not Quite Eating Pork: Culinary Nationalism and Islamic Difference in Millennial French Comedies." *Performing Islam, Intellect*, January 2016, pp. 107–28.
Warshow, Robert. "The Gangster as Tragic Hero." *The Immediate Experience: Movies, Comics, Theatre, and Other Aspects of Popular Culture*. Garden City, N.Y.: Doubleday, 1962.
Weil, Patrick. *Le Sens de la République*. Paris: Grasset, 2015.
Wideman, Dominique. "*La Chine est encore loin*." *L'Humanité*, April 28, 2010, http://www.humanite.fr/node/437258. Accessed June 17, 2016.
Wilson, Emma. *Alain Resnais*. Manchester: Manchester University Press, 2006.
Wood, Robin. *Hollywood from Vietnam to Reagan*. New York: Columbia University Press, 1986.
Yacef, Saâdi. *Souvenirs de la bataille d'Alger, décembre 1956–septembre 1957*. Paris: René Juillard, 1962.
Yacono, Xavier. "La Régence d'Alger en 1830 d'après l'enquête des commissions de 1833–1834." *Revue de l'Occident Musulman et de la Méditerranée*, vol. 1, no. 1, 1966, pp. 229–44.
Yosef, Raz. "Traces of War: Memory, Trauma, and the Archive in Joseph Cedar's *Beaufort*." *Cinema Journal: The Journal of the Society for Cinema and Media Studies*, vol. 50, no. 2, 2011, pp. 61–84.
d'Yvoire, Christophe and Jean-Pierre Lavoignat. *Mesrine—30 Ans de cavale dans le cinema*. Paris: Sonatine Editions, 2008.

Filmography

The following is by no means an exhaustive list of films that treat the Franco-Algerian War. Rather this list includes exclusively the films that this book cites. While I do not include every aspect of their production, I do list principal production sources and state agencies. The films are listed chronologically based on the year of their premier, and within that year, in alphabetical order. Some Algerian films made during the war do not list a production city. Although some of these films made during the Revolution were developed in East Germany and Yugoslavia, I have not always been able to procure this information with precision.

Films Cited

Little Caesar. Mervyn Leroy. Los Angeles: First National Pictures/Warner Brothers, 1930.
The Public Enemy. William A. Wellman. Los Angeles: Warner Brothers, 1931.
Scarface. Howard Hawks. Los Angeles: The Caddo Company, 1932.
Pépé le moko. Julien Duvivier. Paris: Paris Film, 1937.
Germania anno zero. (*Germany Year Zero.*) Roberto Rossellini. Berlin: DEFA (Deutsche Film-Aktiengesellschaft); Sadfi, Paris: UGC, Rome: Tevere Film, 1948.
Afrique 50. René Vautier. Paris: Ligue Française de l'enseignement, 1950.
Los Olvidados. (*The Young and the Damned.*) Luis Buñuel. Madrid: Ultramar Films, 1950.
Une Nation, l'Algérie. (*A Nation, Algeria.*) René Vautier, 1954.
Touchez pas au grisbi. (*Don't Touch the Loot.*) Jacques Becker. Rome: Del Duca Films, 1954.
Rififi. Jules Dassin. Paris: Pathé Consortium Cinema, 1955.
Nuit et brouillard. (*Night and Fog.*) Alain Resnais. Paris: Argos Films, 1956.
Toute la mémoire du monde. (*All the World's Memories.*) Alain Resnais. Paris: Les Films de la Pléiade, 1956.
L'École, Les Infirmieres de l'ALN, L'Attaque des mines de l'Ounza. (*School, The Nurses of the ALN, The Attack of Ounza's Mines.*) School of Cinema under René Vautier, 1957.
Les Réfugiés. Cécile Decugis, 1957. (Reedited with a new audio track in 2011 as *La Distribution du pain*).
Algérie en flammes. (*Algeria in Flames.*) René Vautier. Berlin: DEFA (Deutsche Film-Aktiengesellschaft), 1958.
Gamila el Gazairia. (*Djamilah.*) Youssef Chahine. Cairo: Magda Films, 1958.
Moi un noir. (*Me a Black Person.*) Jean Rouch. Paris: Les Films de la Pléiade, 1958.

Popiól i diament. (*Ashes and Diamonds.*) Andrzej Wadja. Warsaw: KADR, 1958.

Réfugiés algériens. (*Algerian Refugees.*) Pierre Clément and Djamel Chanderli. Cinema Serviceof GPRA (Gouvernement provisoire de la République algérienne), 1958.

Sakiet Sidi Youssef. Pierre Clément. Cinema Service of GPRA (Gouvernement provisoire de la République algérienne), 1958.

58.2/B. Guy Chalon. Paris, 1959.

Hiroshima mon amour. Alain Resnais. Paris: Argos Films and Pathé, 1959.

Moranbong, une aventure coréenne. (*Moranbong, a Korean Adventure.*) Jean-Claude Bonnardot. Paris: Films d'aujourd'hui, Ombre et Lumière, 1959.

La Passe du diable. (*The Devil's Pass.*) Pierre Schoendoerffer and Jacques Dupont. Barcelona: Ibérica Film; Paris: Gamma Film; Rome: Fono Roma, 1959.

Les Quatre Cents Coups. (*400 Blows.*) François Truffaut. Paris: Les Films du Carrosse, Société d'exploitation et de distribution de films, 1959.

Secteur postal 89098. Philippe Durand. Paris, 1959.

À bout de souffle. (*Breathless.*) Jean-Luc Godard. Paris: Les Films Impéria, Les Productions de Georges de Beauregard, and (SNC) Société nouvelle de cinématographie, 1960.

Les Distractions. Jacques Dupont. 1960.

Djazairouna. (*On Algeria.*) René Vautier and Djamel Chanderli. Cinema Service of GPRA (Gouvernement provisoire de la République algérienne), 1960.

Fluct aus der Hölle. (*Escape from Hell.*) Hans-Erich Korbschmitt. Berlin: DEFA (Deutsche Film-Aktiengesellschaft), 1960.

Les Honneurs de la guerre. (*The Honors of the War.*) Jean Dewer. Paris: AKO Films, 1960.

Kapò. Gillo Pontecorvo. Belgrade: Lovcen Film; Paris: Francinex; Rome: Cineriz, Vides, 1960.

Ahmed weine nicht. (*Ahmed Doesn't Cry.*) Berlin: DEFA (Deutsche Film-Aktiengesellschaft), 1961.

Allons les enfants ... pour l'Algérie. (*Let's Go Children ... for Algeria.*) Karl Gass. Berlin: DEFA (Deutsche Film-Aktiengesellschaft), 1961.

L'Année dernière à Marienbad. (*Last Year at Marienbad.*) Alain Resnais. Paris: Cocinor, 1961.

Camping durch Tunesien (*Camping through Tunisia.*) Berlin: DEFA (Deutsche Film-Aktiengesellschaft), 1961.

Chronique d'un été. (*Chronicle of a Summer.*) Edgar Morin and Jean Rouch. Paris: Argos Films, 1961.

Cuba si! (*Cuba Yes!*) Chris Marker. Paris: Les Films de la Pléiade, 1961.

Die Frage. (*The Question.*) Mohand Ali Yahia. Babelsberg: Film University Babelsberg, 1961.

J'ai huit ans. (*I Am 8 Years Old.*) Yann Le Masson and Olga Poliakof. Paris: Les Grains de Sable, 1961.

Mit Kombi. (*Combined.*) Berlin: DEFA (Deutsche Film-Aktiengesellschaft), 1961.

Sorah und Ali. (*Sorah and Ali.*) Berlin: DEFA (Deutsche Film-Aktiengesellschaft), 1961.

Tu ne tueras point. (*Thou Shalt Not Kill.*) Claude Autant-Lara. Belgrade: Lovcen Film, Vaduz Film, Gold Film, 1961.
Yasmina. Mohamed Lakhdar-Hamina. The Cinema Service of GPRA (Gouvernement provisoire de la République algérienne), 1961.
Algérie année zero. (*Algeria Year Zero.*) Marie Loridan-Ivens and Jean-Pierre Sergeant. Paris: Argos Films, 1962.
Cléo de 5 à 7. (*Cléo from 5 to 7.*) Agnès Varda. Paris: Ciné Tamaris, 1962.
Le Combat dans l'île. (*The Fight on the Island.*) Alain Cavalier. Paris: Nouvelles Éditions de films, 1962.
Le Doulos. Jean-Pierre Melville. Rome: Compagnia Cinematografica Champion and Rome Paris Films, 1962.
La Jetée. Chris Marker. Paris: Argos Films, 1962.
Octobre à Paris. (*October in Paris.*) Jacques Panijel. Paris: Comité Maurice Audin, 1962.
Oliviers de la Justice. (*Olive Trees of Justice.*) James Blue. Algiers: *La Société Algérienne de Production des Studios Africa*, 1962.
Paris nous appartient. (*Paris Belongs to Us.*) Jacques Rivette. Paris: Ajym Films and Les Films du Carosse, 1962.
Adieu Philippine. Jacques Rozier. Paris: Rome Paris Films, 1963.
Le Feu follet (*The Fire Within.*) Louis Malle. Paris: Nouvelles éditions de films, 1963.
Le Grand Escroc. (*The Confidence Man.*) Jean-Luc Godard. Paris: Les Productions de Georges de Beauregard, 1963.
Le Joli mai. (*The Pretty May.*) Chris Marker. Paris: Sofracima,1963.
Muriel ou le temps d'un retour. (*Muriel or the Time of Return.*) Alain Resnais. Paris: Argos Films, 1963.
Le Petit Soldat. (*The Little Soldier.*) Jean-Luc Godard. Paris: Les Productions de Georges de Beauregard, and SNC (Société nouvelle de cinématographie), 1963.
La Quille. (*The Keel.*) Jean Herman. Paris: Société franco-africaine du cinéma, 1963.
La Rabbia. (*The Rage.*) Giovanni Guareschi and Pier Paolo Pasolini. Rome: Opus Film, 1963.
La Belle Vie. (*The Beautiful Life.*) Robert Enrico. Paris: Les Films du Centaure, 1964.
Les Parapluies de Cherbourg. (*The Umbrellas of Cherbourg.*) Jacques Demy. Paris: Parc Film, Madeline Film, Beta Film, 1964.
Les Statues meurent aussi. (*Statues Also Die.*) Chris Marker and Alain Resnais. Paris: Présence africaine and Tadié Cinéma, 1964.
Une si jeune paix. (*So Young a Peace.*) Jacques Charby. Algiers: CNC (Centre national du cinéma algérien), 1965.
Fajr al-mu'adhhabin. (*The Dawn of the Damned.*) Ahmed Rachedi. Algiers: CNC (Centre national du cinéma algérien), 1966.
La Battaglia di Algeri. (*The Battle of Algiers.*) Gillo Pontecorvo. Algiers: Casbah Film, 1966.
Le Samouraï. Jean-Pierre Melville. Paris: CICC (Compagnie industrielle et commerciale cinématographique), 1967.
Soleil noir. (*Black Sun.*) De La Palletière. Algiers: Casbah Film and Comacico, 1967.

Lo straniero. (*The Stranger.*) Luchino Visconti. Algiers: Casbah Film, 1967; Paris: Marianne productions, and Master film, Rome: Dio de Laurentiis cinematografica, 1967.

Le Vent des Aurès. (*The Wind of the Aurès.*) Mohammed Lakhdar-Hamina. Algiers: OAA (Office des actualités algériennes), 1967.

Le Voleur. (*The Thief of Paris.*) Louis Malle. Paris: NEF Nouvelles éditions des films, Rome: Compagnia cinematographica champion, 1967.

Hassan Terro. Mohammed Lakhdar-Hamina. Algiers: OAA (Office des actualités algériennes), 1968.

L'Enfer à dix ans. (*Hell at 10 Years Old.*) Algiers: ONCIC (Office national pour le commerce et l'industrie cinématographique), 1969.

Les Hors-la-loi. (*The Outlaws.*) Tewfik Farès. Algiers: ONCIC (Office national pour le commerce et l'industrie cinématographique), 1969.

Les Ajoncs. (*The Gorse Bushes.*) René Vautier. Brest: UPCB (Unité production cinématographique de Bretagne), 1970.

Le Cercle Rouge. (*The Red Circle.*) Jean-Pierre Melville. Paris: Les Films corona, Rome: EIF (Euro international film), 1970.

Elise ou la vraie vie. (*Elise or the Real Life.*) Michael Drach. Algiers: Casbah film; Paris: Port-Royal Films, 1970.

Les Trois Cousins. (*The Three Cousins.*) René Vautier. Brest: UPCB (Unité production cinématographique Bretagne), 1970.

L'Opium et le baton. (*The Opium and the Stick.*) Ahmed Rachedi. Algiers: ONCIC (Office national pour le commerce et l'industrie cinématographique), 1971.

Tahia Ya Didou! Mohamed Zinet. Algiers: APC (Algérie Presse Service), 1971.

Avoir 20 ans dans les Aurès. (*To Be 20 in the Aurès.*) René Vautier. Brest: UPCB (l'Union de production cinématographique de bretagne), 1972.

Le Charbonnier. (*The Charcoal Maker.*) Mohamed Bouamari. Algiers: ONCIC (Office national pour le commerce et l'industrie cinématographique), 1972.

The Godfather. Francis Ford Coppola. Los Angeles: Paramount Pictures, 1972.

La Guerre d'Algérie. Yves Courrière and Philippe Monnier. Paris: Reggane Films, 1972.

Noua. Abdelaziz Tolbi. Algiers: Radiodiffusion-télévision Algérienne, 1972.

Décembre. Mohammed Lakhdar-Hamina. Algiers: OAA (Office des actualités algériennes); Paris: Telcia Films, 1973.

La Guerre de Libération. (*The War of Liberation.*) Ahmed Fadheli. Algiers: CAC (Centre algérien du cinéma) and ONCIC (Office national pour le commerce et l'industrie cinématographique), 1973.

R.A.S. (*Nothing to Report.*) Yves Boisset. Paris: Transinter Films, 1973.

Dupont Lajoie. Yves Boisset. Paris: Sofracima, 1974.

The Godfather II. Francis Ford Coppola. Los Angeles: Paramount Pictures, 1974.

Stavisky. Alain Resnais. Paris: Cerito Films, 1974.

Chronique des années de braise. (*Chronicle of the Years of Fire.*) Mohammed Lakhdar-Hamina. Algiers: ONCIC (Office national pour le commerce et l'industrie cinématographique), 1975.

L'Évasion de Hassan Terro. Mustapha Badie, 1976.

Omar Gatlato. Merzak Allouache. Algiers: ONCIC (Office national pour le commerce et l'industrie cinématographique), 1976.
La Crabe tamboure. (*The Drummer Crab*.) Pierre Schoendoerffer. Paris: AMLF (Agence méditerranéenne de location de films), Bela Productions, TF1, 1977.
La Nouba des femmes de Mont Chenoua. (*The Nouba of the Women of Mont Chenoua*.) Assia Djebar. Algiers: RTA (Radiodiffusion-télévision algérienne), 1977.
La Question. Laurent Heynemann. Paris: Little Bear Productions, 1977.
Hassan Terro au maquis. (*Hassan Terro in the Bush*.) Moussa Haddad. 1978.
Hassan Taxi. Mohamed Slimane Riad. 1978.
Le Coup de sirocco. Alex Arcady. Paris: Les Films d'Alma and Alexandre films, 1979.
Prends 10,000 francs et casse-toi. (*Take 10,000 Francs and Get Out*.) Mahmoud Zemmouri. Paris: Fennec Productions, 1981.
L'Honneur d'un capitaine. (*The Honor of a Captain*.) Pierre Schoendoerffer. Paris: Bela Productions, TF1, 1982.
Les Sacrifiés. (*The Sacrificed*.) Okacha Touita. Paris: Marion's Films, Les Films de l'atelier, 1982.
Serkadji. Hadj Rahim. Algiers: RTA (Radiodiffusion-télévision algérienne), 1982.
La Zerda ou les chants de l'oubli. (*Zerda or the Songs of Forgetfulness*.) Assia Djebar. Algiers: RTA (Radiodiffusion-télévision algérienne), 1982.
Liberté la nuit. (*Liberty the Night*.) Philippe Garrel. Paris: Institut national de la communication audiovisuelle, 1983.
Once Upon a Time in America. Sergio Leone. Los Angeles: The Ladd Company, 1983.
Scarface. Brian DePalma. Los Angeles: Universal Pictures, 1983.
Mesrine. André Génovèse. Paris: G.R. Productions, 1984.
Barberousse mes soeurs. (*Barberousse My Sisters*.) Hassen Bouabdellah. Algiers: RTA (Radiodiffusion-télévision algérienne), 1985.
Bâton Rouge. Rachid Bouchareb. Paris: Lyric International, TF1, 1985.
Combien je vous aime. (*How Much I Love You*.) Azzedin Meddour. Algiers: RTA (Radiodiffusion-télévision algérienne), 1985.
Déjà le sang de mai ensemençait novembre. (*Already the Blood of May Sowed November*.) René Vautier. Brest: UPCB (Unité production cinématographique de Bretagne), 1985.
Les Folles Années du Twist. (*The Crazy Years of the Twist*.) Mahmoud Zemmouri. Algiers: ONCIC (Office national pour le commerce et l'industrie cinématographique), 1986.
Jean de Florette. Claude Berry. Paris: DD productions, 1986.
Manon des sources. (*Manon of the Spring*.) Claude Berry. Paris: DD Productions, 1986.
Le Thé au harem d'Archimède. (*Tea in the Harem*.) Paris: CNC (Centre national du cinéma et l'image animée), Ministre des Affaires étrangères, 1986.
Les Yeux brûlés. (*The Burned Eyes*.) Laurent Roth. Paris: ECPAD (Etablissement de communication et de production audiovisuelle de la défense), 1986.
La Citadelle. (*The Citadel*.) Mohamed Chouikh. Algiers: CAAIC (Centre algérien pour l'art et l'industrie cinématographiques), 1988.
Cher Frangin. (*Dear Brother*.) Gérard Mordillat. Paris: Stéphan films, 1989.
Godfather III. Francis Ford Coppola. Los Angeles: Paramount Pictures, 1990.

Jacquot de Nantes. Agnès Varda. Paris: Tamaris Films, 1991.
Le Silence du fleuve. (*The Silence of the River.*) Agnès Denis and Mehdi Lallaoui. Paris: Au nom de la mémoires, 1991.
Les Roseaux Sauvages. (*Wild Reeds.*) André Techiné. Paris: Ima Films, Canal +, CNC (Centre national du cinéma et l'image animée), 1991.
La Guerre sans nom. (*The War without a Name.*) Bernard Tavernier. Paris: GMT Productions, Canal Studio, 1992.
Les Frères des frères. (*Brothers in Arms.*) Gérard Copans. Paris: Les Films d'ici, CNC (Centre national du cinéma et l'image animée), FAS (Fonds d'action sociale), 1992.
Une journée portée disparue. (*A Day Gone Missing.*) Phillip Brooks and Alan Hayling. Paris: Point du jour for Channel 4, 1993.
Bab El-Oued City. Merzak Allouache. Algiers: Flashback Audiovisuel; Geneva: Thelma film AG; Mainz: ZDR-Zweites Deutsches Fernsehen; Paris: Les Matins Films, 1994.
Des Feux mal éteints. (*Poorly Extinguished Fires.*) Serge Moati. Paris: Canal +, CNC (Centre national du cinéma et l'image animée), 1994.
Youssef: la légende du 7e dormant. (*Youssef: The Legend of the Seventh Sleeper.*) Mohamed Chouikh. Algiers: CAAIC (Centre algérien pour l'art et l'industrie cinématographiques), 1994.
Le Fusil de bois. (*The Wooden Gun.*) Pierre Delerive. Paris: Les Films Princesse, Alizés Films, 1995.
Les Massacres de Sétif, un certain 8 mai 1945. (*The Massacres of Sétif, a Certain May 8, 1945.*) Mehdi Lallaoui and Bernard Langois. Paris: Au Nom de la mémoire, 1995.
L'Arche du desert. (*The Ark of the Desert.*) Mohamed Chouikh. Algiers: Atlas Films, et Le Ministère de la Culture et de la Communication, ENPA (Enterprise nationale de production audiovisuelle); Paris: K-Films, CNC (Centre national du cinéma et l'image animée), 1997.
C'était le 17 octobre 1961: Opération télécité. (*It Was October 17, 1961: Operation Télécité.*) Paris: Alizé Productions, 1999.
Vivre au Paradis. Bourlem Guerdjou. Paris:3B Productions, 1999.
The Bunker. Rob Green. London: Millenium Pictures, 2001.
Dissimulation d'un massacre—17 octobre 1961. (*Dissimulation of a Massacre—October 17, 1961.*) Daniel Kupferstein. Paris: CNC (Centre national du cinéma et l'image animée), 2001.
Guerre d'Algérie, les enfants aussi. (*The Algerian War, Children Too.*) Daniel Edinger. Paris: France 3, 2001.
La Guerre sans nom dans Paris: une nuit d'octobre 1961. (*The War without a Name in Paris: An October Night in 1961.*) Aude Touly. 2001.
Dog Soldiers. Neil Marshall. London: Kismet Entertainment Group, 2002.
Deathwatch. Michael J. Bassett. London: Apollomedia, 2002.
L'Ennemi intime. (*The Intimate Enemy.*) Patrick Rotman. Paris: Kuiv Productions, 2002.
Mémoires du 17 octobre. (*Memories of Ocober 17th.*) Faïza Guène and Bernard Richard. Paris: Les Engraineurs, 2002.

Pacification en Algérie. André Gazut. Paris: Arte, 2002.
Algérie, mes fantômes. (*Algeria, My Ghosts.*) Jean-Pierre Lledo. Paris: Iskra, 2003.
Saw. James Wan. Los Angeles: Evolution Entertainment, 2004.
Avant l'oubli. (*Before Forgetting.*) Augustin Burger. Paris: Quo Vadis Cinéma, Arte, CNC (Centre national du cinéma et l'image animée); Madrid: Elías Querejeta Producciones Cinematográficas S.L., 2005.
Caché. (*Hidden.*) Michael Haneke. Paris: Les Films du Losange, 2005.
La Nuit Noire: 17 octobre, 1961. (*Black Night: October 17, 1961.*) Alain Tasma. Paris: France 3, 2005.
La Trahison. (*The Betrayal.*) Phillippe Faucon. Paris: Kinok Films, CNC (Centre national du cinéma et l'image animée), 2006.
Algérie Tours/détours. Oriane Brun-Moschetti and Leïla Morouche. Algiers: Air Algérie, la Cinémathèque algérienne, CDC (le Centre de diffusion du cinéma en Algérie); Paris: Défi jeunes, Villa Médicis, l'Ambassade d'Algérie en France, the French Minister of foreign affairs, 2006.
Azur et Asmar. Michel Ocelot. Paris: Nord-Ouest Films, 2006.
Beur, Blanc, Rouge. (*Beur, White, Red.*) Mahmoud Zemmouri. Algiers: ENTV (Établissement national de télévision algérienne); Paris: Fennac Productions, CNC (Centre national du cinéma et l'image animée), 2006.
Cartouches Gauloises. (*Summer of '62.*) Mehdi Charef. Paris: K.G. Productions; Pathé, Algiers: FDATIC (Fonds de développement de l'art, de la technique et de l'industrie cinématographique), 2006.
Ghost Dance. Ken Mcmullen. Mediabox, 2006.
Indigènes. (*Days of Glory.*) Rachid Bouchareb. Algiers: Tessali Films; Paris: CNC (Centre national du cinéma et l'image animée), FASILD (Fonds d'action et de soutien à l'intégration et à la lutte contre les discriminations), 2006.
Mon Colonel. (*The Colonel.*) Laurent Herbiet. Paris: K.G. Productions, 2006.
Algérie, les histoires de ne pas dire. (*Algeria, Stories to Not Tell.*) Jean-Pierre Lledo. Algiers: Naouel Films, ENTV (Enterprise national de la télévision algérienne); Paris: Mille et Une Productions, 2007.
L'Avocat de la terreur. (*Terror's Advocate.*) Barbet Schroeder. Paris: La Sofica Uni Etoile 3, CNC (Centre National du Cinéma et l'image animée), 2007.
L'Ennemi intime. (*The Intimate Enemy.*) Florent-Emilio Siri. Casablanca: Agora Films; Paris: Les Films du Kiosque, 2007.
Mémoires du 8 mai 1945. (*Memories of May 8, 1945.*) Mariem Hamidat. Algiers and Paris: HKE Productions, 2007.
La Môme. (*La Vie en Rose.*) Olivier Dahan. Paris: TF1, Légende Films, 2007.
La question: Le Pen et la torture. (*The Question: Le Pen and Torture.*) José Bourgarel. Paris: France 2, 2007.
L'Autre 8 mai 1945, aux origins de la Guerre d'Algérie. (*The Other May 8, 1945: The Origins of the Algerian War.*) Yasmina Adi. Paris:CPB Films (Compagnie des Phares et Balises), 2008.
La Chine est encore loin. (*China Is Still Far.*) Malek Bensmaïl. Algiers: ENTV (Enterprise national de la télévision algérienne); Paris: Unlimited, CNC (Centre National du cinéma et l'image animée), 2008.

Mesrine: L'instinct de mort et Public ennemi no.1. (*Mesrine: Part I the Killer Instinct and Part II Public Enemy No. 1.*) Jean-Paul Richet. Paris: La Petite Reine, CNC (Centre national du cinéma et l'image animée) Support, 2008.

Mostafa Ben Boulaid. Ahmed Rachedi. Algiers: Minister of Moudjahidines, 2008.

Vent de sable: Le Sahara des essais nucléaires. (*Wind of Sand: The Nuclear Tests of the Sahara.*) Larbi Benchiha. Le Mans: 24 Images; Paris: CNC (Centre national du cinéma et l'image animée), 2008.

Gerboise bleue. (*The Blast of Shame.*) Djamel Ouahab. Algiers: Bladi Films; Paris: Kalame Films, CNC (Centre national du cinéma et l'image animée), support from ACSE (Agence nationale pour la cohésion sociale et l'egalité des chances) and Fonds images de la diversité, 2009.

Paroles d'un prisonnier d'ALN. (*Words from a Prisoner of the ALN.*) Salim Aggar. Algiers: ENTV (Établissement national de télévision algérienne), 2009.

Un balcon sur la mer. (*A View of Love.*) Nicole Garcia. Paris: Europa Corps, CNC (Centre national du cinéma et l'image animée), 2010.

Djinns. (*Stranded.*) Hughes and Sandra Martin. Casablanca: Agora Films; Paris: Delante Films, Kare Productions, 2010.

Hors-la-loi. (*Outside the Law.*) Rachid Bouchareb. Algiers: Tessalit Productions, AARC (Agence algérienne pour le rayonnement cuturel), EPTV (Établissement public de television), Ministère Algérien de la Culture (participation); Paris: CNC (Centre national du cinéma et l'image animée) (participation), Canal +, France television, 2010.

Case Départ. (*Tee Box.*) Lionel Steketee and Fabrice Eboué. Paris: Légende Films, 2011.

Ici on noie les Algériens. (*Here We Drown Algerians.*) Yasmina Ada. Paris: CNC (Centre national du cinéma et l'image animée), 2011.

Fidaï. Damien Ounouri. Beijing: Xstream Pictures; Kuwait: Linked Productions; Paris: Kafard Films, 2012.

50 ans 50 femmes. Sabrina Draoui, Kenza Mehadji, Marie-Ange Poyet, Hassene Bélaïd, Nourredine Benahmed, Khaled Benaïssa, Ilyes Bensalem, Hassen Ferhani, Abdelghani Raoui, and Hocine Redjala. Algiers and Paris: HKE Production, 2013.

Les Coulisses Suisses de la Guerre d'Algérie. (*The Swiss Backstage of the Algerian War.*) Pierre-André Thiébaud. Genève: PCT Cinéma et Télévision SA, 2013.

Loubia Hamra. (*Bloody Beans.*) Narimane Mari. Algiers: Allers-Retours, Ministère de la Culture, FDATIC (Fonds de développement de l'art, de la technique et de l'industrie cinématographique); Marseille: Central Electrique; Paris: CNAP (Centre national des arts plastiques), 2013.

10949 Femmes. (*10949 Women.*) Nassima Guessoum. Paris: GREC (Groupe de recherches et d'essais cinématographiques), 2014.

Krim Belkacim. Ahmed Rachedi. Algiers: Minister of Moudjahidines, 2014.

Certifié Halal. Mahmoud Zemmouri. Algiers: AARC (Agence Algérienne pour le Rayonnement Cuturel); Paris: Fennec Productions, ACSE (Agence Nationale pour la Cohésion et l'Egalité des Chances), 2015.

Lofti. Ahmed Rachedi. Algiers: Minister of Moudjahidines, 2015.

Zabana! Saïd Ould Khelifa. Algiers: Laith Media, 2015.

Prisonniers Français du FLN: Algérie 1954–1962. Rémi Lainé. Alégria Productions and France 3, 2016.
Le Fort des fous. (*The Oven for Crazies.*) Narimane Mari. Algiers: Allers-Retours; Athens: Blonde; Marseille: Centrale-Electrique, 2017.
La Bleuïte: L'Autre guerre d'Algérie. (*La Bleuïte: The Other Algerian War.*) Jean-Paul Mari. Paris: France 5, 2018.

Index

Page entries in *italic* refer to figures.

400 Blows (*Les Quatre cents coups*, November 1959) 21–2

Afrique 50 (Vautier) 16, 44
Algeria in Flames (Vautier) 16–18, 44
Algeria Year Zero (*Algérie année zéro*, Loridan/Sergent) 17
Algérie Tours/detours (Brun-Moschetti/ Morouche) 6, 41–7, *46*, 50, 57, 59, 155
All the World's Memories (*Toute la mémoire du monde*, Resnais) 36
Anderson, Benedict 52
archival material, and claims to 35–6
Archive fever (*Le Mal d'archive*, Deleuze) 56–7, 173–4
Armes, Roy 44, 45, 168, 171
Artaud, Antonin 149–50
Association des Vétérans des essais nucléaires (AVEN) 79
Association nationale des Français d'Afrique du nord, d'Outre-Mer et de leurs amis (ANFANOMA) 29
atomic bomb tests (Sahara) 61–3, 75, 78–82, 84–5
Aussaresses, Paul (General) 5, 53, 119, 156, 161, 164, 173, 180
Austin, Guy 37, 90, 91, 100, 171, 176, 178, 185

Bancel, Nicolas 5, 76
Barthes, Roland 77
Baton rouge (Bouchareb) 94
Battle of Algiers, A Film in History (*La Bataille d'Alger, un film dans l'Histoire*) 152
Battle of Algiers, The (*La Battaglia di Algeri*, Pontecorvo) 25, 27–9, 47, 61–2, 66, 91, *92*, 94–6, 102, 104, 106, 116, 134, 145–6, 152, 156, 160, 161, 168–9, 183
Beautiful Life, The (*La Belle Vie*, Enrico) 22–3, 166

Bedjaoui, Ahmed 168, 169, 178
Benjidid, Chanli 36–7
Bensmaïa, Réda 7, 41, 90, 97, 100
Bensmaïl, Malek 48–9, 152, 155–6, 172, 183
Berber Movement (1980s) 12, 36
Betrayal, The (*La Trahison*, Faucon) 6, 62, 82, 116, 151, 201
Black Decade, i.e. Black Years (c.1992–2002) 6, 12, 37–9, 50, 108, 154, 161
Black Night: October 17, 1961 (*La Nuit Noire: 17 octobre, 1961* Tasma) 99
Black Power movement 27
Blanchard, Pascal 5, 76, 116, 121, 164, 175, 177, 179–80
bleuïte, la 18
Bloc Identitaire 151, 183
Bloody Beans (*Loubia Hamra*, Mari) 2, 3, 4, 8, 131, 132, 143–54, 155, 156, 158, 182
bloody week (*semaine sanglante, la*, October 1988) 36
Boisset, Yves 5, 12
Bouchareb, Rachid 34, 89, 94
Boudiaf, Mohamed 37, 161
Boudjedra, Rachid 26–7, 168
Boumediene, Houari 28, 33, 161
Bouteflika, Abdelaziz 156, 161–2
Branche, Raphaelle 5, 119–20, 124, 127, 156, 164, 173–4, 180
Breathless (*A bout de souffle*, Godard) 21, 22, 24, 196

Caché (Haneke) 2, 82, 99, 124
Cahiers du cinéma, Les 21, 49, 94
Camus, Albert 16
Capitalisme et Schizophrénie: Tome 1 and 2 (Deleuze and Guattari) 6–7, 42, 47, 54, 58–9, 90, 93, 95–6, 163, 171, 172, 173, 174
Casbah Films 27, 91
Cassel, Vincent 114–15

Cayrol, Jean 26
censorship 1, 2, 5, 11–14, 17, 18, 19, 20, 23–32, 36, 39, 74, 76, 79, 81, 85, 99, 111–12, 124, 127–8, 156–7, 167, 168, 169
Certifiée Halal (Zemmouri) 34
Charby, Jacques 181 *see also So Young a Peace*
Charef, Mehdi 34, 89, 90, 94–7, 145, 155
Charonne metro station 22, 160
China Is Still Far (*La Chine est encore loin*, Bensmaïl) 3, 6, 41–2, 47–52, *51*
Chouikh, Mohamed 28, 37, 39
Chronicle of a Summer (*Chronique d'un été*, Rouch/Morin) 16–17, 22
Chronicle of the Years of Fire (*Chronique des années de braise*, Lakhdar-Hamina) 12, 21, 27, 31, 34, 39, 44, 89, 90–5, 98, 103, 145, 177, 178
cinéma djidid 31, 91, 176
cinéma parallèle, le 5, 19–21, 24, 26–9, 94, 166, 168
cinéma vérité 22, 49, 52
Ciné-pops 19, 43–5
Cléo from 5 to 7 (*Cléo de 5 à 7*, Varda) 22
Colonel, the (*Mon Colonel*, Herbiet) 62, 63, 95, 173
Confidence Man, The (*Le Grand escroc*, Godard) 25
Coup de sirocco, Le (Arcady) 33–4
Coutard, Raoul 22, 32, 169
Crazy Years of the Twist, The (*Les Folles Années du twist*, Zemmouri) 3, 8, 34–5, 90, 101–9, 137, 178
Croombs, Matthew 22

Dadci, Younès 18, 164
Daennickx, Didier 127
Dafri, Abdel Raouf 8, 114, 117
Dallier, Jacques 123, 124
Daoud, Kamel 1, 2, 3, 4, 163
Dawn of the Damned (*Fajr al-mu'adhhabin*, Rachedi) 30, 36
Days of Glory (*Indigènes*, Bouchareb) 8, 98
De Gaulle, Charles 13, 18, 24, 78, 79, 84, 119, 160, 161
Décembre (Lakhdar-Hamina) 30–1, 33, 62
Declaration of the Rights of Man and of the Citizen, the 1, 2, 19

deterritorialization/reterritorialization 4, 7–8, 90–5, 99, 132
Deutsche Film-Aktiengesellschaft (DEFA) 17, 18, 166
Devil's Pass, The (*Le Passe du diable*, Schoendoerffer) 169
Di Iorio, Sam 22
Djebar, Assia 11 *see also individual films*
Djinns (*Stranded*, Martin) 2, 3, 7, 26, 61, 62, 63, 75–87, *77*
Drummer Crab, The (*La Crabe tamboure*, Schoendoerffer) 32–3, 39, 156,
Dupont Lajoie (Boisset) 169
Dying Colonialism, A (*L'An V de la révolution algérienne*, Fanon) 15

Einaudi, Jean-Luc 124, 127, 156, 177
El Moudjahid (newspaper) 14, 134
Elise, Or Real Life (*Elise ou la vraie vie*, Drach) 28–9, 33, 38
Elsaesser, Thomas 75
Enfants d'Algérie, Les (*The Children of Algeria*, Charby ed.) 134–5, 181
enfumades 125, 159
Enrico, Robert 22, 23
d'Estaing, Valérie Giscard 34
Evian Accords (March 18, 1962) 19, 21, 22, 24, 25, 29, 131, 152, 160, 161, 167

family act 35, 161
Fanon, Frantz 14, 142
Farès, Nabile 101
Fidaï (Ounouri) 3, 6, 41–2, 52–7, 59, 116, 155, 163, 173
First Man, The (*Le Premier Homme*, Camus) 182
Flood, Maria 26
Foucault, Michel *see* heterotopia
Front de libération nationale (FLN) 11, 14, 17, 18, 20, 21, 24, 25, 27, 29, 34, 35, 37, 38, 41, 44–5, 49
Front Islamic du Salut (FIS) 36, 37, 108, 161

gangster-film genre 112–14
Garcia, Nicole 28, 32
Ghost Dance (McMullen) 80–1
Godard, Jean-Luc *see individual films*
Godfather series (Coppola) 99, 113, 115, 122
Groupe Farid 16

Hantke, Steffan 83
harkis 18, 20, 22, 64, 70–1, 116, 118, 156, 180,
Hassan Terro (Lakhdar-Hamina) 34, 102–3
Hennebelle, Guy 18, 134, 164, 168, 181
heterotopia 8, 131, 132, 133, 138–40, 143–4, 147
Higbee, Will 42, 171, 89, 177
Hiroshima mon amour (Resnais) 24
Hirsch, Marianne (post-memory) 58, 74
Hollande, François 2, 162
Holocaust 16–17, 23, 29, 68
Honor of a Captain, The (*L'Honneur d'un capitaine*, Schoendoerffer) 28, 32–3, 39, 156
Honors of War, The (*Les honneurs de la guerre*, Dewer) 14
How Much I Love You (*Combien je vous aime*, Meddour) 35–6

I am 8 Years Old (*J'ai huit ans*, Yann Le Masson Olga Poliakof, and René Vautier 1961) 19, 44, 50–1, *50–1*, 135, 182
image-mouvement and *image temps* (Deleuze) 95, 176
immigration 4–5, 12–13, 28–9, 33–4, 152
Intimate Enemy, The (*L'Ennemi intime*, Florent-Emilio Siri) 2, 3, 7, 53, 61, 63–75, *64*, *66*, 68–9, *72*, 86, 111, 116, 151, 157
Intimate Enemy, The (*L'Ennemi intime*, Rotman) 53, 157

Jenni, Alexis, 62
Jetée, La (Marker) 22, 25

Kapò (Pontecorvo) 27
Khanna, Ranjana 35
Krim Belkacim (Rachedi) 156, 163

Lacheraf, Mostefa 91
Lakhdar-Hamina, Mohammed 21, 104, 108, 145, 178 see also individual films
Lapointe, Ali 46, 47
Last Year at Marienbad (*L'année dernière à Marienbad*, Resnais) 24, 167
Lazreg, Marina 63, 65, 66–7, 68, 70, 71, 73, 74

Le Pen, Jean-Marie 32
Le Sueur, James 5, 14, 15
Let's Go Children ... for Algeria (*Allons les enfants pour Algérie*, Gass) 17, 79
Liberty the night (*Liberté la nuit*, Garrel) 177
Little Soldier, The (*Le Petit Soldat*, Godard) 11, 22, 23, 24–5, 39, 82, 167
Lofti (Rachedi) 156, 163
Loridan-Ivens, Marceline 16–17
Lumière Brothers 44–5, 171

Macron, Emmanuel 1, 2, 3, 4, 32, 162
Maherzi, Lofti 21, 45, 91, 167
Malkmus, Lizbeth 45
Malley, Robert 5
Malraux, André 13
Manifeste des 121 23
Mari, Narimane see individual films
Marie, Michel 21
Marker, Chris 26 see also individual films
Marks, Laura U. 53
Massu, Jacques (General) 29, 70, 156
May 1968 29
Me a black person (*Moi un noir*, Rouch) 19
Megherbi, Abdelghani 7, 164
Memmi, Albert 15
Mesrine, Jacques 8, 117, 121, 126
Mesrine Part I: Killer Instinct (*L'instinct de mort*, Richet) 3, 111–22, *118*, *120*
Mesrine Part II: Public Enemy No.1 (*Public Enemy no.1*, Richet) 3, 111, 112, 115, 122–9
Meursault contre-enquête (*The Meursault Investigation*, Daoud) 3
military-horror film genre 82–6
MNA (Mouvement national algérien) 18, 26, 70, 76, 85, 98, 100, 156, 160, 166, 177, 178
Morag, Raya 63, 68, 72
Moranbong, a Korean Adventure (*Moranbong, une adventure coréenne*, Bonnardot) 13
Mostafa Ben Boulaid (Rachedi) 156, 163
moudjahid cinema 7, 11, 21, 28, 31, 33, 44, 52, 89–96, 98–109, 146, 153
Mouillaud-Fraisse, Geneviève 52, 58
Mudimbé, V. Y. 15, 165

Muriel, Histoire d'une recherche (Claude Bailblé, Michel Marie, and Marie Claire Ropars-Wuilleumier) 26, 168
Muriel or the Time of Return (*Muriel ou le temps d'un retour*, Resnais) 11, 22–7, 30, 39, 62, 82
Muritti, Paul 45

Naficy, Hamid 89–90
Neale, Steve 114
Night and Fog (*Nuit et Brouillard*, Resnais) 17, 23, 26, 165,
Nothing to Report (*R.A.S.*, Boisset) 29–30, 156
Nouba of the Women of Mont Chenoua, The (*La Nouba des femmes de Mont Chenoua*, Djebar) 34–5, 143, 146, 170

OAS (Organisation de l'armée secrète) 22, 24, 32–3, 38, 78, 111, 119–20, 123, 127–8, 137, 138, 141, 144, 146, 151, 152–4, 160, 161, 167, 177
October in Paris (*Octobre à Paris*, Panijel) 17, 20
  October 17, 1961 Paris Massacre 2, 17, 99–100, 124
Omar Gatlato 177
Opium and the Stick, The (*L'Opium et le baton*, Rachedi) 44, 91
Oran 89, 95–7, 106, 159, 178, 183
Outlaws, The (*Les Hors-la-loi*, Farès) 27, 28, 89, 91, 104, 145, 178
Outside the Law (*Hors-la-loi* Bouchareb) 2, 8, 89, 94, 98, 107, 124, 155, 178–9, 199, 201–2
Oven for Crazies (*Le Fort des fous*, Mari) 152, 172

Papon, Maurice 5, 100, 124, 160, 161, 177, 180
Pasolini, Pier Paolo 54
Pierrot le fou (Godard) 25
Pontecorvo, Gillo 45 *see also individual films*
porteurs de valise 14, 18, 20, 24, 134, 177
Positif (magazine) 19, 29
Powrie, Phil 113
Pretty May, The (*Le joli mai*, Marker) 22

Question, La (Alleg, Henri) 14, 22, 25, 71, 164, 167, 175
Question, La (film adaptations) 32, 169

Rachedi, Ahmed 166 *see also individual films*
Rage, The (*The Rabbia*, Pasolini) 54
Rahal, Malika 4
Raz, Yosef 173
Resnais, Alain 23, 168 *see also individual films*
Richet, Jean-Paul *see Mesrine Part I and II*
Ross, Kristin 29
Rothberg, Michael, multidirectional memory, 4, 16, 37, 131
Rotman, Patrick 53, 64, 157
Rouch, Jean 16, 49, 172 *see also individual films*
Roudy Law 35
Roussel-Cubberly, Noëlle 75

Sacrificed, The (*Les Sacrificés*, Touita) 98
Sakiet Sidi Youssef (Clément) 18
Saïd, Edward 71, 76, 100
Salan, Raoul 22, 138
Sarkozy, Nicolas 2, 73, 162
Sartre, Jean-Paul 5, 12, 14–19, 23, 25, 164, 165
Scarface (De Palma, 1984) 114
Schoendoeffer, Pierre *see individual films*
scission, theory of (Derrida) 8, 112, 122, 124, 158
  Shibboleth for Paul Celan 128–9
Secteur postal 89098 (Philippe Durand, 1959) 20
self-censorship 17, 22
Service cinématographique de l'armée (SCA) 13, 18–19, 22, 23, 26, 32, 166
Service de diffusion cinématographique (SDC) 45
Sétif Massacre (May 8, 1945) 45, 99, 106, 159, 177
Sharpe, Mani xi, 22
Silverstein, Paul 5, 11–12
So Young a Peace (*Une paix si jeune* Charby) 3, 8, 131–43, *136*, *138*, *139–42*, 146, 153, 155, 181, 182
Spaces of Hope (Harvey) 4, 132, 143, 150, 153–4
spectre, theory of (Derrida) 63, 77–8, 80, 81, 86, 157
Statues Also Die (*Statues meurent aussi*, Marker/Renais) 36
Stavisky (Resnais) 113
Stora, Benjamin 5, 13, 33, 45, 53, 77, 79, 127, 164, 172
Stranger, The (*L'Etranger*, Camus) 3, 163

Stranger, The (*L'Etranger*, Visconti) 27
Summer of '62 (Charef) 2, 3, 6, 7–8, 89, 94, 94–8, *97*, 101, 105, 106, 107, 108, 109, 145, 151, 155, 156, 179,

Tahia Ya Didou! (Zinet) 30–1
Take 10,000 Francs and Get Out (*Prends 10,000 francs et casse-toi*, Zemmouri) 34, 104
Tarr, Carrie 38
Tea in the Harem (*Le Thé au Harem d'Archimède*, Charef) 94
Thou Shalt Not Kill (*Tu ne tueras point*, Autant-Lara) 14, 20, 26, 168
To Be 20 in the Aurès (*Avoir 20 ans dans les Aurès*, Vautier) 12, 29, 33, 156
total cinema theory 22
Toussaint Rouge 49, 78
Truffaut, François 21, 23
Turim, Maureen 55, 115, 173

Umbrellas of Cherbourg, The (*Les Parapluies de Cherbourg*, Demy) 22

Vautier, René 5, 15–20, 23–4, 27, 41–7, 50, 62, 135, 165–7, 169, 175, 177, 181, 195–6, 198–9

Vérité liberté (journal) 14, 19, 20
Vivre au Paradis (Guerdjou) 99

Warshow, Robert 113
Wild Reeds (*Les Roseaux Sauvages*, Techiné) 38
Wind of the Aurès, The (*Le Vent des Aurès*, Lakhdar-Hamina) 21, 28, 31, 89, 90, 91, 92–6
Woods, Robin 82–3
Wretched of the Earth, The (*Les Damnées de la terre*, Fanon) 134, 137–8

Yacef, Saâdi 27, 91, 134
Yasmina (Lakhdar-Hamina) 21
Youssef: The Legend of the Seventh Sleeper (*Youssef: la légende du 7e dormant*, Chouikh) 36–7

Zemmouri, Mahmoud 11 *see also individual films*
Zerda or the Songs of Forgetfulness (*La Zerda, ou les chants de l'oubli*, Djebar) 36
Zinet, Mohamed 33, 169

www.ingramcontent.com/pod-product-compliance
Lightning Source LLC
Chambersburg PA
CBHW052041300426
44117CB00012B/1924